IBM REDUX

Lou Gerstner and the Business Turnaround of the Decade

DOUG GARR

HarperBusiness
A Division of HarperCollins*Publishers*

IBM REDUX. Copyright © 1999 by Doug Garr. All rights reserved. Printed in the United States of America. No part of this book may be used or reproduced in any manner whatsoever without written permission except in the case of brief quotations embodied in critical articles and reviews. For information address HarperCollins Publishers, Inc., 10 East 53rd Street, New York, NY 10022.

HarperCollins books may be purchased for educational, business, or sales promotional use. For information please write: Special Markets Department, HarperCollins Publishers, Inc., 10 East 53rd Street, New York, NY 10022.

FIRST EDITION

Designed by William Ruoto

Library of Congress Cataloging-in-Publication Data

Garr, Doug.
    IBM redux : Lou Gerstner and the business turnaround of the
decade / Doug Garr.
       p. cm.
    ISBN 0 88730-943-7
    1. International Business Machines Corporation. 2. Gerstner,
Louis V. 3. Computer Industry—United States. I. Title
HD9696.2.U64I254 1999
338.7'61004'0973—dc21   99-31856

99 00 01 02 03 ❖/RRD 10 9 8 7 6 5 4 3 2 1

For Meg and Jake, and for the memory of my father

Contents

A Brand Guy in the Information Age

The cab drivers are busy but unhappy because Las Vegas Boulevard is jammed and morning traffic is crawling. The best craps dealers are calling in sick because the tips are lousy. Casino pit bosses are griping that the gambling tables are slow, the way they are every year at this time. When the computer crowd shows up just before Thanksgiving, a lot of the natives would rather just take the week off. What flows into town is net worth, not cash. The digerati, you see, even the wealthy ones, just don't gamble very much, at least in casinos. Bill Gates plays $25 blackjack. These conventioneers aren't typical tourists; they're geeks and suits who know the odds to the hundredth when they roll the dice. They like action, but they're not stupid. They know they can't beat the house. The people who live in Las Vegas have not yet figured out that the people who earn their living in the world of high technology are high rollers at heart; they shoot craps when they wake up every morning.

The city's biggest convention means fat receipts for the hotels. They are booked solid a year in advance, and the food and the inflated room rentals will make more money than the gambling tables will, an aberration that continues to baffle local economists.

This is the annual worldwide confab of the makers and purveyors of microchips and related wares, hard, soft, middle, and
otherwise. COMDEX, the Computer Dealers Exposition, where a
couple of hundred thousand digital savants converge at the
Convention Center. Hundreds of high-tech companies, from
one-horse outfits to multinationals, clamor for attention. In
hotel conference rooms and trailers in the parking lots outside
the exhibit hall, the industry's power brokers meet and cut deals,
carve up territories, make alliances, plot against Sun or Oracle or
Dell or Compaq—or even IBM, the company everyone loved to
hate until a couple of years ago. Before Microsoft was on the
verge of becoming like IBM.

On the Strip at the Aladdin Hotel Theater, up onstage is Lou
Gerstner, the fifty-three-year-old chairman and CEO of IBM.
He's about to give the keynote address that traditionally opens
the show, the biggest single draw of the four-day event. The video
feed will be piped into the ballrooms of several other hotels.
Unless you're hopelessly hungover or closing the deal of a life-
time, you're tuned into this speech.

The "Voice of God," convention lingo for the words from an
anonymous technician at the mixing console, introduces the
speaker.

Gerstner is not a casual guy. He doesn't go onstage in khakis
and a sweater. He is wearing a perfectly pressed dark suit, white
shirt, beige print tie. His suit coat is buttoned, and it will remain
that way until he sits on a stool. His style differs from most other
industry luminaries, who try to outdo one another at COMDEX
with elaborately staged theatrics. The stage is sparse. There is a
simple background of vertical brown and white and gray panels,
with downlights illuminating them. No pyrotechnics, no multimedia for this CEO. No giant company logo either. Gerstner is
larger than life only on the projection screens on either side of
the stage. Just the stool and a glass of water off to the side on a
modern, stylized group of rectangular pedestals. This simple
approach is deliberate. After considerable discussion and debate,
it was suggested that one way to distinguish Gerstner from the

technology clutter was to send him out there without any fanfare, without the usual gizmos or props.

This is Gerstner's most visible public appearance since he took the reins of the failing computer company two and a half years earlier. He has meticulously avoided high-profile events like these, mainly because he feels uncomfortable in front of a crowd of technology devotees. His most visible industry peers and rivals, Andy Grove of Intel, Bill Gates of Microsoft, Scott McNealy of Sun Microsystems, and Larry Ellison of Oracle, are guys who like working under the hood, getting their clothes full of the grease of computing. Gates and Grove are technology lifers, pure wonks within their own firms, at ease among the eccentrics, the engineers and scientists and programmers. McNealy, who would stimulate a good deal of the Internet's growth with the Java programming language, is outspoken on any topic, especially when prodded about his dislike for Microsoft's monopolistic tendencies and strong-arm marketing tactics. Ellison, the often flamboyant purveyor of large system database software, is a Silicon Valley original and something of a loose cannon—his highly controversial personal life rivals Ted Turner in his worst bad-boy moments.

All four of those CEOs have an intimacy with technology, and a certain healthy disdain—but not disregard—for IBM, a company that is squarely in recovery but which they still think of as well past its innovative prime. They respect Big Blue but they do not fear it. They haven't been afraid of it in years, ever since the monolith began to melt. Even Gerstner, a man with a considerable appetite for achievement, admits that IBM will never be an omnipotent presence again. He is hoping for something less: consistent growth and profitability and a leadership role in the burgeoning networked world.

No, Lou Gerstner never looks under the hood. He doesn't speak the language of the digerati, and he's never going to learn it. Therefore, he is something of an outsider. He isn't a CEO who hangs out with the design guys and listens to their rhapsodies on processor speeds, memory capacity, bandwidth, and applets.

He hates that stuff, and he makes no secret about it. And you couldn't measure his contempt for any twenty-eight-year-old T-shirt-clad Silicon Valley multimillionaire whose motto is "Failure is cool."

Gerstner also tries to distance himself from other high-tech companies because IBM is more mammoth, more global, more of an industrial concern than any of the other firms. He prefers to be grouped with GM or Exxon or DuPont. The Suns, Microsofts, Ciscos, DECs may keep him awake at night, but none alone can torpedo IBM. He runs the aircraft carrier in the high-technology fleet. The other guys are on the bridges of battleships and cruisers. Gerstner's company is still *Big* Blue. Bigger than everyone else. If IBM is a country, its 1995 revenues, just under $72 billion, are larger than the gross national products of places like Venezuela, New Zealand, or the Philippines.

So for many industry observers, including some IBMers, this is Gerstner's debut, a coming-out of sorts. He greets the audience and dispenses with the small talk. He gets right into it: "Every now and then, a technology or an idea comes along that is so profound, and so powerful, and so universal, that its impact changes everything. The printing press, the incandescent light, the automobile, manned flight. It doesn't happen often, but when it does, the world is changed forever."

It's clear that this isn't going to be the usual sales pitch. Photographers' strobes are pop-pop-popping so fast that you think perhaps the old man himself, Tom Watson, had entered the building.

He continues. "Now, I joined this industry and IBM because I believe that information technology has that potential. I'm more and more convinced that IT is the defining technology of the end of this century and will be well into the next century." His hands emphasize this point, palms outward, preparing to deliver a sermon. "That's why everybody is at COMDEX. Because when you get past all the glitz, this event is really about two things: it's about enthusiasm for our industry and a keen interest in its future."

He is ready for this day, for this speech. You can tell right away. In fact, he has memorized much of it. He steals only an occasional glance at the floor-level TelePrompTers. He paces the stage deliberately, his arms waving like a conductor to emphasize points.

His optimism and passion are radiating from the Aladdin stage now. "What do I think after thirty months on the job? I think this industry has an incredible future. My expectations have been exceeded. I see no limits for at least a decade for the underlying technologies that drive our industry. Processor power, memory, disk capacity, bandwidth, the trajectories will continue without any scientific limits for at least a decade or more."

But Gerstner is also temperate to a fault. Behind the enthusiasm lurks a taskmaster. He has no problem criticizing a business that is making him an extremely wealthy man, even though he is a hired hand and not the latest Silicon Valley entrepreneur with an Internet company whose hot IPO was a triple run-up on the first trading day. In fact, he sprinkles some sarcasm out in the crowd. "When the show opens in about an hour," he reminds everyone, "we'll be bombarded by extraordinary products and lots of promises. . . . Oh yes, lots of promises of dazzling innovations that are just around the corner. You just have to find the corner." He pauses after the last line, but it doesn't get a laugh.

Not only is Gerstner a lingering technophobe, he still has a healthy distrust of the business. "I'm not here at COMDEX to win this year's industry's pied piper award," he declares. He certainly is not. In fact, he views boxes of microprocessors and packages of diskettes as nothing more than shrink-wrapped commodities. They are not unlike the cookies and crackers and cigarettes he peddled at RJR Nabisco, and the scary part is, they have about the same shelf life, maybe shorter. Worse, the depreciation rate is like no other business. Six-month-old PCs that clog inventories are often sold for zero profit—if indeed they can be sold at all. Less than a stale box of Oreos, if you're really cynical.

Today, finally up on center stage in the world of computers, he cannot resist a shot at the dreamers. "One of the things I've discovered about this industry is that it absolutely thrives on hype," he exclaims. "It just loves hype. It's constantly prowling for the next big thing to promote with the presumption that everyone will instantly move to the next wave, and all that preceded it is dead. It's the most brilliant example of planned obsolescence I've ever seen in any industry."

Gerstner sees so many announcements where products are never released—"vaporware," as they're known in the trade—he complains that his lawyers told him he'd be arrested if he tried this tactic in his previous enterprises. If you want the latest software upgrade with dozens of new features you will never use, you are compelled to buy a new one. Why? Because the older version cannot run on a newer computer. Or the newer release cannot run on an older machine. This is intentional, of course, and it's one of the pumps that primes this fascinating business.

Gerstner is still an outsider, but he is charming the audience, reveling in this mock exasperation, asking the right rhetorical questions, pointing out all the little foibles that still grate on everyone's nerves except for the pure hackers who understand the nuances and secrets of computer code. Those guys aren't here listening to Gerstner anyway. The audience is smiling and chuckling. He is talking about us. And he's right! Some of us have approved vaporware press releases. Lou Gerstner is saying we should be ashamed of ourselves. Give him a few more years.

Meanwhile, half the people in the audience are old enough to have watched IBM brought to its knees by the U.S. Justice Department's protracted antitrust suit. Microsoft is just beginning to spend millions of dollars on legal fees and a few years inveighing against overzealous government intervention. IBM has been there and done that to an order of magnitude Bill Gates does not yet fathom. It fought similar accusations for more than a decade. The IBM antitrust suit dragged on from 1969 to 1982, with Justice finally giving up with an unceremonious and abrupt withdrawal of the charges. It was as if the old Gilda Radner character from *Saturday Night Live,* Emily Litella, walked into the courtroom herself— *Never mind.* I'm sorry. No breakup, no consent order, *nada.* There is wonderful irony here. The industry's wise elders—the guys in their fifties and sixties who sold computers with punch cards—know that many years earlier IBM practically wrote the handbook on many of the things Gerstner was carping about. And because they know he is right, they like him. He's a quick study.

Gerstner goes on to admonish technology purveyors for their intrinsic love of complexity, confessing a fascination for the fact that an entire segment has flourished because the stuff is still too difficult. Once a consumer finally masters it, voilà!—a newer version invariably comes out. Gerstner is a guy who really understands why there is still an "ESCAPE" button on the top left corner of every computer keyboard. Has he been reminded that it was an IBMer who first put it there?

Though Gerstner is not the type to scan a technical journal, he is a willing victim of the subtle seduction of the gadgets he sees in his labs. Recently briefed on a new optical microscope invented by IBM, he says, "It has the potential of imaging a single atom that could be viewed in visible light. Unprecedented. I was thinking about this. What do we do with it? How do we turn it into a product? It turns out it could be used for incredibly dense storage devices, a hundred times more than today's. It has the potential to put all 16 million volumes of books in the Library of Congress on a diskette the size of a penny."

This is a terrific bit. But then Gerstner wonders why anyone would want to carry around the entire contents of the Library of Congress in his pocket.

He tells about one of the projects he has seen at the MIT Media Lab. "It's called 'Things That Think.' The idea is to put intelligence in every form of inanimate object. Furniture, glasses, even shoes. A computer in a shoe. Actually it's not such a crazy idea. As I understand it you power the computer with every step you take"—he crosses the stage with exaggerated steps and then stops—"and you shake hands with somebody who's also wearing a shoe computer, you establish a low-voltage electrical connection, and you exchange information through the handshake. Sort of a personal area network. Maxwell Smart, eat your heart out.

"What happens next is you download to your shoe the person's title, who they are, where they work, their phone numbers, even a digital photo or video clip. Now, if you think that's nutty, think about it tonight, before you hit the sack. Try to remember the names and the faces of everyone you meet here today. Empty those pockets of all those business cards you collected, and then . . . look at your shoes. It's not such a wacky thought after all." Gerstner must have liked this gadget. It would not be long before he would hire the guy away from MIT to continue to develop the personal area network at IBM.

He also was shown a prototype of an impressive new digital imaging color screen on a ThinkPad. The display is dazzling in its sharpness. Another laptop he is shown has the same image, only it has a magazine page pasted on the screen. He is challenged to a taste test, and he confesses that he honestly cannot tell the difference. "They went on to talk to me about pixels and all the rest of that, and I said, 'Forget it, just get it to me. I need it today.'" If there is one thing Gerstner has learned since he took the job, it is the phrase "speed to market." This CEO has a sense of urgency that the industry has not yet seen at IBM.

When you peek under the polished exterior, Gerstner is just a brand guy in the information age, a conventional, conservative, button-down CEO who wants people to know that he does not understand how computers work. Just that they *do* work. This is his great strength, he feels. He remembers his chronic frustration when he was at American Express and had to write big checks for computers and hoped they would do what the companies that sold them swore they would do. Sometimes they did, but then he prayed they wouldn't be outdated in six months. When he called IBM and complained that their computers didn't do what he wanted, Big Blue had just the solution. What you need is . . . another box! It drove him crazy.

Too often the industry is focused on megahertz, gigabits, and multitasking. Technology for technology's sake; IBM has platoons—no, *regiments*—of those types still lurking around sites the world over. There is a disconnect between taking on technical challenges and meeting the customer's needs. Yes, there is a difference between applied research and *über*-science. (So far, that optical microscope has not done much more than spell out IBM's logo in atoms. But it certainly looked impressive in the newspaper clips.)

Gerstner does not want anyone to forget that "I was a customer of this industry for twenty years. I've also led consumer-oriented companies, and I can tell you we've got a lot to learn." It is a sermonette that he likes to repeat. "At this very important juncture in our industry's history, I'm reminded of something Dickens wrote in *A Christmas Carol,* maybe because the holidays are upon us. Remember when Scrooge encountered that last ghostly spirit who revealed the future. Scrooge asked, 'Are these the things that will be or might be?' I think we're looking at the same thing in our industry. We can see the future. It's there before us. The question is, will it happen? I think it will, but only if we step up to certain responsiblities as an industry. If we don't, we won't grow as quickly as we'd like, and we will not realize the potential of our technology no matter how impressive it might be. All these challenges fit under one banner . . . listening to our customers."

The CEO continues pacing. He takes a sip of water. He makes it clear that he—as well as the customer—doesn't much care for the industry's labels and conventions and abbreviations. When Gerstner heard his managers refer to LOBs, or "lines of business," he scoffed at the jargon and immediately had it struck from the IBM vocabulary. "Business unit" will have to do. IBM's internal computer system has a useful feature called "whatis," a dictionary of thousands of obscure acronyms and abbreviations used by both the company and the high-tech industry. New IBM recruits spend hours deciphering the company's jargon in memos, amazed to discover a reference to some arcane computer architecture or networking protocol that has long been jetti-soned everywhere except within the company infrastructure.

Gerstner ridicules the naming of software with all its upgrades, version three point whatever, and so on. It's almost like . . . don't get me started. He walks faster and turns away when he says this. He wonders why a computer product doesn't simply have a name rather than a number. Give him credit. "Warp" certainly has a lot more zip than "OS/2." Who can argue with that?

Gerstner, who is not known for his modesty, especially in pri-vate, adds a touch of humility for this speech. It is a natural ora-torical device, and it tempers his criticism and forms a credible foundation for his more caustic observations.

So when it comes to bad-mouthing a turkey, Gerstner looks no further than his own warehouse, showing one of the TV ads for the PC Junior that ran in 1983, when half the people in the audience were still watching cartoons. The ad, now running on the twenty-foot projection screens, features tree-lined sidewalks in suburbia, a real *Leave It to Beaver* neighborhood. The PC Junior, the low-cost family computer with its chintzy Chiclet keyboard, was released only a couple of years after the best-selling IBM PC. The IBM PC was the front-runner in a multibillion-dol-lar business. It helped perpetuate the second industrial revolu-tion. Junior, alas, was one of IBM's most public failures.

The friendly voice-over in the commercial booms, "What can you do with it?" A perfect cue. Gerstner interrupts, "Enough of you told us what we could do with it." The half of the audience that remembers this awful excuse for a computer laughs. He then extracts from behind the lectern an IBM PC Convertible, a fourteen-pound machine that was dubbed the "loveable lug-gable." Released in 1986, it had no hard drive but had two three-and-a-half-inch disk drives. Never mind that it had no parallel port. If you need to connect it to a printer, well, take your diskette over to a friend who has one. Again, customers told IBM what they could do with it.

His speechwriters have supplied him with amusing anecdotes, but his timing and delivery often allow them to slip from his lips unnoticed. Generally, Gerstner is an effective public speaker, occasionally wry and funny, but it's usually spontaneous. One of the few loud laughs he gets comes at the expense of his own workforce after he describes another piece of advanced research. Scientists at Yorktown demonstrated a new speech technology interface that went beyond voice recognition. There is nothing especially new about that, he says. "We have products that do that today. This interface understood what I was saying, it extracted the meaning, and it delivered some information in response . . . something, I might add, that some IBM managers still can't do when I talk to them." This is vintage Gerstner, reinforcing his reputation for having no patience for weak or muddy thinking. He'd heard one too many IBMers try to explain their way out of a tight spot with technobabble. They forget he does not understand the dialect.

His neatly matted gray and white hair glistens in the lights, his short, broad-shouldered, tree-trunk build strides effortlessly across the stage. He is chunky but solid. He exudes confidence. You immediately understand why people say that attention is diverted toward him when he enters a room. His butterball face contains the icy eyes of a man who senses that sloth is the worst of the deadly sins. Even his posed pictures reveal reluctant smiles, not quite insincere, not quite smirks, but just the kind of expression that tells the viewer that smiling for Lou Gerstner isn't fun and requires a degree of effort. Smiling may even be a waste of time.

As he slowly moves about, he sometimes places his hands together, and you can see the index and third fingers on his right hand. Gerstner suffered a freak accident when he was a young man. He was mowing his lawn and a stick or a rock or something got stuck in the blade, and he reached down to clear it. The standard story is that he wrapped his bloodied fingers, rushed himself to a doctor, and while receiving medical attention insisted that he could not cancel an important business meeting on Monday morning. It is difficult to understand this toughness, this stoicism. Perhaps it comes from his strict Catholic upbringing, his struggle to make it big from a modest middle-class background in an era when modest meant that you didn't have that much. "The man is driven in ways that do not seem to be particularly healthful," one fifteen-year IBM veteran who worked with him says. "But maybe that's what it takes to be as successful as he is."

The accident was also a revelation, however, according to a longtime McKinsey colleague, now retired, who knew him when it occurred. Gerstner nearly had a nervous breakdown, not because of the damage to his fingers, but because the *idea* of the accident was so incomprehensible. There was an intellectual breakdown that caused it. This is a guy who analyzes and plans and agonizes over details. He should have anticipated the risk, he should have known that a lawn mower blade could jam and then quickly begin whirring again. "He was just absolutely crushed by the stupidity of that act," said the McKinsey associate. "And he gradually got over it, and now when you shake hands with him, he covers it up."

Gerstner continues, exasperated with yet another phase of the business, one that impresses him with its collective stupidity as well. Incompatibility, especially among operating systems, is a constant peccadillo. High technology, he complains, is the only industry he knows of that refuses to deliver open industry standards to its customers. He cannot understand this. It is so simple. It is ridiculous. The same gas runs any car; why can't the industry apply this theory to computers and operating systems and software? With all of this intellectual might lurking out there in this Las Vegas crowd, he wonders how this can be.

He turns to the audience and asks, "Would you buy a telephone that only dials certain area codes, or a television set that has only odd-numbered stations? I wouldn't." He says that having proprietary or closed systems—the path that IBM had followed so successfully for so many years when it dominated the industry—is a losing strategy. "I bet you thought you'd never hear that from IBM. But having had a near-death experience, we know what we're talking about." There are a number of polite snickers in the front rows. He is encouraged to see that customers are demanding and the industry appears to be embracing open standards. IBM can no longer create its own rules and expect every other company to observe them.

And while the old IBM had missed many market opportunities, he is determined not to let this happen again. Obviously, the playing field is different. "We went from a few large companies to sixty thousand niche players, and in the process, that nearly blew IBM up. I know, I was there as a customer. I even helped light some of the fuses."

With that line about the "near-death experience," Gerstner gives an ever-so-subtle reminder of the failed strategy of his predecessor, John Akers, who had been forced out by the board after posting progressively record losses between 1991 and early 1993. Only a short while ago, a graph of IBM's profits resembled a *New Yorker* cartoon, the line heading off the easel toward the floor. The caption could have read, "I think we were a little light in Europe this year, sir." After posting record profits in 1990, IBM lost $2.9 billion the following year. It followed that with red ink of $5 billion and $8.1 billion, respectively. In three years, IBM lost $16 billion, and the wonder was how it remained afloat while hemorrhaging so much money. (The last huge loss in 1993 came under Gerstner's watch, but he was still cleaning up Akers's mess.)

Along with his cogent observations and curmudgeonly comments about all the challenges this industry faces, Gerstner still needs a pronouncement, something cautiously upbeat. He must tell the technology universe what he thinks things look like from IBM's perch.

Lou Gerstner is bullish on the next wave of technology, the Internet. He wholeheartedly embraces this grand new phase of computing, beginning with businesses and filtering down to consumers. He feels it is a natural progression from the first phase of technology, with its large centralized computer systems, and the second phase, where people now have on their desks the computing power of a ten-year-old mainframe. At IBM the new wave is called "network-centric computing," a term Gerstner would grouse about in his own annual report just five months later. "I'll admit it's a cumbersome name, if not out-and-out dull. I'd like to come up with something snappier, but I think it's too late." (It apparently wasn't. IBM eventually dropped the "centric" and just called it "network computing" like everyone else.)

"So I hope you get the idea that we're taking network-centric computing very seriously at IBM. I'd say that we're betting much of our future on it," he says.

Gerstner pauses, and he casually steps back from the commerce part of his pitch, and launches into his cause, which is the improvement of education. "A while ago, I met with Nelson Mandela and I was talking to him about the greatest challenges facing his country. One of the legacies of apartheid is that the best educational infrastructure is concentrated in a few cities. What were formerly the homelands have very little infrastructure. It will cost millions and millions to build it, and it will take years. We got into a discussion of distance learning, about bringing teachers in cities to students in the homelands by networks. I saw a lightbulb go off. He's very interested in this as a possible solution to the problem."

With all the hosannas about the Internet, Gerstner knows he must also wax sincere about the criticism. "Our industry operates in a free space. It's part of the reason for its success. This freedom must be honored and protected, but it also must be earned. We've got to come to grips with the fact that the proliferation of our technology raises some very provocative and serious societal issues. Some people feel that the Internet is getting out of control. The information highway, it's a dangerous pipeline for pornography, intellectual property theft, and a serious threat to privacy and commerce. Governments are going to be increasingly concerned with the impact our industry has on the nation-state. . . . People are concerned about universal access, about creating a society of technological haves and have nots." He presses all the right buttons on this issue. Then he says the industry must self-regulate. He is a conservative Republican from Connecticut. He doesn't trust big government unless he has to.

Gerstner warily eyes the convention-goers and warns them about another defining technology of a few decades ago. Nuclear power. "It too was going to change the world. It promised energy as cheap as water. There would be reactors to power spacecraft and automobiles. There would be inexhaustible supplies. Those grand visions were never realized. Why? Was it because of bad science? Disappointing technology? Not really. While that industry focused on megawatts and reactor cores, communities worried about the implications of the technology, and they stopped the industry dead in its tracks."

After pontificating for nearly an hour, he prepares to deliver his closing benediction.

"Our industry has some grand visions. We're talking about changing the world in nothing less than fundamental ways. Yet too often, what are we focused on? What will you hear here at COMDEX? Megahertz, gigabits, multitasking. There's a disconnect between our priorities and those of other people and governments."

He pauses and strolls. "The printing press, the incandescent lightbulb, manned flight. It's an extraordinarily rare and humbling opportunity to earn a place in history. I for one think we will. I think we'll make our visions reality. I think we as stewards of our industry will step up to the challenges of social responsibility. We will improve the world, and the way we work, the way we communicate, live, and learn as people. We have grown, we have innovated, have prospered at a rate unsurpassed by any other. It's been an amazing and breathtaking ride. It can continue and accelerate if we remember that our future rests on how well we respond to the total needs of society and of our customers all around the world."

This is the story of how IBM underwent change and how an executive who had previously dispensed management advice, cigarettes, cookies, and traveler's checks affected that change. It will explain what was broken, what was fixed, and what still eludes Gerstner's considerable talents and abilities. It's about a company that was lost and eventually found its way out of the dark. But it's also about a company that's still struggling to make its mark in the world of technology for the twenty-first century, wondering if it can ever regain the industry leadership it once had. The question remains: Is Gerstner returning IBM to the company it once was, or is he reinventing a completely new Big Blue?

When Lou Gerstner was appointed the chairman and CEO of IBM, critics scoffed and asked, could he make the elephant dance? Gerstner has had a profound effect on IBM; he has fashioned one of the most dramatic recoveries in America's corporate history. This is indisputable, even to his detractors. In fact, many observers speculated that after he had righted the ship, when IBM was safely in the black, Gerstner, who had never worked in a high-technology company, would leave and seek a new challenge. But in the fall of 1997, he signed a new five-year contract. He said he had unfinished business, and shrewd observers agreed. The elephant was back on the dance floor, but there were other animals in the high-tech kingdom that were dancing so much faster and more gracefully.

IBM's rebound has come at considerable cost. Gerstner dramatically accelerated mandatory layoffs, and the remaining employees endured changes in the workplace that were akin to China's cultural revolution. In six years, Gerstner brought an intensity and urgency to the company that none of its previous leaders ever had.

Clearly, there have been three distinct epochs of Big Blue. The first was defined by the Watsons, the founding father and his son, in which IBM automated the nation's offices. It was Watson Junior who took the great big leap into computers in the 1950s and 1960s. It took years before any company could catch up. Then, of course, everyone did. The second was transitional, where four homegrown CEOs tried to navigate through a murkier, more competitive period as technology innovation accelerated at an unpredictably fast pace. And IBM's de facto monopoly abruptly ended.

The third epoch began in 1993. An outsider's company for the first time, it can truly be called "Gerstner's IBM." He is writing the first chapters of this period.

Many observers, both employees and ex-employees, think IBM under Gerstner is not really a better—or worse—place to work, or even that it is much different from its earlier incarnation. Some things at IBM have changed, and others have stayed the same. Yes, the IBM of today is "not the IBM your father worked for," to repeat the cliché. Those remaining IBMers—many of whom have seen their relatives excessed—maintain a love-hate relationship with the new leadership. They miss the paternal atmosphere of old—where "respect for the individual" was a human resources mantra—but they've resigned themselves to the fact that the company probably could not have survived under the old regime. In fact, so many were insulated from IBM's most serious problems that when they learn how close the company came to collapse, they refuse to believe it. Those same complainers begrudgingly admit that he has done more to boost stock prices than they ever dreamed possible. They are looking forward to a comfortable retirement. Others, of course, those doers who didn't quit in disgust during the bad days, think Gerstner was what IBM so desperately needed. Developers can finally get products out the door without genuflecting to a dozen committees.

Still, there are those who have a distaste for the strong, centralized nature of Gerstner's management structure. Despite the inherent imperfections of a hierarchy—Gerstner is always talking about the "matrix"—the structure now works, far better than it has in years. Anyway, it's like democracy. Until something comes along that's better, he's sticking with it. Maybe Gerstner is just an able technocrat, an administrator. But at least he's an effective one.

Most IBMers agree that company morale is substantially higher under Gerstner, though it will never reach the height it did in its glory years. Gerstner's idea of esprit de corps is creating and sharing wealth, and you can skip all that spiritual bonding. IBM will never resemble a Silicon Valley high-tech firm—nobody expects lunchtime volleyball games and hot tub parties under Gerstner's watch—but it's behaving as if it wants to be welcomed back to the fold. It wants respect, and appears to be getting it again. While Big Blue did not make *Fortune* magazine's list of the Ten Most Admired Companies in 1998, it was number one in the "computer, office equipment" category (moving ahead of both Compaq and Hewlett-Packard from 1997).

Obviously, the final grades on Gerstner's IBM will not be turned in until he retires, probably sometime in 2002 or shortly thereafter. The picture of what kind of company IBM will be at that time is still somewhat fuzzy, but it is gradually coming into sharper focus.

Would Anyone Want This Job?

ARMONK, NY—January 1993

A few months before Lou Gerstner agreed to assume the stewardship of IBM, the company endured the longest, eeriest winter in its proud and illustrious history. The New Year was hardly a call for celebration. From January through late March of 1993, the vast parking lots at IBM headquarters in Armonk looked like the concrete equivalent of Death Valley. As the days grew longer, fewer people showed up for work, and rumors circulated throughout the building that the company might be in serious danger of going under. Longtime IBM managers shuffled aimlessly on the tangerine-colored carpeting, sleepwalking the wide corridors, wondering what would happen next.

The company's chairman and CEO, John Akers, no longer drove into the Armonk parking lot in his jaunty Mercedes sports car, only to slip into the elevator and disappear into his bunker-suite on the second floor in a corner of the main building. Akers had already packed his $5 million parachute and bailed out, landing in exile at IBM's "transition" offices on the Stamford, Connecticut, waterfront.

He did, however, leave behind a considerable amount of carnage. From 1990 to 1993, shareholders saw nearly $6 billion in equity evaporate as the stock plunged by some thirty percent. In the final years of Akers's reign, he cut IBM's workforce by a quarter, closing ten plants and trimming manufacturing capacity by forty percent.

A palpable sense of failure permeated IBM's headquarters. Already intellectually drained and bankrupt of ideas, the company was now leaderless and rudderless for the first time in nearly eighty years. Since nobody was in command, nothing was happening in corporate headquarters. Traditionally, executives and managers took off the last week of the year, returning refreshed and anxious to begin anew. But that winter no feeling of urgency existed, no project deadlines loomed. In fact, for most of the Armonk bureaucrats, there simply was no real work. To borrow a phrase from technology advertising guru Steve Hayden, IBM faced a state of "total entropic meltdown."

IBM's board had been in a black hole for some time. It had backed the chairman for as long as it could—far too long, in retrospect—before succumbing to pressure from institutional investors and the business press. Jim Burke, the former chairman and CEO of Johnson and Johnson, and a longtime IBM board member, finally led the other seventeen directors to realize there had to be a change at the top. IBM's rubber-stamp board was dysfunctional as well. For years, IBM's CEOs had dictated strategies and policies, and for years the directors had nodded their heads without question. "The board was of absolutely no help to John Akers, no help whatsoever," confessed a former IBM director, who included himself in the statement. Did Akers ever ask for the board's input? "That's a good question," he replied. "Probably not." Either way, the board was hopelessly out of touch with modern technology. Only two directors—former Defense Secretary Dr. Harold Brown and Wellesley President Nannerl Keohane (and now president of Duke University)—used personal computers.

Burke knew that IBM without a leader was like an infection that would fester and spread, making a protracted search for a successor—the standard practice of many other companies—unacceptable. IBM needed a new CEO immediately, preferably before the April annual meeting. Burke enlisted fellow director Tom Murphy, the head of Cap Cities/ABC, to help him scour the business universe for Akers's replacement. Though there was a formal search committee consisting of five board members, including Burke and Murphy, the two did not ask for, or were not offered, much input from the others.

Only one thing was certain: The board insisted on a candidate who wasn't an IBMer, someone without the baggage of the company culture. This was a classic turnaround problem, probably the most challenging in recent American corporate history. The board felt strongly that what was wrong with IBM couldn't be fixed by an IBMer.

A couple of nominations were casually tossed out by board members, including GE's Jack Welch, one of the nation's most revered CEOs in recent memory. IBM's board was so enamored of Welch that it even considered proposing a merger, however briefly, going so far as to have one of its finance people run the numbers. Like everyone else, the finance executive felt that IBM would benefit from the merger because it would be getting Welch as well as the company. In principle, such an alliance would be GE-IBM, and not IBM-GE. Jack Welch was an asset that was difficult to overvalue, but he wasn't interested in the job. He had spent his entire career at GE, and he wanted to finish it in Fairfield, Connecticut, and not Armonk.

Burke enlisted two of the top executive search firms, Heidrick and Struggle and Spencer Stuart, to draw up a list of candidates. Using two firms for such a highly public search was unusual, and it reflected the board's desire not to overlook anyone. Between the two, every available and qualified CEO could be considered. Burke even made a courtesy call to Redmond, Washington, to take the pulse of the billionaire software magnate, Bill Gates. Gates, of course, was not interested in the job; he could never leave the company he'd cofounded. Nonetheless, Burke asked Gates to encapsulate what was wrong with IBM. Gates wasn't sure anyone could save the company, at least in its present form.

The short list quickly became very short: John Sculley, who was CEO of Apple; Larry Bossidy, AlliedSignal's CEO; George Fisher, fifty-two, CEO of Motorola (now the head of Kodak); John Malone, fifty, CEO of Tele-Communications; John Young, sixty-one, CEO emeritus of Hewlett-Packard; and Lou Gerstner Jr., fifty-one, CEO of RJR Nabisco.

John Sculley was an early front-runner until he proposed an IBM-Apple merger. Nobody on the board thought this was a good solution. When news of Sculley's candidacy leaked to the press, it put him in a potentially embarrassing spot with his own directors, even though he had followed protocol and quickly informed them of Big Blue's overtures. IBM eliminated him at about the same time he withdrew his candidacy.

Of all the realistic candidates, Larry Bossidy topped the list, the search committee's unanimous choice. He had recently become a star in the business world. A protégé of Jack Welch, he had risen to become the number two man at GE, and he had been credited with building GE's financial services and leasing businesses into huge profit streams. But Bossidy had not been at AlliedSignal very long. An IBM director asked Sculley if he could ask President Clinton to make a call to Bossidy to persuade him to take the job. Sculley did not think that saving IBM was a national priority, however, and he declined. Sculley did agree to call Bossidy himself, however, and though the AlliedSignal CEO was flattered, he gracefully turned the offer down. Bossidy felt that resuscitating IBM was next to impossible. He later described the ideal candidate as someone "who is thirty-five years old, knows computers, and can clone himself twenty-five times."

After Bossidy bowed out, Jim Burke must have realized just how unattractive the job was to almost anyone qualified to do it. IBM had suffered so many wounds, the task was so arduous, and the position was so high profile that the person who took it and failed probably would be forced to call it a career.

Why would anyone want this job?

With Wall Street and the press waiting anxiously for a puff of smoke from the Armonk spire, articles began appearing in *USA*

Today, the *Wall Street Journal,* and the *New York Times* speculating rampantly about IBM's search. Reporters concluded that the remaining contenders were Fisher, Young, and Gerstner. Later, the *Washington Post* astutely remarked that the search was a "media circus" of business luminaries who said they were offered the job and then turned it down.

Lou Gerstner, though always under serious consideration, was not IBM's first choice. When first approached by the search committee, he said that he was not interested in leaving Nabisco. Burke had sounded out Gerstner early in the recruitment phase. "That's not for me; I'm happy where I am," he reportedly told Burke. He had even told one of the recruiters that he didn't want to be interviewed on company time. When asked when it would it be convenient, he balked. The implication was that every waking minute was company time. Later, he said that he thought IBM was in some kind of "death spiral." But some insiders say that his early indifference was merely posturing. They claim he was avidly interested in the job, even when the board was actively courting other candidates.

IBM was desperate, and the candidates undoubtedly sensed this. After at least two others—and possibly more—had said no, Burke decided to aggressively go after Gerstner. He played the civic responsibility card. He told Gerstner that it was important to the economy, and it was crucial that IBM be restored to its position of prominence in the industry. The company was as important to the technology industry as Chrysler was to the automobile industry.

Gerstner's record was nothing less than impressive. He'd had only three jobs in his career, but they had been significant and progressively bigger. He had a stellar record as a consultant with McKinsey and Company, and had had an eleven-year run with American Express, where he rose to be president and the number two man under chairman James Robinson III. For the last four years he had run the food and tobacco conglomerate, RJR Nabisco, for Kohlberg, Kravis and Roberts, after Henry Kravis engineered the largest leveraged buyout in American business history.

Gerstner spearheaded a brilliant turnaround at Nabisco, according to some observers. Four years earlier, he had landed at the newly formed company handicapped with $29 billion in debt. Gerstner had whittled it almost in half. He'd sold off several divisions of the company. Anything superfluous to the business was jettisoned. He'd scotched the plans to build unneeded factories. He sold off a fleet of corporate jets and company apartments used by executives. He was a bottom-line CEO, paring fat right to the bone, but he was also a smart, cerebral manager. He scratched out $300 million in profit at Nabisco in 1992, the first black ink the company had seen in four years. Though his job at Nabisco was largely unfinished, perhaps he was the savior IBM so desperately needed. He was not a loveable manager. He fired a few thousand RJR employees. But Wall Street had a deep affection for unloveable managers.

Gerstner had never run a computer company, and this significant gap in his background could be interpreted either as a plus or a minus. Some observers—mostly industry insiders—thought it was a huge disadvantage. The computer business was like no other, the reasoning went. It moved at a faster pace than other industries; competition came from sharklike venture capitalists and Stanford or MIT graduate students and fanatics who thrived in the often quirky and murky world of digital chaos. It had a garage mentality. There was a strong argument to be made that an understanding of technology was a prime requisite. The very best leaders in the industry possessed both management and technical skills. And the technical company founders who didn't have management skills were usually smart enough to recognize their limitations. They hired a real boss to run their company.

On the other hand, IBM's problems were not intrinsically technical. The place was teeming with scientific brilliance. It was simply in a two-year funk, albeit a serious one. It had all the tools; it merely had performance anxiety.

Gerstner made no claims to computer knowledge, but he was passionate about management and business. He was known as a classic McKinsey type. Perhaps an outsider with little or no knowledge of the computer business could turn this inherent weakness into an advantage. IBM wanted a capable businessman with fresh ideas. Technological creativity was secondary. It also needed a CEO who could penetrate the corporate culture and change the company's insular way of thinking and operating. A strict disciplinarian. Someone who could return its focus to the customer. Gerstner was foremost customer-focused, and there were thousands of unhappy IBM customers in more than a hundred countries.

Jim Burke was convinced that Gerstner was the man to do it, but the candidate was still skeptical. So Burke asked Paul Rizzo, IBM's retired vice chairman, to walk Gerstner through some of the problems he'd face as head of the company. In early March, Burke arranged for Rizzo and Gerstner to meet secretly in a Washington, D.C., hotel room where the two talked for three and a half hours. Gerstner wanted to hear all of the grisly news before he seriously thought about leaving Nabisco. This was important to any candidate who had ever been involved in a turnaround. Often the problems are understated. Rizzo, however, did not make the task any less daunting than Gerstner suspected. He would have to contend with a complex infrastructure; "managing change" was a major priority.

After the meeting with Rizzo, there were two additional meetings at Heidrick and Struggle chief Gerry Roche's second home in Hobe Sound, Florida, a small but exclusive vacation community where, coincidentally, Gerstner also has a house. Hobe Sound is run with the efficiency and secrecy of an elite Fifth Avenue co-op. A private police detail discreetly patrols the streets in golf carts. Not everyone can own a home there. Provenance and status are more important than money; running a big company is a good credential. The Jupiter Island Club, with its intentionally antiquated decor, is where guests and former homeowners stay. Winter reservations must be secured well in advance, and the club must approve guests. You might see David Rockefeller spending the winter holiday on Hobe Sound, or former Secretary of State Cyrus Vance, or George Bush's family. Former New York Governor Averill Harriman once had a home there. Lou Gerstner now owns Harriman's home, as he likes to remind visitors.

During the first meeting, on March 12, Gerry Roche, Jim Burke, and Tom Murphy spent hours discussing with Gerstner Akers's plan to dismantle IBM into smaller units. Gerstner wasn't sure this was wise. It was an issue he'd study if he took the job. Many of Gerstner's concerns centered on how much leeway the board would allow him to make significant changes, especially in terms of top officials. It was a sensitive subject, but Gerstner wanted to choose his own board, as well. Obviously, some directors who were loyal to Akers would resign; others would be asked to leave. Gerstner, whose considerable ego was well known, was also clear that he wanted the twin titles of chairman and CEO. He wasn't sure he wanted to appoint a president, which would add another layer of management between him and the senior staff.

In short, Gerstner wanted free rein. At this point, the board had little choice but to agree. He might be the last best hope.

By now, Gerstner was strongly considering the challenge. He spent the next couple of weeks continuing to research IBM's woes. He read the recently published book *Computer Wars*, by Charles H. Ferguson and Charles R. Morris, which not only detailed IBM's decline but also analyzed some of the sea changes in the computer industry. It's difficult to imagine how he felt when he read the authors' comparison of IBM with the former Soviet Union. They wrote, "Now the Armonk *Nomenklatura* sits like a dead weight on the company's soul." His friends offered their counsel. Vernon Jordan, a golfing partner and bunkmate on fishing trips, encouraged him to take the risk.

During the last two weeks of March, when Gerstner's name was mentioned in almost every major news story as perhaps the leading contender for the IBM job, his boss, Henry Kravis, the nation's leveraged buyout king, asked him whether he was a candidate. Gerstner denied the press rumors. He told Kravis he was staying at RJR.

By the second Hobe Sound meeting, Gerstner was leaning toward yes, ready to discuss his pay package. He asked Joe Bachelder, his New York lawyer, to phone into the Florida meeting. Bachelder was the ranking heavyweight employment attorney with several of the nation's top CEOs for clients, including CBS's Michael Jordan. Pitching his services, he once had brazenly sent letters to the CEOs of the top hundred companies in the United States, suggesting that they might be underpaid. He was famous for drafting gargantuan pay packages for company heads. And he knew IBM was certainly not in a strong bargaining position. Among other demands, he told IBM his client wanted a signing bonus of $5 million, a first-year base salary of $2 million, performance bonuses of up to $1.5 million, and 500,000 stock options. He also wanted a commitment for guaranteed gains on unexercised Nabisco stock options of at least $9.9 million. Gerstner did not want to leave money on the table at his old shop.

At least one observer viewed the pay package with skepticism. Graef Crystal, a compensation consultant and newsletter publisher with a cynical view of excessive CEO compensation, said, "It looks like, when he comes to his own salary, Gerstner is pretty much risk-averse," he said. "It's set up so he does pretty well, no matter how IBM does. This is the hallmark of Joe Bachelder's negotiating style, which is to load you up with a pay package so that even if you fail you're going to be very rich. And if you manage to hit it out of the infield you'll be richer still. But you'll not be poor under any circumstances."

What particularly bothered Crystal was not the total pay package but the structure. It is customary that when a board brings in someone from the outside, they're required to pay a premium. It's almost like free agency in baseball. What was excessive was the $2 million in salary. Under the tax laws, anything over $1 million in base pay is not deductible. That's an immediate net loss to IBM of about $350,000. "There's any number of ways to get that compensation back in the package," Crystal says. "Forrest Gump could figure out ten ways in five minutes. So right away he sends out a signal that he's careless with the shareholders' money." Also, Gerstner required the board to pay for Bachelder's not insubstantial negotiating fee.

Considering IBM's pay to previous CEOs (Akers's base salary was $925,000 when he resigned, less than half of Gerstner's), the board appeared to be generous. It would be taking a calculated risk, and it wasn't the $20 million it would cost if things didn't work out. If Gerstner bombed, it would be an incalculable public relations disaster for IBM, and enticing a qualified replacement would be virtually impossible. The company would probably not survive in its present form.

Gerstner's career was on the line as well. If he failed, it might be his last job. If IBM recovered, he stood to benefit greatly—more prestige, not to mention the money. Instead of remaining an ordinary rich CEO at a large cookie and cigarette concern, he had the opportunity to become extremely wealthy selling computers and related technology. Now he would be joining a very exclusive club, the CEO of a Fortune 10 company.

Henry Kravis seethed when he heard the news. He'd believed Gerstner when he said he wasn't interested in the IBM job. Kravis shouldn't have been surprised, however. Four years earlier, when Gerstner left American Express to take the RJR job, he couldn't have been more abrupt. He gave his boss, CEO and chairman Jim Robinson III, less than a day's notice.

Lou Gerstner's formal coronation as the new leader of IBM was set for the Mercury Ballroom at the New York Hilton on the last Friday morning of March 1993. Joe Bachelder showed up late with Gerstner's contract. It wasn't signed until after the ceremony. For some, it was a strange, discomfiting scene. There were underpinnings of a kind of requiem. At center stage, outgoing chairman John Akers stood stolidly facing the audience—mostly financial analysts, reporters, and a few executives—his corporate game face all but gone. His resignation three months earlier, after a firestorm of criticism, had left him beaten and drained. Also somewhat relieved, according to some.

Those who were close to Akers, those who had watched his rise through the ranks to lead the company, felt badly. Here was an ex-Navy pilot who had landed jets on aircraft carriers at night, a warm, personable executive who had barely stumbled in his thirty-three-year career at IBM. He was the consummate Big Blue salesman, once the overseer of some 420,000 employees. The epitome of the blue suit, eager and ready to greet customers with an accommodating smile. But his can-do attitude had faded. Somehow his ship had lost its way, and he was the last man on the bridge. All of his efforts, all the technological strength of his research labs, all the intellectual might of his senior staff had not been able to reset the compass.

He introduced his successor indirectly, through Jim Burke, and shortly after he did, he slid quietly into a chair at the edge of the stage. For Akers, a tall and engaging man, it was a cruel and humiliating end to his career.

At the podium, waiting to assume command, was Louis Vincent Gerstner Jr., the first outsider to claim the executive suite.

To the technology pundits, it was a risky, unsettling choice. To reporters, it was an awkward moment. There were a lot of questions, and it was too early to hope for any substantive answers. During the press conference, as strobes bounced off the curtains, Gerstner vowed to "seek to create brilliant strategies and seek to execute them brilliantly." He couldn't be any more vague and McKinseyesque. It was a statement that he'd success-fully road-tested in the past. It was nearly the exact same thing he'd told an *Institutional Investor* reporter when he was the subject of a cover story five years earlier. "What's in the Cards for Lou Gerstner?" asked the headline of American Express's rising star.

Gerstner himself leaked the story of his IBM appointment to *Business Week* late in the magazine's production cycle. It was cer-tainly the biggest business story of the week. Over the weekend, editors ripped up the cover and replaced it with the Gerstner story. This wasn't exactly a surprise, because *Business Week* had published editorials calling for a change at the top of IBM.

Months earlier, the magazine had spearheaded a campaign that took aim at poorly managed public companies that some had termed "corporate governance by embarrassment." IBM had been embarrassed. Akers's removal was the validation of their views.

A few business writers and technology pundits applauded the appointment; Gerstner had a reputation for being a tough, disciplined, and demanding manager, just what IBM needed. Others were not as encouraged about the company's prospects, given the new CEO's background and lack of experience competing with lean, nimble, ambitious Silicon Valley firms.

Scott McNealy, the jovial CEO of Sun Microsystems, said, ". . . the shelf life of biscuits and technology is about the same. And they won't have to change the logo—International Biscuit Maker will still fly." It was a typically clever McNealy remark, uttered most likely without knowing much about Gerstner's considerable business skills.

If the new CEO could be accused of being technologically challenged, he was guilty as charged. But he wasn't the complete Luddite critics implied, certainly not like other CEOs who had never touched a computer keyboard. Gerstner said he had a computer on his desk as early as 1980, a year before the IBM PC had been introduced. When asked which brand, however, he said he didn't remember. He'd also been an engineering major as an undergraduate, although that was in the early 1960s, the prehistoric age of electronics. There weren't any microprocessor illustrations in the pages of his textbooks.

He was cautious when asked about his plans. "This is not going to be a short-term fix," Gerstner said. "This is going to take time." But in response to another question, Gerstner allowed that he did not intend to be a conservative leader. He'd had a reputation as a prudent risk taker, and he was not going to change that aspect of his management strategy. He quoted an aphorism he'd seen stitched on a throw pillow: "Watch the turtle. He only moves forward by sticking his neck out."

Dan Mandresh, a former IBMer and the chief financial analyst for Merrill Lynch for the past eighteen years, watched these proceedings and had only cursory thoughts about the meaning of the moment.

The king was dead, long live the king, thought Mandresh. That's life in the corporate world. It's just another change in another corner office. We'll see how this guy Gerstner performs.

Let's find out how far out his neck goes.

3

A New Man in Armonk

2

2ENWICH, CT—April 1993

Early in the morning on the first day of the month, Lou
Gerstner left his thirteen-room mansion in the tony, gated
Belle Haven section of Greenwich to report for his first official day of work at IBM. He told his driver that he wanted to stop
just a few houses away down Field Point Road. He would be calling for the seventy-nine-year-old Tom Watson Jr., the son of the
founder and the man who had guided the company into the
computer age some half century earlier. This modest meeting on
the drive to Armonk would make good newspaper copy—a company legend would be informally dispensing goodwill and
advice to the seventh chairman and CEO. Watson dutifully followed up the public relations gimmick with a letter to Jim
Burke, the IBM director who had headed the search. It read:

> Dear Jim,
>
> Gerstner is a superb selection. I rode to the office with him today
> as a courtesy. This was just his first day at Armonk. After twenty
> minutes of conversation I'm convinced that you and your
> committee have made a brilliant choice. IBM's problems can be
> solved by good leadership, and you and the committee have taken

the first major step. Congratulations and thanks. Please pass on my
feelings to the rest of your committee. As in many things in the past,
you have done a superb job.
    Sincerely,

    Tom

While this missive was a strong, syrupy vote of confidence,
there was little doubt about the pressure put on Gerstner (and
Burke for so strongly influencing the board's choice) to bring
IBM back to the land of the living. Burke wisely did not make the
letter public or share it with Gerstner until two years later, when
IBM was safely on its way to recovery.

It was probably just as well that Gerstner didn't read the platitudes from Watson. A vote of confidence from the son of the
company founder would not solve the company's problems.
Besides, he didn't need any more pressure. In less than thirty
days, the incoming CEO would have to introduce himself to tens
of thousands of skeptical IBMers worldwide, many worrying
whether they would have a job by year's end; face angry, perplexed, and demanding shareholders at the annual meeting; and
begin to sketch in a few new players in the senior management
boxes on his organization chart. He was an outsider; the honey-
moon traditionally afforded incoming CEOs would be much
shorter, given the pressing circumstances. At a cocktail party, no
less a luminary than Joshua Lederberg, the geneticist and Nobel
laureate, told Gerstner, "Do you know that you have one of the
great technical treasures in the world at IBM? You better not
blow it." David Wu, an analyst with S. G. Warburg, bluntly told a
trade journal, "Lou Gerstner will go down in history as the guy
who saved IBM or the guy who doomed it."

His first day on the job, John Akers introduced him to his
dozen or so senior managers, and he spent about a half hour
telling them what was expected. Since he didn't know any of
them, he explained that the scorecards were erased. He told them

he'd meet with them individually to review their businesses with them. He would not waste any time.

One of his first moves was to stabilize the ranks of the high-level managers. He immediately asked the IBM board to approve an incentive plan to keep valuable members of his workforce from fleeing the company before the new administration was in place. Gerstner had learned from experience four years earlier. When he took over RJR Nabisco after the infamous leveraged buyout, Gerstner had called to speak to some RJR officials, unaware that they had already departed. He had gone through a nightmarish few weeks as nearly all of the two dozen senior executives resigned en masse.

He could not afford to allow a similar exodus at IBM. Gerstner also was well aware that competitors had compiled lists of key IBMers they wanted to recruit. And those who had IBM stock options were tempting targets because they were "under water," or worthless, because the stock had dropped so precipitously.

So Gerstner decided to allow 1,200 managers the opportunity to rewrite their stock options at the current strike price of $47 per share. Or they could stay with the options they had. This was a magnanimous gesture, almost a gift, but with it Gerstner extracted a commitment. The old shares could be exchanged only at a ratio of two and a half to one, and they could be vested only after two and four years and only when the stock climbed back to at least $70 per share. (The two dozen top senior managers, who had large blocks, however, were not allowed to participate in this plan.) It was a fairly liberal plan, and it was not wholly original, but it wasn't the total giveaway that was common in so many small Silicon Valley firms.

The new CEO had barely settled in when he discovered that he was getting a couple of hundred e-mails a day from IBMers who sent their best wishes, complaints, and advice. This was part of Gerstner's homework for the first few weeks. It was refreshing to many IBMers that Gerstner actually read their messages, even though they didn't expect him to personally cope with the company's worldwide internal network. The antiquated intranet was a computer system known as PROFS (Professional Office System) where you needed to know a recipient's "node" (a designated location) as well as his user name (in his case RHQVM20/Gerstner). Gerstner's online companywide response: "You've told me that restoring morale is important to any business plans we develop. I couldn't agree more." Mostly, many first-line managers and the rank and file working in the factories felt encouraged; there actually was a functioning body in the corner office. Others worried about impending layoffs.

Gerstner suspected that at least some of Akers's management team was likely to be more a part of IBM's problems than its solutions, so he quickly wanted to bring in some high-level people who "understood his shorthand," according to one IBM executive. He had been considering two positions even as he was leaving Nabisco.

As a formerly disgruntled customer, he didn't need anyone to remind him that IBM's image was tattered. He wanted an executive who could take a fresh look at the company's advertising strategy and devise a completely new approach, a corporate makeover. Gerstner would look for someone he had worked with, someone who wouldn't be constricted by the company's past, an executive who could bring fresh thinking to the problem of restoring IBM's once respectable name.

He also needed a topflight communications officer, someone loyal, and someone he could trust to get his messages out to the press. Gerstner was now in a high-profile position where his image had to be constantly shaped and spun. Also, IBM had been pummeled with impunity by technology and business journalists for the past two years. Gerstner wanted an executive to deflect the incoming missiles, especially during the first year, when he would be scrutinized with particularly thick reportorial lenses.

Gerstner's decision to ask David Kalis to be his first hire as top communications executive was an easy, obvious choice. It surprised nobody who knew Gerstner. Kalis had molded Gerstner's image at both American Express and Nabisco for more than a decade. In fact, when Gerstner was introduced publicly as IBM's new chairman, Kalis already was working the Hilton ballroom press conference, making sure key journalists knew he soon would be following his boss from Manhattan to Westchester. He already was crafting his strategy, deciding which business reporters and media outlets would be given time with the CEO during his first months on the job.

Kalis is one of a handful of Gerstner confidants. Colleagues agree that he is one of the few people who can anticipate Gerstner's thoughts and needs and cope with his sometimes mercurial, impatient style. He understands Gerstner's short-hand. One company manager said that after two decades together they know each other so well, they even communicate with grunts. Nobody knows what they're talking about but those two. A former IBM communications manager said that Kalis is a clone of Gerstner, cut from the same strand of DNA, and often just as mercurial. He's the gatekeeper to Gerstner's office.

Physically, the mustachioed Kalis is a strapping and imposing man, somewhat narrower than Gerstner but a head and a half taller. He favors suspenders and monogrammed shirts. He grew up in a small town in Ohio, and he studied for the priesthood, first planning to become ordained as a Franciscan monk. Instead, he opted for a stint in the Peace Corps and lived in Asia before shifting his career to corporate pitchman. One former PR man who worked for him described him as brilliant but "a little inscrutable. It's hard to tell what's on his agenda."

Kalis is hardly a slick press agent. He prefers to work behind the curtain. Kalis is usually very reserved, very serious, though once he surprised a subordinate after a meeting by allowing that he col-lected classic comic books (Little Lulu and Walt Disney, in particu-lar), a revelation that seemed completely out of character. He wan-ders the hallways in Armonk, head hunched slightly forward, eyes straight ahead, like a horse with blinkers on, deep in thought, rarely returning a greeting to a passing colleague. The body language sug-

gests that he's unapproachable while he's perambulating. One former staffer was always puzzled by this. "How can the head of communications not communicate with his own people?" he wondered.
IBMers who now work for him explain this idiosyncrasy by claiming
he's shy, preferring to concentrate on the single critical task of negotiating access to Gerstner's suite.

When a particular journalist has earned Kalis's approval on a
number of pieces, Kalis has been known to boast gleefully about his
success. Preferential access to Gerstner may be the reward. On the
other hand, those who have written prickly stories about IBM or
Gerstner have been on the receiving end of angry phone calls from
him. "It's almost like the Nixon enemies list, the way they decide
who in the press is friendly to them, and who isn't," another former
IBM PR manager said of Kalis's style. "Kalis is very bright, very vin-
dictive," says a press officer who worked in the Armonk headquarters. "He reminds me of a young Dick Nixon during the McCarthy
era. He's very suspicious-minded, looking for a conspiracy behind
the bush. He has vendettas and agendas all the time." A business
editor agrees, saying that Kalis relishes the "cloak and dagger"
aspects of dealing with the press. Yet a former corporate speechwriter with a particularly bitter dislike for Kalis was forced to admit,
"If there's a better PR man than David Kalis, I don't know who it is."
Though he is rarely quoted as a "spokesman" for IBM, he is one of
the most powerful corporate flacks in America.

"David's very good at sensing where the land mines are," marvels a retired PR man who worked for him at IBM. He leaves
nothing to chance. Once Gerstner was scheduled to do a short
videotape after a morning breakfast meeting with education officials at IBM's offices in Manhattan. When it was determined that
it might make a nice effect to tape the CEO seated on the edge of
a large conference table, Kalis asked the crew whether it was
strong enough. After being assured there was no way the massive
piece of furniture could collapse under the weight of one man,
Kalis himself tested it by bobbing on the edge.

Inside the company, he is a cold, calculating manager, say
some former PR hands, and he can be incredibly rude and unfor-

giving. He has been known to banish underlings to unsung out-posts for a singular misdeed. "The guy is just like . . . the culture of fear," explained one IBMer. Every one of the dozens of high-level divisional press officers at IBM knows that there's an invisi-ble line—or a dotted line, as IBMers like to say—in the company's myriad organization charts that connects to Kalis's office.

While Kalis's image to some of his staff is that of flack-as-torpedo, he is also known as the boss's courtier. Kalis has an unfettered loyalty to Gerstner, and he's in awe of the CEO he serves. Gerstner tries to do the little things to acknowledge his faithful commitment, but it's a difficult effort. When Kalis's father was gravely ill, Gerstner would call Kalis periodically, ostensibly to find out how he was holding up under the strain. But if Gerstner and Kalis have anything in common it's that both tend to be socially reserved. It is telling that when Gerstner made those calls he never directly asked about Kalis's father's condition. He just simply called, something that the CEO does not often do in the workplace. He does not have the warmth that other CEOs like Jack Welch work hard to display. Still, one observer said that Gerstner was almost like a father to Kalis even though they are roughly the same age.

Like a dedicated Secret Service agent's duty to shadow the President, Kalis's mandate is to protect Gerstner from the media. He never forgets this, and implies as much to others. New hires for top PR slots in IBM divisions go through pro forma meetings with Kalis and are told to remember two things: first, if a press inquiry directly concerns Gerstner, Kalis takes charge personally, and second, "no surprises." He does not want to read bad news about IBM or his boss in the next day's newspapers, or worse, see it on the evening news before being told about it per-sonally. A former IBM spokeswoman said, "I remember him say-ing in management training school that you're going to get fired if you ever do anything that I don't know about that I should have known about." Kalis then informed the trainees that he'd just happened to fire someone in Atlanta for a particular PR transgression.

By the time Kalis introduced himself to his new staff at IBM, his predecessor, Mary Lee Turner, had been shipped off to China. Literally. She did a stint consulting for IBM in Beijing. She was no longer responsible for corporate communications policy.

Turner's sendoff might have been construed as crude behavior under previous administrations at IBM, yet it sent a clear signal throughout the executive offices. Kalis's appointment represented a huge discontinuity in the way that corporate communications were viewed internally at IBM. Kalis was the first PR *professional* to head corporate communications at IBM. Historically, Turner and her predecessors were marketing executives for whom the department had been a grooming post, a way station where executives on the rise would go and get their passports stamped "Armonk." But they were marketing people, and in IBM terms that meant salespeople, and they typically didn't have a whole lot of prior experience in any of the communications arts. They weren't versed in advertising, speechwriting, or public relations. There was always some marketing executive in the job, and he or she did not care much about it, and cared even less about the press. All they thought about was their next job in the company. This was the pattern all the way back to the Watson days.

Because IBM had a sorry history of releasing so much blather and hoping it would be construed as news, Kalis's strategy was to consolidate major announcements and drastically reduce the number of press releases. If there was something he really wanted to leak, he knew he could post it on the company's internal bulletin board, I-News. Some employee would be sure to call a friend in the press. But in the beginning at least, no news, for the most part, would be good news. Underpromise and overdeliver. It was a verse in the Gerstner scripture. No longer would just any new product announcement rate a hoo-hah laser show and outsized buffet in a midtown New York hotel ballroom. In order to rebuild credibility with journalists, less was more, Kalis concluded.

Kalis opened the door for two important interviews with Gerstner, the first with *Fortune* magazine, which recounted his first thirty days on the job, and the second, a six-month review with the *New York Times*. Gerstner told *Fortune*, "We are going to be very, very parsimonious about talking, and we are going to be maniacal about doing what we want to do." He was also equally terse in his answers. When asked if IBM's great strengths reduced his sense of crisis, he replied, "I don't have a sense of crisis." He also said that rightsizing was the first of four short-term priorities. (The other three were to spend more time with customers, figure out the big strategic issues, and restore employee morale and incentives.)

Marketing and branding, however, still constituted a pressing matter, if not a crisis, and this was one of Gerstner's strong suits. One of his first phone calls after leaving Nabisco was to Abby Kohnstamm, his former executive assistant at American Express in 1986 and 1987. Born in Los Angeles, Kohnstamm earned a degree in the East, at Tufts University. She also had two master's degrees, in education and business, from NYU. A friend and roommate who knew her early in her career said that Abby was definitely ambitious, but she and the other two roommates never thought Abby would go so far in her career. Kohnstamm had come from a privileged background, and she was memorable in that she whined when she didn't get her way. "Abby liked to be admired and well thought of," recalls the roommate. "I remember her mother for some reason as being kind of hard driving. Abby thought she was superior to all of us, and probably she was."

Kohnstamm joined AmEx when she was twenty-five, and had spent her entire career there. She held a variety of marketing positions as she steadily rose through the executive ranks. Her latest job was senior vice president for AmEx's entire cardmember marketing operation. Perhaps more than anyone else's, her thinking about brands dovetailed with Gerstner's. Also, she was well respected by Madison Avenue. Brad Johnson of *AdWeek* magazine described her as a "smart, aggressive marketer. In the world according to advertising agencies, there are good clients and there are bad clients. Abby is known as a good client."

Gerstner asked Kohnstamm if she might be interested in making the change from the charge card business to technology.

The terrain was enormous; the budget substantial; advertising, promotion, market research, sponsorships, trade shows. This would be a major leap in responsibility, holding sway over an annual budget of $500 million to $600 million. Of course, she'd also be under considerable pressure. Kohnstamm was interested, saying she'd give it some thought.

She is a quiet, unassuming and genial thirty-nine-year-old executive. She has a neat, short hairdo and favors conservative suits. She is not a particularly dynamic public speaker—she doesn't veer much from the prepared remarks—but she is a solid businesswoman and a sound thinker. An advertising executive who works with Kohnstamm described her: "Abby projects a really nonthreatening, plain exterior. You don't expect her to tell a great joke or an anecdote. My theory has always been that this is just a bit of camouflage to move her agenda forward. There's an iron fist in the velvet glove. She's very analytical and extremely creative, and when the big boys in the industry discover this, they're sort of shocked."

There was a small irony in Gerstner's choice for this job. Kohnstamm's father, Charlie Francis, once had it. Francis had been IBM's senior advertising executive for many years. He saw the glory and the collapse. Now he was semiretired, running a small consulting business in Chappaqua, New York. While Francis did not know Gerstner, he did know IBM. At first, he hesitated to encourage his daughter, wondering why she would want to move after fourteen years with the same firm. She had been doing very well at AmEx. It would be a risk. In the end, Kohnstamm recalled a Winston Churchill quote she had read while vacationing in England and visiting the Normandy beachhead, a reminder that the glory goes to those who take chances. She joined IBM two months after Gerstner did, on May 1, reporting to David Kalis. (Later, however, Gerstner would remove her group from communications, and Kohnstamm would report directly to him.)

With two executives on board whom he had known for most of his career, Gerstner had two fewer things to worry about.

The most critical hire, however, undoubtedly would be the CFO.

Gerstner needed someone who could help him assess IBM's mammoth worldwide businesses, scour the financials in much greater detail than ever before, and instill fiscal discipline in the company. (This search actually began at the same time Akers was ousted. The board also asked Frank Metz, his chief financial officer, to step down.) The search committee asked A. D. Hart, a partner at Russell Reynolds, a headhunting firm, to begin looking for candidates they could present to whoever would become the new chairman. Hart had scoured the top fifty U.S. companies for financial officers, and he had pruned his list to five possibilities.

One candidate who stood out was Jerome B. York, fifty-four, who had a long, distinguished résumé with a wide range of experience in manufacturing, engineering, and finance. Well known in Detroit business circles, York had held top positions at General Motors, Ford, and Chrysler. He had run the Hertz Equipment Rental division, and he had been managing director of Chrysler's Mexico operations for three years (becoming fluent in Spanish). He had risen to CFO of Chrysler, and he had played a key role in the company's closely watched government bailout and rescue from bankruptcy. In his last three years at Chrysler, York had overseen a $3 billion cost-cutting effort, supervised a $2.4 billion stock offering, put in motion the renegotiations of credit agreements with banks, and sold off some $3 billion in assets, including the sale of Gulfstream, the executive business jet maker, and a consumer finance division. In fourteen years at Chrysler, he had lived through two major industry downturns. He was accustomed to immersing himself deep in the muck of a company's problems, and he relished a challenge.

When York received the first call from Hart, he knew it was a job he could do, and one that he probably wanted, despite his long love affair with the automobile industry.

York flew to New York on April 13, spending an hour and a half at IBM's New York City offices meeting with Gerstner and Paul Rizzo, who had been asked by the board to return to IBM as acting CFO. Gerstner made it plain that he was looking for a CFO who had a lot of experience in restructuring a company, who wouldn't shirk from making difficult cost-cutting decisions, and most of all, who would be a key partner in turning a sick company into a healthy one.

Gerstner was impressed enough with York; he asked to meet with him for a second interview. Two weeks later, while on a business trip in Tokyo for Chrysler, York received a call from A. D. Hart telling him that IBM had narrowed the field to York and one other unnamed candidate. In a couple of days, Gerstner decided on Jerry York; the announcement was made on April 29.

York's owlish appearance—he is short and slightly built, with thinning hair—belies his reputation as a bulldog and a maverick. He has been married four times, his second and fourth time to the same woman. His personality is anything but diminutive. No polite fiction from York, he is in your face if you don't deliver. One former IBMer called him "that profane little Marine who gets the job done." He had survived and flourished in an intensely stressful atmosphere, working for an intimidating boss, Lee Iacocca. York operated the same way as Iacocca. He was result-oriented, a tough, take-no-prisoners manager, and he had a reputation for using fear as a motivator. This was a guy, Gerstner knew, who would have few reservations about taking a blowtorch to any part of IBM where it seemed necessary.

York's and Gerstner's reputations had been well documented in their previous jobs, so IBMers expected nothing less than severe discipline. The top two officers of Big Blue possessed the same degree of sagacity and instinct to cut to the nub of a given issue. Both Gerstner and York knew just how much debate was necessary before making a decision and rapidly implementing it.

Their management styles were not similar, however. While they were both nothing if not direct in their dealings with executives who reported to them, York's threshold of impatience was far lower than Gerstner's. Gerstner's style was to confront the issue first. He gave the executive in charge plenty of room to maneuver and a reasonable period of time to implement change.

If you failed Gerstner, reprisals didn't occur all at once. He began ignoring you at meetings. Then he sent a messenger to explain that things weren't going as well as he had expected. There was a strategic impulse at work here, even in dealing with his direct reports.

York, however, relied greatly on initial reactions and gut instinct. Jim Cannavino, IBM's chief strategist at the time, whose office was across the hall from York's, described his style as that of a baseball manager with a quick hook for any starting pitcher who gave up a few hits in the first inning. Said Cannavino, "If you make a bad first impression with York, even if you're a good guy, you're toast. He did not have the patience to go back and look a second time. He will eventually find the right guys, it's just that his bar is a little higher. And you lose a few guys, but it saves you a lot of time, and he doesn't have any time." Indeed, his scheduling habits were akin to Mussolini's. When York called a meeting, it began precisely at the appointed minute and never took longer than the allotted time. Unlike marathon meetings that IBM managers were accustomed to attending, York's were mercifully brief. He was short on rhetoric and long on extracting commitments. According to one former company official, he made sure that the division heads knew that "if they don't make their targets, I want them jumping through their assholes."

Along with his considerable skills and talent, York also brought profanity to IBM, which gave a sometimes amusing contrast to a company that always had been unfailingly polite. Once, after a particular litany of cursing, York looked around the conference room at a bevy of flushed faces. When he realized why they were blushing, he asked, "Doesn't anyone curse around IBM?" If it was anathema to IBMers, it was cathartic to York. There certainly was a lot to swear at in this company, at this time. Maybe if they threw a few expletives around, they could jump-start some somnolent brains. After Jerry York arrived, even women managers and executives could emphasize their viewpoints with a few well-chosen, well-timed four-letter words. And some did.

Born in Memphis, York grew up an Army brat, living in some fifteen different states. He originally wanted to become an engineer, and he set his sights on Cal Tech or MIT. But his high school girlfriend was the daughter of a West Point graduate, and her father—as well as his own—had a great deal of influence on him. He received an appointment to the U.S. Military Academy at West Point, and while at the Academy seriously considered becoming a career Army officer. But he fractured his spine in a gymnastics injury during his plebe year, and by the time he was a senior his injury was considered permanent, and left him physically unfit for an officer's commission and active duty.

So engineering looked like the safe fallback. York scrambled to get into graduate school, and he received a master's degree in structural engineering at MIT. The automobile industry beckoned; General Motors was king at the time, owning nearly half of the worldwide market. And while he enjoyed engineering, he quickly realized that he wasn't going to get near the top management of a company if he came up through the technology ranks. While working for GM's Pontiac division designing engines, he went to night school and earned an MBA from the University of Michigan. He then began to steadily scale the management ranks.

Like Gerstner, York had no experience in the computer business, but it wasn't much of a handicap. He could stroll through an IBM plant, inspect the assembly line, and know precisely what questions to ask. Technical guys at first would mistake York for a mere bean counter, or a messenger from Armonk, or simply "Lou's hatchet man." He played all of these roles, but much more. IBMers were taken aback when he asked questions that involved engineering. York didn't mind wending his way through the endless details of projects that only first-line managers dealt with.

About nine months after he arrived, he bluntly told Bruce Claflin, "I hate IBM executives." Claflin, a long-time IBM executive who was responsible for the launch and success of the ThinkPad laptops, was stunned by his candor and asked why. York explained, "Oh, you all look so pretty, and you have nice suits and white shirts, and your shoes are shined, and you give great speeches, and you have wonderful charts. But you don't know the goddamn details of your business." Claflin said, "At first I resented it, but then I thought about it, and I knew he was right."

York summarized a manager's business as simply as possible. If you had good products and solid revenues and you weren't making any money, then there was something wrong with your expense structure.

York was not going to be your typical IBMer.

He was certainly going to know the details of his business. It was York who began poring over seemingly small invoices and expenses that appeared to have limited or no impact on IBM's bottom line. Amy Wohl, an analyst and newsletter writer from suburban Philadelphia, recalled that one day an IBM consultant relations representative called on her, asking to examine her IBM invoices. She was mildly surprised that Big Blue was auditing someone whose company was as small as hers. What she didn't know was that York had called for a wide-ranging probe into IBM's hundreds of consultants and vendors.

Bob Djurdjevic, an ex-IBMer living in Phoenix who had several long-running consulting arrangements with the company, made the fatal error of placing York on his mailing list. Djurdjevic's newsletter, the *Annex Bulletin,* began appearing in the CFO's inbox. And York, ever meticulous, read everything. He thought Djurdjevic's analyses of Big Blue were either way off base or lacking in depth. York audited his newsletter. When he discovered that IBM was paying hundreds of thousands of dollars annually for this kind of insight, he refused to renew the contracts. IBM's senior executives resisted, however. They were afraid of Djurdjevic's influence and possible repercussions. A vice president in corporate headquarters at IBM said, "York went really crazy; why are we pissing away this money, he wondered?"

York was intent on examining everything and saving nickels wherever he could.

In late April, less than three weeks after Gerstner took charge, IBM reported $285 million in losses for its first quarter of 1993.

47

IBM's dividend was reduced by more than half, from $1.21 a share to 54 cents. The cut made shareholders unhappy, and IBM had to borrow to pay the reduced dividend. IBM's board could never consider suspending the dividend because the company's reach was so great. Large pension funds like CALPERS—which held the retirement investments of California's public employees—had huge positions in IBM, and their bylaws typically specified buying only the stocks of companies that paid an annual dividend. There were 770,000 IBM shareholders and it was the second most widely held stock in America. The stock was foundering in the $40s, and there was always the danger that a hasty sell-off by institutional shareholders could cause the stock to crater even further.

The first quarter loss had occurred under Akers's watch, but the news still sent a chill through the workforce (technically, the company was leaderless for that fiscal period). Gerstner hadn't been at IBM long enough to deliver any major pronouncements. But more red ink undoubtedly meant more layoffs. The rightsizing priority on the CEO's short list of initiatives meant that 25,000 and as many as 40,000 IBMers would lose their jobs by year's end.

In the past, the Watsons' policy of full employment was perhaps the most important part of the company's makeup. It was well known that IBM was the one American company that most duplicated the best elements of the Japanese concept of a cradle-to-grave job. In fact, many Japanese companies learned much from IBM in management-employee relations. In the postwar economy, when Japan became the most significant economic power in the Far East, workers never worried about downturns. It was management's responsibility to worry about business cycles. (Though in the late 1990s, Japanese businesses are beginning to see that full employment is no longer a viable philosophy.)

Now, in order to become competitive again, IBM would abandon this credo. Still bloated, it required a personnel chief who could help the company get through a difficult period. Gerstner wanted a progressive executive who understood modern human resources, one who could preside over the worries of the remaining workforce—one that was still the size of a pretty large city. IBM had never competed; now it was struggling to survive. Someone had to instill a new attitude that promoted aggressive, winning behavior within the workforce. It would take a combination of psychology and genius to create esprit de corps among the business units, which until this point were happier when they weren't talking with one another.

Now that Kalis, York, and Kohnstamm had been picked, choosing the head of human resources would complete Gerstner's first steps in reorganizing and reenergizing the high command.

Just before he left Nabisco, Gerstner had asked Gene Croisant, the company's chief personnel executive, to recommend someone who could fill the same role at IBM. Croisant, a former banker, sensed that Gerstner wanted to have someone with general business skills in that job. He suggested an ex-colleague, Gerald Czarnecki. Gerstner did not look much further.

Czarnecki (pronounced *char*-nuh-kee), fifty-three, was appointed IBM's new senior vice president of human resources a week after Jerry York. A banker with thirty years' experience, he had a broad management background. He had held a number of executive jobs in Chicago, Houston, and Mobile, Alabama. But his career break occurred when he worked for former U.S. Treasury Secretary William E. Simon. When Simon's group bought Honolulu Federal, Czarnecki was asked to run it. At HonFed Czarnecki was credited with transforming a lagging S&L into a profitable bank. He cut HonFed's staff by thirty-five percent and strengthened its consumer and real estate lending operations. He wasn't a personnel specialist per se, but he was more than a banker. He had the critical restructuring experience Gerstner was looking for in any outside hire he didn't already know.

Equally important, Czarnecki had an item on his résumé that appealed to Gerstner. He had a lot of experience as an IBM customer. He'd been a chief technology officer for several banks, and he'd lorded over their information technology, or IT, departments, as companies like Hewlett-Packard and Digital Equipment stole business away from IBM. He'd witnessed Big Blue's steep decline from the same vantage point as Gerstner.

Early on, Czarnecki described his job as "one of the harder human resource jobs in the country," probably an understatement, given the minions who were about to be hauled to the guillotine. His challenge was to "continue the downsizing of the organization and protect the values of the company."

He referred to his job function as "chief of staff." This was an ambitious description to some who felt that Gerstner's chief of staff was really Jerry York. Also, Gerstner purposefully did not appoint a president or chief operating officer, who in other companies traditionally would handle the day-to-day running of a large enterprise.

Czarnecki's assumption that this unofficial role—chief of staff—was pompous. In retrospect, his inflated view of his job description was a small indicator that things would not go smoothly for him at IBM. The headhunter's reference check on Czarnecki had been largely favorable, but there was a single caveat emptor that turned out to be telling. According to an IBM vice president at corporate headquarters who read it, one reference who was interviewed by the search firm thought Czarnecki had an outsized ego and probably wouldn't be a good fit with IBM. This likely wasn't enough of a red flag for Gerstner; his ego was somewhat outsized, and he was as much of an outsider as IBM could imagine. Also, the outgoing human resources head, Walt Burdick, was a fervent champion of old company values where the employee came first. It was important to Gerstner that IBM's personnel chief be a non-IBMer.

What Gerstner did not yet realize was that Gerry Czarnecki would be a problem almost as soon as he arrived at One Old Orchard Road.

Czarnecki's office was adjacent to York's. The decor was certainly unconventional for a senior executive. He had an immense "stand-up" desk, as if he were the kind of man who wouldn't be caught lazing around in an office chair. On the wall he had hung the kind of plaques with hokey aphorisms you see in the gift shops of rest areas along interstate highways. The kind with cheap wooden frames that read, "When the going gets tough, the tough get going." Or, "Quality is number one." If you've ever wondered who buys those kinds of signs, it is someone like Gerry Czarnecki. He had bad luck in another respect. It seemed that whenever York or Gerstner needed him most, he was away on a fact-finding trip to some IBM outpost. Meanwhile, Gerstner was desperate for a plan to reevaluate and restructure his workforce.

Czarnecki's quasi–New Age approach to the workplace made York crazy. The human resources head was someone who smiled, gently persuaded, and used whatever touchy-feely tactics he could muster to communicate with IBMers. York's management style was much more direct. He divided people into two categories: those who got the job done, and those who didn't. Once York was running a meeting with several top people when a secretary appeared at the door, waving to get Czarnecki's attention. It's standard courtesy, of course, to be excused for an important message. When Czarnecki rose to meet with her, he asked York for permission to step outside for a moment. York bellowed, "This is a meeting." Czarnecki sat down. It was clear who was in charge.

Czarnecki had a mandate to revamp human resources and build it into a vital organization that would attack IBM's corporate culture problems. Despite his pronouncements about the company no longer accommodating a philosophy of full employment—IBMers would have to prove their value to the company—Czarnecki was more like an old-style blue suiter than anyone might have imagined. Czarnecki wanted to preserve the warm and fuzzy management mentality that had pervaded IBM since it began selling butcher scales and mechanical tabulating machines back in 1914. Gerstner wanted morale restored, but he wanted it done quickly. Czarnecki was all psychologist but no drill sergeant. And IBM needed tough love.

He did not act swiftly on serious transgressions, and this infuriated York and Gerstner. One deficiency quickly discovered

51

through the audit staff was that IBM was losing as much as a couple of hundred million dollars a year through internal fiscal chicanery—employees who were receiving kickbacks from outside vendors. This is a constant threat to large corporations, and IBM still had a lingering reputation among hundreds of vendors for being a soft touch. Before Gerstner and York arrived, IBM never had the need to get competitive quotes on many jobs, and if purchasers did ask vendors for bids, they didn't feel compelled to award a contract for the lowest bid. This left a lot of room for illegal gratuities. When a Big Blue purchasing agent called a vendor, you could almost smell the price rising through the phone. Sometimes it was IBM's own fault. In the pre-Gerstner days, a former IBMer and now a meetings-and-conventions contractor said he once tried to return a $20,000 overpayment, but IBM resisted because of the paperwork involved. For IBM to accept the refund, somebody in the company would have to take the responsibility for the overpayment. It was a mistake that could be costly in a performance review. So nobody was willing to be dinged for such a small amount of money. He was told to just keep it.

With IBM still suffering rampant losses from kickback schemes, it wasn't difficult to uncover midlevel IBM managers who had become confederates with longtime suppliers. Corruption had reigned for years under the old regimes. Says a former senior finance official, "You would catch somebody stealing and the HR organization would say, 'Well, we ought to just pat this guy on the hand and let it go at that.' My experience has always been, when you catch somebody stealing, you fire them. If you don't, the rest of the organization thinks you're stupid, and anyone who's stealing says, 'Well, I guess I can keep doing it.'"

Czarnecki could not bring himself to act quickly and fire those who were guilty of such transgressions. It was as if he were running a twelve-step program for IBMers who were chronic thieves. If this was his way of "protecting the values of the company," they weren't the same ones York and Gerstner wanted to protect.

Czarnecki was more like a friendly salesman, or a "gregarious loan officer," according to one IBM vice president. "Ultimately, there was no *there* there," he said. Still, it took a year before IBM showed Czarnecki the door. Just before his resignation was made public, a press officer made a courtesy call to Czarnecki's office to let him know that it might be useful to draft a list of accomplishments; reporters would be calling within minutes after the announcement was faxed to the business press. Czarnecki couldn't think of *anything* significant. It was difficult to come up with the standard polite response for those press-release-driven personnel changes. "I don't think this job maximized my strengths," Czarnecki said. Gerstner was equally terse in a short statement he released to IBM's managers: "Gerry is a high-energy executive who probably will be much happier out-side . . . IBM."

The reality was something else. In the end, Gerstner and York had not been able to get Czarnecki to actually *do* what they thought needed to be done. Czarnecki was just a very nice guy, too nice for the new IBM.

4

First Months, First Moves

It was hardly good timing. Gerstner had been on the job for only twenty-four days. And Florida was not the best choice of venues, because of a greater likelihood of a hostile audience, but it was too late to change. The crowd was predominantly gray-haired. Many attendees were distraught IBM retirees whose pensions were wrapped up in the company's performance. So when IBM senior officials and directors flew south for the April 26, 1993, annual meeting, they knew they were about to face an unhappy group of investors. And there were a lot of them. A crowd of 2,300 shareholders—triple the normal turnout—awaited the arrival of Gerstner and the team of directors who had caused so much distress over the past two years. Red ink had been running on IBM's quarterly financial reports for nine straight quarters. The stock price, which had once hit the $170s, was now $48.

At the Tampa Convention Center, each stockholder passed through an airport-style metal detector, and given the situation, this normal precaution probably was a cause for relief to IBM officials. A protestor who walked the convention floor with a sign reading "IBM—I've Been Mugged" was quickly hustled out the door by security guards. By the 10 A.M. start, the atmosphere was contentious as shareholders anxiously waited for a chance to seize a microphone for the Q&A part of the meeting.

Gerstner's opening speech offered little in the way of plans or strategy; he hadn't yet wrapped his arms around the company's problems. He talked a lot about the "pain," and he said he understood their pain, and he regretted it, and he would do something about it. He sounded like a cautiously upbeat politician, and this was at least partly by design since IBM's head speechwriter at the time was Bentley Elliot, who had run the White House speechwriter's office for Ronald Reagan.

The meeting lasted two and a half hours, and the Q&A portion was particularly brutal. Gerstner, of course, wasn't the cause of the audience's rancor, he was the only convenient target. "IBM's stock no longer provides for your old age," shareholder Bill Steiner told Gerstner, "but it certainly hastens its arrival." One woman noted that IBM's stock had actually dropped a few points after the new CEO had arrived. Replied Gerstner, "I'm sorry that my selection didn't raise the price of your stock—and now my stock price. I'm what you've got, at least until they decide they don't want me anymore."

At this annual meeting, Gerstner revealed perhaps the most important strategic decision of his first year. When asked by a shareholder if he would continue Akers's plan of splitting IBM into a group of smaller companies, he said no. While he had already told his senior executives, this was his first public announcement of that decision. And it wasn't an easy one. Gerstner admitted that he was by nature a "decentralist." He believed in autonomy among divisions, to a degree. As long as a business strategy was sound, he didn't tamper with a division that was performing.

It was the first major departure from previous IBM strategy, the first real difference between his and Akers's view of where the company fit in the technology universe. Gerstner believed that IBM could marshal great strength from its global presence, its sheer size.

Many observers, even those who disagreed with the abrupt reversal of course, think Gerstner's first major business decision was also his most important one.

Two years earlier, when Akers had announced the formation of the "Baby Blues," he hoped that IBM's parts might resemble the "Baby Bells" that remained after the forced breakup of AT&T, which occurred in the mid–1980s. The spun-off regional phone companies had thrived independently.

Wall Street had endorsed Akers's breakup plans, too. How could it not? IBM had lost market share and its competitive edge in just about every one of its businesses, even its flagship mainframe computers. The strong divisions would survive. Weaker ones could find partners. Wall Street investment firms smelled cash in situations like this. Their M&A departments stood to earn large fees.

More important, the Baby Blues were heartily endorsed by IBM general managers in the United States who felt crushed by the weight of the company bureaucracy. They longed to run their own fiefdoms. (IBM's foreign units operated with near total autonomy.) When Akers informed them they would be semiautonomous, the general managers immediately dropped the word "semi." There was a sense of euphoria that could only be compared with Martin Luther King's famous speech, recalled an IBM manager. We are free, free at last, free from the bonds of Armonk. Executives in IBM divisions felt that the dictates from corporate headquarters only interfered with their businesses. If you needed funds for plants or advertising or new hires or to develop a new product, only then did general managers want to cope with the corporate hierarchy. The powers in Armonk controlled their budgets, not their business strategies.

There was a good deal of support for these "independent silos" because IBM's divisions were famously territorial. Say there was a medium-sized company whose CIO needed a technology solution somewhere between a stack of servers and large-scale enterprise computing. The CIO might find himself pitched by two different IBM divisions. In such cases, the mainframe division's sales force was often competing with the server division's sales force. They did not want to acknowledge the existence of each other because there were so many overlapping products and only so many customers. The divisions were forced to vie with one another for business. Factionalism was the logical outgrowth, and it existed within IBM to a far greater extent than most other companies.

As with AT&T's Baby Bells, the plan was to divide the company into separate business units—the Baby Blues—each with its own sales force, its own marketing staff, its own R&D, its own administration—even its own name. They would become, in effect, IBM's stepchildren. Operating independently, they could eventually float their own IPOs, and even behave as if they were feisty Silicon Valley start-ups.

It was not widely known, but the Baby Blues plan was all but official. Akers's strategy to decentralize IBM already was well under way when Gerstner took over. Some IBM units already had disconnected themselves from the mother ship, at least in name. The printing division was renamed "Pennant." The IBM storage systems division, which manufactured disk drives and magnetic tapes, became "AdStar." In San Jose, where the division was located, the giant sign with the blue eight-bar IBM logo had been removed. It was replaced with the AdStar logo. A small sign under it read, "An IBM Company," as if it were an afterthought. This was a conscious effort to remove the identification with IBM. With all IBM's financial woes, some divisional leaders felt its name was more of a liability than an asset.

Under Gerstner, the signs were removed. These companies were IBM, and IBM only, once again. He would unify Big Blue.

When they returned to Armonk after the annual meeting, both Jerry York and Lou Gerstner knew the remaining eight months of 1993 were going to be arduous. They had to take the first decisive steps that could begin their rescue operation and stabilize the company. They planned to cut expenses through layoffs, restructure internal finances, close plants, sell off any superfluous business units, and establish credibility once again with key customers. Changes would also be made on IBM's board of directors.

Their work was broadly divided into two areas. York was responsible for the expenses, and Gerstner took charge of the top line.

York mainly concentrated on a single task: cost restructuring. To do this, he had to focus on analyzing IBM's individual business units. Not only would he spend the next eight months trimming the company's legendary fat, he'd identify businesses that weren't core to IBM and sell them off. Bolstering IBM's cash position was paramount.

The CEO was the company's top salesman, so it was incumbent upon Gerstner to repair bonds with former customers, forge relationships with new ones, and instill in his workforce the belief it could succeed once again. He did a lot of listening, not just to customers, but to the legions of analysts and technology pundits. His philosophy was sparse but his calendar was jammed. He spent sixty percent of his time with customers. Gerstner displayed behind his desk a maxim from a John le Carré novel: "A desk is a dangerous place from which to view the world." This was a major departure from John Akers's modus operandi. Akers had been more of a courtly chairman. He presided over board meetings and had lunches with senior executives. He did not log anywhere near the time in company jets that Gerstner did.

Jerry York made an extended road trip as well. His was not to customers, however, but to IBM outposts.

Between May and July, York scoured the numbers of all the business units. He was dismayed with what he found. IBM's operating margins had been reduced from fifty-five percent to about forty percent. Operating expenses were out of control. Coupled with R&D, the company was spending eleven percent more than its rivals. Benefits, warranty, and purchasing expenses were rising. Many of the write-offs were due to excess inventory. IBM's own data processing expenses were more than triple the industry average—seven percent versus two percent. This alone was embarrassing.

York decided that not only was an overhaul of IBM's finances necessary, but also a complete reengineering of the business processes of the various units. One of the first tasks was to complete a benchmark study that compared IBM's expenses with competitors. Each division's figures were pitted against the company's principal competitors. For example, services was up against Electronic Data Systems; the storage division was compared with EMC; microelectronics with other chip producers like Intel and Motorola; the PC Company with Dell, Gateway, and Compaq. More than forty competitors were used in the benchmark studies.

The benchmark results indicated IBM had an expense-to-revenue percentage that was far too high—forty-two percent. York needed to shave nine points off that figure. The total SG&A and R&D component was $26.8 billion in 1992, and this needed to be reduced to $20 billion for IBM to be competitive. In sum, IBM was too fat by nearly $7 billion. The goal was to reduce expenses by this amount in three years.

At the study's conclusion, more than thirty discrete reengineering projects in elevent different categories were initiated. The categories included everything from hardware and software development, production and procurement, human resources and information technology, as well as finance. The vice president of quality and reengineering, Wilson Lowery, spearheaded the program. Results were visible early, and the speed with which cost reductions occurred surprised everyone.

"IBM had a reputation for having a strong finance organization," recalled York. "And that's what I found when I joined the company—extremely bright, capable individuals. However, some were part of the solution, and some were part of the problem despite their capabilities. What do I mean by this? Well, some were just too caught up in preserving the status quo for their individual units. That is, they didn't have a total corporate point of view. Data submitted to Lou and me early on frequently would be presented in the best possible light with problems buried in the company's intercompany pricing system. Some individuals just didn't seem to want to get to the bottom line and fix problems, at least not in their own units."

The York prescription meant that he needed every business unit's buy-in to the cost-cutting plan. Those who ignored it did so at their own peril.

An IBM vice president recalled one revealing Saturday morning meeting in Armonk. York had gathered his top finance people together, ostensibly to review the current health of the company and unify a cost-cutting strategy that could be presented to Gerstner. As soon as he walked into the conference room, the manager marveled at the contrasting scene. The IBM finance guys were dressed casually, in slacks and open-collared shirts. York showed up looking like an aging biker from *The Wild One,* the 1950s Marlon Brando movie about a motorcycle gang. He was wearing blue jeans and a tight-fitting black Harley-Davidson T-shirt with a pack of cigarettes rolled up in the sleeve. This, uh, was the CFO of IBM?

York listened attentively to his subordinates' analyses; they had carefully run the numbers on their calculators. They were coming up with plans to shave a few bucks from this project, a few from that unit. There were a couple of different scenarios. York didn't need to hear this because he already knew what had to be done. From his preliminary workup, he told them, IBM was bloated beyond their worst guesses. We have to swallow the whole lousy-tasting pill almost all at once, he said. We must cut at least $6 billion out of its expenses over the next three years, maybe as much as $7 billion. And we may have to do it in even less than three years.

It was a memorable scene, said the IBM vice president, who had been with the company for several years. York's procedure was yet another departure from the old IBM, where John Akers and CFO Frank Metz politely discussed "problems" with "soft sales" in IBM's foreign units, known as the "geos," for geographies. There would be more meetings and more grim looks, and then nothing would happen. Here, a biker rides in on a Saturday morning with a new fiscal plan, plops it on the conference table. He tells a bunch of straight-arrow bean counters at the world's largest technology company what needs to be done. This was a

Jerry York imperative. You guys want to debate it, debate it. But from my point of view, there's no debate.

Meanwhile, with IBM's stock price floundering, Gerstner knew that he had to get the company to begin marching to the cadence of Wall Street. Shareholder value was one of his first priorities, and Gerstner's work style reflected a fresh approach to IBMers. "Lou and the senior team arrive in Armonk really early," said one former manager. "They have read all the morning papers, they have looked at all the overseas dispatches, they're in tune with the marketplace. The stock market opens at 9:30 a.m. in New York. By the time the market closes late in the day, these guys are going home. They've already put in their eleven or twelve hours by 5 o'clock because their day starts really early. And that's significant in the following way: Akers was the apotheosis of the IBM culture of the salesman. He was definitely a nine-to-five guy. He marched to internal IBM rhythms. Meanwhile, the primary responsibility of a CEO to [his] shareholders was being completely ignored under Akers, and it was a disaster."

By mid-July of 1993, after absorbing all the figures from IBM's vast network of worldwide business units, Gerstner had a fair idea about IBM's fiscal strategy for the remainder of the year. Another large block of employees had to go. A buyout program approved by the board earlier in the year had already authorized cutbacks of 40,000 to 50,000 workers. Now another 35,000, mostly from foreign operations, would be asked to leave.

The announced layoffs were different from the "voluntary" surgical strikes, a few thousand at a time, performed by John Akers. Even those had been difficult. For Akers, it had been "like Luther leaving the Catholic Church and starting the Reformation," said Bill Grabe, a former manager for marketing and services at IBM. "Are you going to be the first CEO in a long line of guys who says full employment is over?"

Gerstner couldn't afford any further slide in company morale. He wanted it known that one big swing of the scythe was preferable to the "Chinese water torture" tactics—a phrase that popped up constantly—of the past regime. Still, in a July 27, 1993, memo to IBM employees, Gerstner wrote, "I know you have heard this before, and each time you thought it was the last time. . . . I know these actions may be bigger and deeper, and may take longer, than many of you anticipated. They certainly have kept me awake at night."

Contrary to what many think, Akers fired far more IBMers than Gerstner, as many as three times more employees. It just seemed far more Draconian under Gerstner because he made the biggest single slices. Also, Akers was laden with the burden, and subsequent guilt, for dismantling a system—a corporate dictum that was built around the concept of "respect for the individual." Akers's early buyouts were generous by Gerstner's standards; longtime employees had received as much as two years' salary. In 1993 under Gerstner, twenty-six weeks' pay was the maximum payout, and IBM paid for only up to six months of additional medical insurance.

The new round of layoffs also was less sensitive than the past ones, perhaps because of Gerstner's penchant for urgency. There were pockets where IBM's efficacy seemed absurd. Steve Schwartz, a retired senior vice president, said that his daughter was excessed when she was eight and a half months pregnant. She was a top performing IBMer, and she had just received a cash award from the company for her marketing work on the Coca-Cola account in Atlanta. Five days later she received a pink slip. Another IBMer got his layoff package while he was in the hospital. He couldn't read it, however. He was comatose from a brain tumor.

Not only did employees have to go, so did the level of benefits. Those who survived the cutbacks were subject to austerity measures. Pay increases were reduced, cash bonus awards—once an almost guaranteed part of employee paychecks—appeared far less often, and employees were asked to contribute more to their health plans.

Cutbacks in health plans were particularly emblematic for many long-term employees. It was a signal difference from the

IBM welfare state of yesteryear. One IBMer, who put in fifteen years with the company and retired at the end of 1996, was particularly bitter about this. His wife had cancer, and the plan no longer reimbursed a wig expenditure due to hair loss from chemotherapy treatments. "There were other reductions, and the cost of the health care plan is going up again," he complained. "We're getting less care. People like me were made promises by a company, that if you put in so many years, certain things will happen. And now these promises are eroding, particularly in areas where we're most vulnerable. We're getting older, and we're getting sick. So it's getting hard when you have to spend $400 for a wig, and you're not getting any money on it."

The payroll cuts gave Jerry York a glimpse of a much better financial picture for late 1993 and early 1994. But he still hadn't attacked IBM's arcane internal business practices and its convoluted accounting system.

In 1990, Akers had implemented a fairly elaborate "transfer-pricing" system within IBM. This was an arrangement where the buying and selling of goods and services from within the divisions was done as if each unit were independent. IBM had become notorious within its own ranks for internal price gouging. Overcharging one another became an intramural sport at IBM, but there was one important motive behind the practice. A division upped the prices it charged so it could make its own sales goals, even if they came at the expense of another IBM unit's bottom line. This created more problems than it solved, mainly because IBMers found that the easiest way to make money was to get a better transfer-pricing arrangement with another IBM unit. Put simply, it turned out to be competitive, grossly inefficient, and expensive. To an honest accountant, it was a disaster.

The transfer-pricing system was so Byzantine, it took York three or four months to fully understand it. He called it the "wooden nickels" deal. It meant there had to be an agreed upon pricing mechanism when one IBM unit did business with another. For example, if the AS/400 division needed to buy parts from the Microelectronics division, a price had to be negotiated. York was furious because he knew it didn't do a thing for IBM's overall P&L statement, and that an enormous amount of time and energy went into the negotiations for these pacts. A company vice president recalls, "York said, 'Now wait a minute, we're all working for the same fucking company.'"

Transfer-pricing made it difficult to ascertain a given division's actual financial performance, as well. For example, the PC Company had a joint venture with a large Japanese electronics manufacturer to supply computer parts, and the partnership continued to lose a lot of money. But the way it was structured, the losses were absorbed by IBM Japan rather than the PC Company, obscuring the true bottom-line contribution of the PC Company. Thus, the PC Company's balance sheet appeared to be healthier than it was.

York reformed the worst aspects of the financial reporting system. Intercompany price markups and the bickering that accompanied them were ended or greatly reduced. IBM Japan still does warranty work for the IBM PC Company, for instance, and it bills the work appropriately. "From time to time, you'll get somebody who has the feeling that the billing isn't fair," York said. But at least he was able to accurately pinpoint nonperforming units.

The European portion of IBM's business gave the company even more headaches. Some operated with complete disregard for modern business principles, with sweetheart quid pro quo deals that cost IBM large amounts of money in needless interest payments. Since IBM had so many banking customers, the banks insisted on keeping IBM on as a borrower, even when it wasn't necessary. The deals were implicit: *If you pay off the loans, we won't buy any more computers from you.* When cash flow improved, IBM never bothered paying off the loans. "They had just fallen into this habit over the years," a former official said. "They didn't want to offend the banks by repaying the loans."

What York found out about bookkeeping techniques in IBM divisions in other countries was even more alarming. IBM had independent accounting firms all over the world examining the operations of every foreign division. But York kept getting insufficient data. He would get an income statement from IBM Brazil, for example, and it would have just four numbers on it: revenue, cost of goods sold, expenses, and profit. Any CFO, especially one like York, if he's going to understand a business needs a lot more detail.

Another problem was reporting speed. The geographies took forever to send Armonk quarterly results, and this was one reason Akers had been blindsided. He didn't know until it was too late when the numbers were bad. And more than half of IBM's revenues come from abroad. In one meeting at Armonk in the early 1990s, Akers had been asked to approve a press release that included the fact that IBM lost $2 billion in Europe. Astonished, Akers peered over his half glasses in front of twenty or so of the company's highest-ranking executives and asked the writer of the press release whether there was a typo. He was hoping there were fewer zeros, perhaps. There were not. CFO Frank Metz, whose responsibility it was to keep the chairman informed about such matters, said, "We were a little light in Europe." It was a defining understatement of old Big Blue.

The income statement was compiled on a consolidated basis about four weeks after the end of the quarter, but the balance sheet that had the updated details wouldn't arrive for more like six weeks. That left what could be a critical two-week gap. If an analyst asked about certain balance sheet figures during that period, they were simply unavailable. Of the slow reporting schedule, especially from the foreign divisions, York said, "This can be a bit risky, because when you get the balance sheet, if you find an error on it, there is the possibility that fixing this balance sheet error might affect the income statement. So you kind of hold your breath and hope nothing material will surface when the balance sheet comes together." Gerstner and York demanded all the statements at the same time, and got them earlier. This kind of urgency in bookkeeping was something new among the divisional finance departments.

Today, the system is not without problems. Though much improved, the procurement machinery is still complex and often frustrating. Much of this stems from the fact that the fiscal controls are now so stringent that IBMers must submit some of the smallest purchases to a supposedly simplified procurement process. Many new hires must attend two-day seminars, where the intricacies of the "simplified" purchasing system are explained. Once, an aide who attended such a seminar was asked by the executive he supported what, if anything, he learned. "If I ever have to buy a pencil for IBM, I'm in deep shit," he replied.

Even experienced finance managers are sometimes overwhelmed by the new system, wondering why they received "escapes"—electronic notices that indicate entry errors—on their MSREQs (requisition forms) or POs (purchase orders). The same aide who expressed wonder at the procurement seminar said he tried to buy a new color printer for his office through the IBM internal purchasing mechanism. After coping with a number of escapes that perplexed a finance worker for five months, he had no success. Finally, his secretary suggested he call CompUSA. He charged a $399 Hewlett-Packard model on his credit card, perhaps saving IBM $200 or more. It was delivered in three days.

When Lou Gerstner was not meeting with customers, he was polling industry experts to delve into key issues facing IBM. Two particular meetings held on the same day made an impression on him.

In early July of 1993, Gerstner met with Sam Albert, a long-time IBMer, now in his sixties, who had retired in 1989 after thirty years with the company. Back in the 1960s, Albert sold IBM computers to Nathan's Famous in Brooklyn to manage its hot dog inventories. Albert was still loyal to the company and yet was considered a sensitive, constructive critic.

Now he appeared to know everybody important in the industry. If there ever was an award for "most frequently quoted" IBM watcher, Albert would win with a show of hands. Working from his home in Scarsdale, New York, he still earned modest consulting fees—less than $30,000 annually—from IBM, according to company sources. When Big Blue hiccuped, whenever there was an executive firing or restructuring, or some crisis in a foreign division, reporters called Albert. He was always ready with an incisive, pithy comment. When senior executives left IBM for new jobs, they sent their updated résumés to Albert in case the *Wall Street Journal* called. If you were looking for a high-tech job, you called Sam Albert. Some days he felt like a headhunter.

The new CEO obviously was an attentive listener. Albert recalled that Gerstner took five pages of notes in their short meeting. When Gerstner asked Albert what he thought was IBM's gravest problem, he had a ready reply. IBM had been telling customers about "reads, speeds, and feeds," a reference to the technical data from the old punch card days. When Gerstner appeared confused, Albert explained that IBM's customers didn't want to be fed jargon and the endless statistics about computer performance. IBM had not changed its selling paradigm in twenty years. Horsepower was long since irrelevant. Customers wanted IBM's help to solve their IT problems; they wanted solutions. Gerstner already understood that. He told Albert that just a day or two earlier, he had visited the Yorktown Heights labs, where a young researcher tried to impress him with the technical data of a new product. Gerstner confessed that he didn't understand a word. He could have been listening to a spiel on reads, speeds, and feeds.

After meeting with Albert, Gerstner sought advice from three important financial analysts who tracked IBM for Wall Street; Dan Mandresh from Merrill Lynch, Steve Smith from Paine Webber, and Steve Milunovich from Morgan Stanley (who would succeed Mandresh at Merrill after Mandresh retired). Each of these three had the kind of clout to move Big Blue's stock up or down, depending on their reports.

When they found themselves in Gerstner's conference room, they discovered that the CEO was going to be asking the questions, and not the other way around, which was the usual protocol.

Gerstner, notepad ready, wanted to know what they thought of the company. He did not want to dwell on past mistakes, missed opportunities, blown markets. What was their perception of IBM now? What were its strengths, its weaknesses? Where was the business going? It was as if he were a McKinsey consultant once again, picking the experts' brains.

Steve Milunovich wasn't shy about his opinions. He told Gerstner he was disappointed that IBM no longer was a role model. It no longer was an industry leader. It seemed awkward and strange to Milunovich that he never called IBM to take the technology industry's pulse. If he wanted to explore where the IT business was headed, he called on IBM's competitors—Sun, Cisco, and Hewlett-Packard. He was always headed for Silicon Valley or Boston or Austin. Someplace other than Armonk. "IBM had surprisingly little to say about trends in the industry, and they weren't first in new product categories," Milunovich said.

Of course, the three analysts did not want the meeting with Gerstner to be an overlooked opportunity to do research for their own reports. They asked Gerstner what moves he would make within the business units. Gerstner balked. Steve Smith recalled Gerstner complaining, " 'You guys, all you want to do is talk about IBM's internal plumbing. We don't need to talk about the plumbing, that's our issue.' He got a bit rankled about Wall Street's focus on the way IBM is structured."

But Smith insisted this was a significant point. He argued that IBM had the vainglorious habit of protecting its businesses from one another. For example, Smith said, all the software IBM wrote for mainframes could also be used on Unix machines and other platforms. IBM had the best database technology in the world, despite Oracle's and Sybase's taking advantage of holes in the marketplace. What IBM was doing was protecting its hardware business by not making database software available on these other platforms. This tired business model—where a company was afraid to eat its young, where everything was proprietary—no longer worked in today's technology world. Smith believed IBM had to have a business where every individual unit thrived on its own merits. It was advice that Gerstner eventually followed.

Gerstner revealed very little of his own plans—he was still fact-finding, after all—but he did say some things that hinted at his thinking. First, he couldn't believe there weren't advantages to IBM's being big and global. Milunovich said, "You certainly had the sense that he was thinking, 'IBM has some advantages, how do we start leveraging them?'"

Gerstner suspected that IBM had lost its competitive edge because it was slow to market. It wasn't moving products quickly into the pipeline. This tardiness stemmed from IBM's long-standing policy never to ship anything until it was absolutely bug-free perfect. High quality is a wonderful ideal, but Big Blue's competitors weren't tinkering with their products for as long.

This practice did little to build credibility with IBM's own sales-force, which continually made promises that it had to reneg on. IBM's sales force was hopelessly muddled, especially abroad. It was structured in an antiquated fashion that required representatives to deal with every facet of the product and services line.

After Gerstner returned from several business trips where he polled his customers, he realized that while IBM had hordes of salespeople, it had no specialized sales force. Each unit had its own sales force; each foreign subsidiary did, as well. Despite the company's once hallowed reputation for salesmen with glossy wing tips who knew the names of their customers' children, they had precious little knowledge of the products they actually sold.

Though the AS/400 midrange computer had been one of the company's big successes, there weren't that many people in the organization worldwide who really knew the machine and how it rated against its competitors. If a customer in Taipei wanted to buy an AS/400 system, he didn't have a clue who in IBM to call. There was a sales rep in Taipei, but he didn't have any AS/400s. And often the sales rep didn't know where to go.

This led to a corollary theory of why IBM had slipped so suddenly. Large corporate customers became exasperated waiting for price quotes. Bids took two weeks or less at Hewlett-Packard, Sun, and Compaq. IBM customers were lucky to have a salesman call back in two months. He couldn't just work up the figures; he might have to get input from three or four different business units. He might have to gain approvals from several layers of management, layers the competition didn't have.

So Gerstner insisted on creating sales specialists. He wanted lists of candidates before the Christmas season. By early December of 1993, he heard IBM Europe could not comply in time. He went absolutely ballistic. A former senior finance official put it this way: "Lou said, 'Either the list will be here by January second when we open for business in 1994, or there's going to be lots of new people.'" They worked through the holidays and made their deadline. But this official said there was still a lot of "malicious obedience," which meant, "I'll say yes to Gerstner and the other powers in Armonk but continue conducting business as usual."

IBM's foreign subsidiaries were among the biggest practitioners of malicious obedience. In the past, they had been cash cows for the company, and they had always operated with little direction from corporate headquarters. A bad quarter in the geos was written off to "macroeconomics," or currency fluctuations or a temporary downturn in the economy. That was about all the explanation general managers like Nick Temple (UK) and Hans-Olaf Henkel (Europe) felt they had to offer to corporate headquarters in the past. Why should they change now that Gerstner was in charge?

As it turned out, Gerstner made an example of Hans-Olaf Henkel, a stern, tough-minded German who had the longest title of any senior executive. Henkel was head of IBM World Trade Europe/EMEA (which included the Middle East and Asia, but not the Pacific nations like Japan, Singapore, Thailand, or the Philippines). It was one of IBM's most important geographies. Gerstner did not accept the simple excuses for soft results his predecessor had. He wanted to rein in the geos, because York had reported their costs were way out of sync with revenues.

Worse than the United States and most other foreign units. Every country under Henkel had a full stand-alone staff, which meant endless redundancy. Henkel's units were unable to get the SG&A to a realistic and ultimately profitable level.

Henkel was ordered to trim his considerable staff and consolidate, but he resisted, or he was too slow. The European work cycle ran so much more casually than the internal one in Armonk. Henkel was a bright, capable executive, according to an IBM vice president, but he was too stubborn to see that Gerstner would ultimately prevail. "When you really cut through it all, he didn't want to change the way business was being done over there," a former senior executive said. "He had to be dragged kicking and screaming."

When Henkel was asked to resign, the system of worldwide fiefdoms, which had flourished within IBM for so long, officially ended. Henkel's demise signified that power at IBM was now consolidated in a way that it had never been before. A greater degree of accountability was instilled among IBM's foreign general managers. Every decision affecting a geography's businesses would now emanate from Gerstner's office in Armonk.

Change was about to occur everywhere, even the boardroom.

Gerstner had pledged to retain tight controls everywhere in his organization, and the IBM directors saw this firsthand. He did not waste time reconfiguring the board. They were hopelessly out of touch with current technology, holdovers from Akers's board, and even earlier CEOs. Dick Munro, the former Time Inc. CEO, was sixty-two, and as a close friend of Akers he thought it was time to step aside. He felt IBM needed "younger legs. Lou should have the right to choose some people he knows, respects, and who are much more attuned to the industry."

Edgar S. Woolard Jr., who was the CEO of DuPont, eventually gave up his IBM seat to join Gil Amelio's board at Apple. Gerstner, Woolard had implied to Amelio, wanted only "prestige" board members who would not vigorously challenge his decisions. "He wanted to go someplace where he'd be very involved as a director, and he didn't want to just go there as window dressing," Amelio said. "And that was the feeling he got at IBM, so that's why he left." Woolard says that Amelio's recollection is faulty and just plain untrue. He said that he never experienced any rifts with Gerstner. "I was now retired, and I wanted to be on a smaller board, and I wanted to be an active participant," Woolard said. "I had been on larger boards where the actions were simply to ratify management's proposals. This had not become a problem at IBM."

Stephen D. Bechtel Jr., sixty-eight, former chairman of Bechtel Corporation, quit as well. Helmut Sihler, retired president of Henkel, a German chemical company, had retired a month earlier, and now Gerstner had a few openings. He named one new director, Charles F. Knight, fifty-seven, who headed Emerson Electric Company. Also, Alex Trotman, who ran Ford, and Cathleen Black, the head of Hearst Magazines, who were contemporaries of Gerstner, would follow as new directors. The IBM board was soon reduced by a third, to a dozen members.

Gerstner's new directors had at least some understanding of IBM's core businesses and the technology business of the 1990s.

One of their first tasks was to examine the company's "non-core assets," divisions that Gerstner felt did not fit in with IBM's long-range plans. IBM Credit Corporation, its finance arm, was considered. Should IBM be in the banking business, they asked? The company did not have a stellar reputation as a lender. One reason was that Akers's team had used the unit to offer very aggressive financing terms to help bolster the sales of hardware. They had given customers extended payment terms, and this led to dramatic cash flow shortages. Also, IBM Credit had been having a difficult time trying to wrest business away from competitors like Comdisco, GE Capital, and AT&T Credit. After some discussion, Gerstner and the board concluded that IBM Credit would stay. When the company's financial outlook improved, IBM Credit could play an integral role in financing large technology purchases for its customers. It could become competitive again.

But after a couple of months of analysis, York was asked to quietly put IBM's defense business—the Federal Systems Company—on the block. Federal produced software for radar warning systems, antisubmarine warfare, satellites, and air traffic control systems. What made the defense business attractive was IBM's contract with the FAA to upgrade the nation's air traffic control web. Already ten years old, the contract was worth $2.5 billion.

Three companies decided to bid: Hughes Aircraft, Northrop Grumman, and Loral, a huge military contractor. At that time, Hughes was run by Mike Armstrong, an ex-IBM senior executive who had been in line to succeed Akers. York had served on the Chrysler board with Kent Cressa, who headed Northrop, and he had once tried to sell Northrop Chrysler's defense business. Hughes and Northrop made offers—Northrop's was slightly higher—but Bernard Schwartz, who had shrewdly built Loral into the nation's leading defense contractor, preempted both bids with a $1.58 billion offer. By mid-December of 1993, a deal was struck.

By the second half of 1993, IBM was beginning to show signs of life once again. Its condition went from critical to stable. The dividend was once again cut in half at midyear, from 54 cents a share to 25 cents. Cash flow was a problem. IBM had to borrow to pay the dividend.

The company announced it would report a small gain, $382 million in net earnings in the fourth quarter. It was a pretty significant milestone under Gerstner. It was the first positive earnings the company had in a year, and it was a huge reversal from the $5.4 billion loss in the fourth quarter of 1992.

Midway through his first year, Gerstner, who had pledged to act maniacally and speak parsimoniously, made one remark that would haunt him for months. At an informal press luncheon at the St. Regis Hotel in New York City, the questions had focused on his problems, the downsizing, plant and office shutdowns, and the record second-quarter loss.

Again, he was vague about his plans. He couldn't make specific comments until he saw how well IBM would perform in the coming months. "There's been a lot of speculation on when I will deliver a vision," Gerstner told reporters. "The last thing IBM needs right now is a vision. What IBM needs right now is a series of very tough-minded, market-driven, highly effective strategies in each of its businesses." It was a bland but candid assessment of his company's situation, and it didn't seem like the kind of comment that could cause a CEO regret. But unfortunately for Gerstner, he was widely quoted out of context. Many large newspapers, including the *New York Times,* picked up only the ten-word middle sentence of the quote. In fact, it was reported as if this lack of a vision was a central Gerstner shortcoming. In September, the *Times* reminded Gerstner again about his statement, comparing it with a similar gaffe made by President Bush who was regularly roughed up by the press about "the vision thing."

A Vertical Vision
of Reality

Lou Gerstner probably had every right to feel that the press comments on his vision statement, or lack thereof, in or out of context, was something of a cheap shot. Too much emphasis was placed on the vision thing in technology anyway. Vision in this business implies a godlike clairvoyance, an ability to spot trends where others could not. A true Silicon Valley prophet can see the next killer app with remarkable acuity—the tech product that will dazzle the digerati, dominate the category, and squash all one's competitors. Marc Andreessen and Jim Clark are such visionaries; they dreamed that Netscape's browser would catalyze the Internet. Or Jerry Yang, a Stanford Ph.D. dropout who at twenty-six cofounded Yahoo! In short, a visionary can find a niche, fill it at megahertz speed, and magically woo the market toward his portal.

If this is what it takes, then Gerstner is not a visionary.

When it comes to personal goals, however, Gerstner is much the visionary. His intelligence, drive, and ambition are boundless, and it is apparent to some who knew him as a youth that he someday would scale great heights.

Lou Gerstner was an early achiever. Joseph Giarputto, a classmate of Gerstner's, recalls his extraordinary focus and sense of himself when the two were in junior high school in the 1950s:

"My recollection, and it's the recollection of a thirteen- or four-teen-year-old kid, is that Lou was a pretty fully formed person at thirteen. He came from an extremely close-knit family, a religious family, and he had a tremendous work ethic. He just worked damn hard, and he had talent. It was almost as if work was an end in itself, not to particularly accomplish anything, although he certainly did. He was a smart guy."

Another schoolboy chum, George Allman, grew up with him and lived one block from the Gerstners. He recalled that Lou was very industrious "even back then." Gerstner was a very bright "normal" kid and "regular" guy. After school, Allman played stickball or sandlot baseball with Gerstner, and shot baskets at the backboard on Allman's garage. Occasionally, they played a scruffy game of tennis. The Gerstner household was quite strict. Gerstner did not have the run of the neighborhood, and he had to be home after school by a certain hour. His was a "classic fifties family."

Gerstner was born on March 1, 1942, and grew up in Mineola, New York, the second of four sons to Louis V. Gerstner and Majorie Gerstner. His father worked as the night traffic manager at the Schaefer Brewery (now owned by Stroh's). His mother had a job in the registrar's office of a local community college and was also a real estate agent.

Mineola is one of the small working-class suburban neighborhoods only a few miles into Nassau County just outside of Queens. An enclave populated mostly by lower level white-collar workers and tradespeople, it has little ethnic diversity other than a small Portuguese population. It is a town where people from New York City go when they want to escape crowded outer-borough apartments, hoping to discover a little piece of paradise on Long Island.

Lou Gerstner was raised in a modest two-story red-brick box with a sloped, shingled roof on Fairfield Avenue. There are two second-story gabled windows facing the street and a one-car garage set in the rear of a narrow lot. For a family of six, it is anything but spacious. The lawns on the block are well kept but barely large enough to toss a ball. Cable TV is available but it appears to be a luxury. There are still plenty of conventional TV antennas on Fairfield's roofs. American-made pickup trucks and vans line the street. The odd foreign car is a Toyota Camry. From just in front of the Gerstner home, a few blocks farther to the west, you can see the city water tower. Gerstner's parents are still in the neighborhood. Now retired, they appear to live the middle-class life they always have. They also own a very simple single-story brown-shingled wood-frame summer house in Southampton, a resort town on eastern Long Island. That home, which has four bedrooms and two bathrooms, was last appraised by the tax assessor in 1990 at $184,400.

About a mile from Fairfield Avenue is Chaminade, the Catholic high school that educated all of the Gerstners' children and was the center of their teenage lives. Chaminade—as well as his parents—had a profound impact on Lou Gerstner's formative years. He endowed the library at the school in honor of his parents in June 1991; there is a bronze plaque on the wall commemorating the donation. He has since made two other gifts totaling $800,000 to the school's scholarship fund, earmarked for students with financial need.

In the 1950s, when Lou and his older brother Dick were students there, tuition was $300 to $350 a year; today, it is a manageable $4,050, the least expensive Catholic school on Long Island, according to school officials. Yet it was a stretch for the Gerstners to pay even a low tuition, and this is one reason his mother worked in an era when women were traditionally homemakers. "My parents worked enormously hard to put four children through college," Lou Gerstner told *Fortune* magazine in 1997. "We didn't have a lot of money." Gerstner earned extra money by working at a local diner. When one of Chaminade's coaches saw him mopping floors and busing tables, he asked him whether he was a waiter. Gerstner said that he hadn't risen yet to that job but that he hoped to one day. (He never did.)

Chaminade is a demanding parochial school. The physical plant is impressive, a well-preserved main building with polished wooden doors. There is marble trim along the entrance hallway. New wings have been added; there is a modern natatorium, a courtyard where students can eat lunch during the warm season. The Marianist Catholic Brothers in residence—so named for the order of the Society of Mary—do much of the routine maintenance work themselves when school is not in session.

Students must pass an entrance exam, and the course work is rigorous. Joe Giarputto, now a business magazine publisher, graduated in the same class as Gerstner at both Chaminade and Harvard Business School. Comparing the two, he said, "It was a hell of a lot harder work at Chaminade than at Harvard. Back in the fifties, it was demanding, disciplined." Latin was mandatory in Gerstner's era. Now it's optional, but a language requirement remains. Brother George Endres, the school's director, said, "We've never had a student not get into college."

Behavioral standards were adopted when the school was founded in 1930; today, they are strictly adhered to and violated at one's peril. Students are required to wear jackets and ties and standard-issue gym shorts and T-shirts. Talking in study hall is prohibited, though a similar library prohibition was rescinded about ten years ago. The Brothers confessed that this was a progressive change; book circulation immediately increased fourfold. There is a computer lab at Chaminade, too, but there are no IBM machines among them. Cheaper PC clones line the desks. Chaminade officials are so appreciative of Gerstner's past generosity, they'd never think to ask him for IBM Aptivas or ThinkPads.

Misbehavior of any kind is deeply frowned on. Back in Gerstner's era, it wasn't uncommon for the Brothers to strike a student for a particularly grievous offense. A Brother might slap a kid hard in the face or on the side of the head. You were expected to take it, recalls one student. In those days, parents of kids didn't object to mild corporal punishment. If you violated a school rule, you received a "green slip," and reported after school to the Dean of Discipline, who was sent the stub of your slip. There was usually a line of boys waiting outside his office. This dean would be seated behind his desk with ominously low lighting. He asked you to confirm your misdeed and then delivered a stern lecture along with the appropriate number of demerits. Students with demerits were punished by putting in hours policing the grounds or washing the cafeteria windows. If you received ten demerits in an academic year, a letter was sent home to your parents. If the total reached twenty, suspension was the result. Thirty demerits meant expulsion. Chaminade's administrators do not recall whether Lou received any demerits. The likelihood is that he didn't, they say.

Gerstner played freshman basketball in 1956 and football for four years, and while his yearbook, the *Crimson and Gold*, called him "an outstanding athlete," this was a slight exaggeration. His classmates remember him as athletic but not a star. George Allman recalls: "He was a quarterback on the sophomore [junior varsity] team. He threw a pass that cost me my career. I remember it very vividly. He overthrew it, and it was intercepted. I was out of the play, just standing there. A guy came out of nowhere and hit me, and something had to give because my spikes were firmly in the ground. My knee gave, [and] I tore the ligaments. When he made the varsity, they switched him to halfback, maybe because he couldn't throw accurately." Also, with Gerstner's thick neck and short, stocky build, he was more suited to play halfback than quarterback.

Though he wasn't considered an egghead, Gerstner probably would have been called a "grind." He was vice president of the National Honor Society chapter, senior class treasurer, a home room officer for four years, and he made the honors program. Brother Richard Hartz, who graduated with Gerstner in the class of 1959, and is now the school's director of development and alumni relations, recalled that Gerstner was merely a smart kid who worked very hard. Hartz insisted that Gerstner's work ethic wasn't necessarily greater than others. Gerstner, however, produced standout results. He graduated as salutatorian, second in his class of 308, with a 95.6 average. *Crimson and Gold* summarized him as "without a doubt, one of the leading men of the senior class." Clearly, religion was important. He was vice prefect of Sodality, the Catholic society. When he had achieved business success, he was asked to return and speak with the students. He assured them that his religion helped him every day. Today when he travels, IBM aides provide the name and address of the Catholic church nearest to his hotel.

Chaminade's roster of graduates has its share of luminaries, and they include Robert Wright, the president of NBC; Brian Dennehy and George Kennedy, the actors; and Alfonse D'Amato, the former three-term U.S. senator from New York. Photos of the graduating classes hang in the hallways. Lou and his brothers Dick and Jim are wearing tuxedos, the commencement tradition of the day, while the youngest, Joe, who graduated in 1969, has on the more casual suit and tie. They all sport the popular pompadour hairstyle of the day.

In an interview with the *Chaminade News*, Joe Gerstner said the school "instilled in me a desire ever to excel—to be the best you can be and not be satisfied with less than one hundred percent effort." None of the Gerstner boys would disappoint their parents. Today, Joe is a lawyer at Westinghouse—he joined the firm in 1981—and he specializes in labor issues, including collective-bargaining agreements, grievance, and arbitration. Jim Gerstner was an honor roll student for four years at Chaminade. He rose to executive vice president and international general manager at the pharmaceutical firm Bristol-Myers Squibb (where Lou Gerstner serves on the board). Jim died of complications from stomach cancer in November 1992.

Dick, the oldest of the Gerstner boys, was also an excellent student, but he wasn't the achiever Lou was. At Chaminade, he made the honor roll, joined the science and math clubs, and was a member of the bowling team. Dick earned a chemical engineering degree at Villanova and a master's from Stanford. He appeared to have more of a technology bent than any of his younger brothers.

Until the mid-1980s, anyone might have picked Dick Gerstner to become CEO of IBM. In fact, Dick Gerstner, not Lou, was the first family member to work for IBM. A lifer who joined the company in

1960 as an engineer, Dick became a classic company man. He rose steadily through the executive ranks, and by the late 1980s, he was the company's top man in Asia. In September 1988 he was brought back to the United States to become the general manager of the Personal Systems Group, heading several of IBM's businesses that included the PC Company. Dick was affable and well liked by many in Armonk, and company observers felt he was a serious candidate for the CEO job.

In 1987, however, Dick's career began to unravel through freakish circumstances. One morning in Tokyo he awoke with severe back and neck pain. At first doctors diagnosed the problem as something caused by a demanding travel schedule and long hours. For three years he worked through the pain, shuttling from doctor to doctor, eventually undergoing surgery to remove a cervical disk. The pain was intermittent, however, and he gamely continued on. He went on steroids, he even had a second back surgery. One day he collapsed in a meeting; everyone thought he'd had a heart attack, but it wasn't the case. His condition, despite exams by doctors in the most accomplished pain clinics, remained a puzzle.

After two years of misery, Dick Gerstner could no longer work. He retired from IBM in 1989, his hope of one day leading the company coming to an end. It wasn't until early 1992, when his wife bumped into another IBMer's wife, that the mystery was solved. She described Dick's symptoms and the woman immediately recognized it as Lyme disease, a debilitating condition caused by deer tick bites. It is common in Connecticut and Long Island, and it can become serious and potentially fatal if not detected early and properly treated. Unfortunately, the steroids exacerbated his condition.

With antibiotics he felt well enough in February to take on a three-month consulting contract with an IBM division. It ended just a few weeks after Lou Gerstner stepped into the corner office in April 1993. During this overlapping period, there were rumblings throughout the organization that Lou might ask Dick to return in a high-level position. Everyone liked Dick; they didn't know his brother. But the practical senior managers knew that Lou was in an untenable position. If he hired his brother, he would be open to accusations of nepotism. If he didn't, he would appear to be insensitive.

The speculation that Dick might return was short-lived. Those who know them have two slightly different takes on their relationship. The polite version is that the two are not particularly close. "He was kind of private about that relationship," said an ex-IBM executive who knows Dick well. "I got the feeling they were kind of competitive." Lou never mentioned Dick or any of his siblings, according to longtime business associates. The two don't socialize. Some sources claim their dislike for each other is quite intense. A former IBM manager adds, "With Lou, there probably was room for only one Gerstner."

Whatever level of *froideur* that exists between them is known only by the two Gerstners. One former IBMer said, "I know [Lou's appointment] must have hurt Dick tremendously." Dick has been gracious about the situation. He has spoken publicly only twice about it since his brother began running the company. He told *Fortune* magazine, "It was a little spooky for both of us. Lou and I both felt it didn't make sense for me to stay. I was ill. I hadn't worked much in three years. I was part of the team that had messed it up. The last thing Lou wanted was somebody from the old guard who happened to be his brother." In the *Wall Street Journal,* he said, "Whether I am or not, I'm sort of identified with the crowd that got IBM in trouble, right?"

Though the faculty is now more broad-minded, in Lou Gerstner's day Chaminade's advisors made a great effort to guide their graduates away from the secular schools toward the better Catholic universities, like Holy Cross, St. John's, Notre Dame, Boston College, or Georgetown. (Today, however, Chaminade officials claim this is not their policy.) As far as the Brothers were concerned, one Chaminade graduate only half joked, not attending a Catholic university meant placing one's soul in jeopardy. So school officials were obviously disappointed when Gerstner decided to accept a scholarship from Dartmouth.

Gerstner was no less industrious, and no less Catholic, as an undergraduate in Hanover, New Hampshire, than he had been on Long Island. If anything, becoming an Ivy Leaguer in 1959 increased his drive. One of his suite mates during freshman and sophomore years was Paul Binder, the founder and director of the Big Apple Circus. Binder's main recollection of Gerstner was how little he saw of him in college. "Lou was the guy who got up before everyone else in the morning and left to go study and came back after everybody was asleep," Binder said. "He was studying all day. He was what we called the classic booker." Another former student recalls that he "literally lived in the 1902 room" in Baker Library, a spot where the bookers reserved chairs. Binder also remembered that during their freshman year one of the Dartmouth deans regularly invited him to his home for dinner. The story was that the dean's wife worried that he was skipping meals because he was putting in so much time at the library.

As an engineering science major, Gerstner was completely focused, and he knew fairly early that he was interested in a business career. He was named an Alfred P. Sloan National Scholar, and in his junior year, he received the Scott Paper Company Foundation Award.

Gerstner had only limited time for the frivolities and leisure activities of campus life. He was either not big enough or not good enough to play Ivy League football. He rowed on the freshman crew team and worked at the campus radio station during his first year. He joined a fraternity, Kappa Sigma. One Dartmouth classmate, Chris Miller, became an advertising copywriter and eventually a comedy writer. Miller was coauthor of *National Lampoon's Animal House,* a 1970s comedy loosely based on the wild fraternity scene at Dartmouth. It wasn't likely that Gerstner spent much time at toga parties, though he wasn't a complete stoic, certainly not a nerd. At least one fraternity brother recalls playing a lot of "beer-pong doubles" at Kappa Sigma parties with Gerstner. Robert Baxley Jr. told the *Dartmouth Alumni Magazine,* "That's where you set up glasses of beer on the four quadrants of a Ping-Pong table. If you hit the other guy's glass when you served, you had to drink the whole glass. He was competitive."

Gerstner's assertiveness and single-mindedness were revealing even in social situations. Brendan Kelly, a Long Islander who had several friends in common with Gerstner, recalled how Lou tried to crash one of his parties. "I lived in Port Washington," Kelly said. "I invited a bunch of college friends, and my dad said that absolutely no one who is not invited to the party gets in. I invited fifty or sixty people, and I didn't know Lou well enough to invite him. About nine o'clock Lou shows up at my front door with a date. The thing I remember about it was that I wouldn't let him in. And he was so tenacious—he wasn't overbearing or anything— he just tried to persuade me. I never did let him in, but I must have talked to him for thirty-five minutes. Most people would have gone away, but that's Lou, I guess."

By the time Gerstner reached his senior year at Dartmouth, he had built an impressive résumé of student activities. He had been class treasurer during his freshman and sophomore years. He was active in student government and a member of the Undergraduate Council's Judiciary Committee. He was named chairman of the Judiciary Committee, a powerful student post. This meant he presided over all the disciplinary proceedings adjudicated by undergraduates. He was a four-year member of Newman, the Catholic society. In the 1963 yearbook, Gerstner can be found in the middle of the Kappa Sigma photo, looking pensive and serious.

His academic record and solid work in student government were the compelling credentials that got him elected to Casque and Gauntlet, Dartmouth's prestigious senior honor society. Casque has the reputation at Dartmouth that Skull and Bones has at Yale, except it isn't a secret society. Unlike Bones, whose members are required to leave any room when the society's name is spoken aloud, Casque's thirty-odd members pose en masse for *Aegis,* the Dartmouth yearbook. They are solemn. It is an exclusive club, however, as only high achievers are tapped, but there also is an effort to recruit a diverse mix of student talent. (Outgoing seniors pick the outstanding juniors.) Nelson Rockefeller had been a member. The actor Michael Moriarty was in Casque during Gerstner's year, 1963.

Casque was modeled after King Arthur's Court, and each member was given a knightly nickname by the group. Stephen Spahn, who today is the headmaster of the Dwight School in Manhattan, recalled only a couple of the Casque sobriquets. His own was Sir Alexander and Gerstner's was Sir Kay. In medieval lore, Sir Kay was the "rude and boastful" knight. As a young man of twenty-one, it was apparent that courtesy and humility were not Gerstner's strong suits.

Spahn said that Gerstner's early schooling and his unprivileged background likely helped shape the future CEO's thinking. He was, after all, surrounded by a lot of preppies, well-heeled kids, many of whom came from a crusty, upper-middle-class lineage. "I thought of his coming from Mineola as having this tough, Catholic background, almost a Jesuit kind of approach," Spahn said. "The hard work was more important than raw brainpower. He expected everybody to be that way. He had little regard for people not living up to what he believed was the correct standard."

After graduating magna cum laude from Dartmouth, Gerstner moved southeast to Cambridge and enrolled in Harvard Business School. While he earned his MBA, Gerstner made one of his first valuable business contacts, although he probably did not know it at the time. A teacher named John McArthur taught Gerstner in his first-year finance class and immediately recognized him as an outstanding student. McArthur eventually became dean of the business school.

An MBA from Harvard was—and is—a powerful launching pad for a business career, especially a student with Gerstner's potential. In 1965, he decided to join McKinsey and Company, one of the nation's most prestigious management consulting firms. Gerstner began in the firm's New York City office. McKinsey was much smaller then, and while today it recruits perhaps sixty from the Harvard Business School, in Gerstner's year it took only six. Job interviews at McKinsey can be uneasy experiences, according to some who have been through them. An applicant must survive several rounds of scrutiny, first by a recruitment group, then by the firm's senior partners. Odd, even bizarre questions—those with no "correct" answers—are asked to examine the applicant's analytical thinking and approach to problem solving. Applicants are known to spend weeks preparing for McKinsey interviews.

The company's advancement policy is much more rigid than the typical white-shoe law firm, where if you do not make partner in a specified time, you do not stay with the firm. At McKinsey you move "up or out" within the first five or six years. Unlike the most prestigious brokerage and law firms, McKinsey partners do not receive tenure. Their performance is periodically reviewed until they retire.

There is no question that Gerstner rose steadily at McKinsey, and his first couple of promotions were fairly rapid. There was a lot of talk about how talented Gerstner was; on the other hand, there also was a lot of buzz about how young and brash he was. At McKinsey, the firm carefully calibrates their newcomers' progress, watching how they interact with people and their clients over a period of "studies" or engagements with clients to see how well they perform.

When the twenty-eight-year-old Gerstner was elected a principal in 1970, he had been with the firm five years and one month. The average time it took to advance to principal was about five years, two months, so Gerstner's first promotion occurred right on schedule. Harvey Golub, who is the CEO of American Express (and was also a Gerstner colleague there), was elected a McKinsey principal after only four years, two months—the fastest first promotion ever. Another McKinsey consultant, Philip Purcell, now the head of Morgan Stanley Dean Witter, made principal four months faster than Gerstner. Purcell and Gerstner were the youngest partners at McKinsey. Purcell was also twenty-eight, a month younger than Gerstner. McKinsey's entry class of 1965 was certainly an extremely talented one.

When Gerstner was promoted to director, the next rung on the firm's ladder, it also happened slightly faster than average. He did become one of the younger directors at McKinsey, but as one of Gerstner's mentors, J. McClain "Mac" Stewart, noted, "There's nothing spectacular about Lou's election both to principal and director."

Mac Stewart and Ron Daniel, who was managing director of the New York office and later managing director of the firm (now treasurer of Harvard), looked after Gerstner's career at McKinsey. As with most companies, unless there are one or two senior managers who take an interest, you won't move. It was up to Daniel and Stewart to see that Gerstner got high-profile assignments. Among the clients he worked for at McKinsey were Mobil, Wachovia Bank in North Carolina, ABC-TV, Food Machinery Corporation (a Midwestern firm), and Pan American. Later, Stewart recommended Gerstner to company boards and to the membership committees of high-profile country clubs.

Gerstner handled his early assignments with enthusiasm and diligence. His disciplined approach to problem-solving impressed many at McKinsey. Linda Levinson, the first woman who was elected principal at McKinsey, said of Gerstner, "He goes directly for the jugular in any problem-solving exercise. He really has a finely honed analytical ability to spot the logical flaws. He's perfectly happy to dive into an argument and challenge. And part of that is to see how strongly held your conviction is of whatever you're propounding, to see if you've got the factual basis to support that argument.

"Sometimes he's digging and challenging just to see if you've got it, but in the course of that digging, if there's a flaw in your logic, he will absolutely find it. So you need to be able to go up against him in those arguments. It's an intellectual free-for-all. He's not easy, because his style isn't easy. If you're a wimp, and if you don't know what you're talking about, I'm sure you think he's very unpleasant." Gerstner's confrontational nature would become his trademark, and those who succeeded with him learned not to take it personally. In a meeting, when Gerstner churned over an issue, he attacked the logic and not the messenger.

Gerstner could be characteristically blunt with clients, too. Once, he made a major presentation, and brought up some important issues, but the executive in charge said that his calendar was so busy he couldn't discuss it for six weeks. Gerstner wrote him a letter that said if he couldn't address it any earlier, then either "we were working on the wrong problem" or he "was focusing on the wrong issues," Levinson recalls. Writing a strongly worded letter was somewhat unusual, according to some McKinsey practitioners. But apparently it jogged the client. The following week the executive met with Gerstner.

Mac Stewart said that Gerstner had the startling talent to make himself look like an expert on subjects he knew nothing about. One day, Gerstner and Stewart were on the R.J. Reynolds company jet when the tobacco firm's president asked the McKinsey pair about CEO succession. The president was upfront about his motive: he wanted to accelerate his boss's retirement so he could assume the top position. Stewart had done a lot of important succession work for several large McKinsey clients—formal strategies for chairmen and CEOs to choose and groom their heirs. At large corporations, the process is usually long and arduous and more delicate than one suspects.

Stewart naturally assumed the president's question was directed at him and not Gerstner. "Without pausing to take a breath, Lou launched into a discussion about how you do a study of succession in a company," said Stewart. "And while he'd never done it before, he wasn't far off. But it just surprised me because here I was sitting next to him, and he really knew what he was talking about. I didn't get a chance."

Despite Gerstner's sharp mind, he had a propensity to assure people about his abilities and high level of intelligence. One McKinsey partner said, "He did have this tendency to boast and to brag. This question of pomposity. He can't help it. It must have something to do with the fact that his father worked in a brewery. Because he's always trying to let you know how important he is." Gerstner was reminded about it many times by this McKinsey colleague. He never seemed to tone down his public self-assessments, however. The McKinsey partner recalled writing Gerstner a letter when he was appointed CEO of IBM. He told Gerstner that now, finally, he could stop with the boasting.

This character trait, however odious at times to his peers, did not stand in the way of Gerstner's career. McKinsey is functionally divided into what it calls "practice groups." The Finance Practice Group was formed by Gerstner in the New York office. It was a significant test for the young consultant because he had to develop a specialty while also servicing his accounts. Gerstner hired a few outsiders who had finance backgrounds. Four who joined McKinsey to work in Gerstner's group were John Wooster, who had been in corporate finance at Exxon; Linda Levinson; Bob Schmitz, and G. Richard "Rick" Thoman. Gerstner became a mentor to many in his group and was admired for this role. "They were devoted to him," Mac Stewart said. "The sun rose and set with Lou, and he looked after them. He saw to it that they got good assignments." Thoman would be associated with Gerstner for many years when they worked together at American Express, RJR Nabisco, and IBM.

John Wooster recalls Gerstner revealing his plans to him after he had arrived at McKinsey. "We both went to Dartmouth, but I didn't know him there," Wooster said. "Here was a relatively young guy— he'd hired me—and he was younger than me by a couple of years. McKinsey would have these whole staff meetings, and we had one at the Westchester Country Club. There was a dinner, and I went walking outside with Lou afterwards. He was talking about his vision. I remember being struck by Lou's enthusiasm for building his practice, the Finance Group. I'm sure he had decided that this was his way to have an impact at McKinsey. This was virgin territory. And he was going to fill it."

Though it wasn't a revenue-producing department, the Finance Group gave Gerstner more visibility, and equally important, a reputation within the firm. Two other clients under his aegis, however, gave Gerstner a chance for visibility outside the McKinsey box: the Penn Central Railroad and American Express. The Penn Central was a natural fit because his former Harvard B-School finance professor, John McArthur, was partly responsible for restructuring the bankrupt railroad. (Ron Daniel says that Gerstner's connection with McArthur at Harvard was not related to his work on the bankruptcy.) The Penn Central was a messy dissolution. It had complex holdings. It was Gerstner's job to advise the company in evaluating the nonrailroad assets so they could be sold. Among them were several office buildings and other real estate holdings in New York City, and a minority interest in the New York Rangers hockey team.

When the Penn Central reemerged as Conrail, Gerstner had demonstrated his prowess on the most demanding assignments. One significant account, however, defined his career as a consultant and laid the groundwork for his next job. Mac Stewart was the senior McKinsey partner in charge of the American Express account for many years, and he was a close advisor to the chairman, Howard Clark. Clark was getting ready to retire and James Robinson III was about to become his successor. At McKinsey, relationships with key clients are critical, the bedrock of the firm. They can mean the difference between a short-term assignment and business that can last for decades. Stewart needed someone at McKinsey to continue his work and eventually form a similar bond with the new chairman. American Express was one of its largest clients, so it was an important decision, given the transition in leadership. After discussing it with Ron Daniel, Stewart gave Gerstner the plum American Express account.

In 1968, Gerstner married Elizabeth Robins Link, a Southerner from Danville, Virginia. Robin, as his wife is known, is the antithesis of Lou's personality. While Gerstner is shy, abrupt, and socially lacking on occasion, Robin is outgoing, warm, gracious, and charming. Friends and associates who are clearly uncomfortable talking about the abrasive side of Gerstner immediately brighten when Robin's name comes up. The Gerstners have two children, Louis III, born in 1973, and Elizabeth, who is three years younger. Louis III earned a degree at Princeton, graduating cum laude, and is a candidate for a master's degree at Columbia University. He was married to another Princeton alumna in the spring of 1999. Elizabeth, who graduated from Brown, is a medical student. (Gerstner's private foundation has made a donation of $500,000 to Elizabeth's medical school.)

Business associates and friends of the Gerstners always cite Gerstner's deep family commitment, especially his close watch on his children's education—and now that they're grown—their careers. Determined to be an active parent, Gerstner reportedly always left work early when Louis III and Elizabeth's report cards were due. His children's grades endured the same careful scrutiny of his McKinsey subordinates. Gerstner put in long days at McKinsey, and he was so focused that his work consumed him. Linda Levinson, who worked alongside Gerstner for several years, said, "We were traveling all the time, and he came into the office one day really upset because his son, who was then a kid, had apparently asked Robin, 'Why doesn't Daddy live here anymore?' It was because we were on an out-of-town assignment, and he wasn't home a lot. He was appalled that his little son felt that way, so he worries about that stuff."

His work on the American Express account pleased everyone at McKinsey, but more important, Howard Clark and Jim Robinson thought he could be a permanent asset in building the company's charge card business. In 1978, Robinson offered him a job running a company division. He had wanted to start at the head of the Travel Related Services group (TRS)—which included Traveler's Cheques and the American Express Card, among an array of smaller businesses—but Robinson and a group executive, George Waters, to whom Gerstner would report for a year, felt that he needed management seasoning. In his long tenure as a consultant, he had never run a business. So he began by running the card unit. When Waters retired, Gerstner would head the TRS division. Gerstner's signature would be on every Traveler's Cheque issued by American Express.

When Gerstner left McKinsey in 1978 after more than twelve years there, many partners were extremely disappointed. They had felt he might someday lead the firm. Gerstner probably had been thinking about leaving for some time. Once, he had tried to persuade a client that his company needed to undergo a massive restructuring. Gerstner prepared an elaborate presentation, but he was unable to persuade the client. "I went home and said I no longer wanted to be the guy putting slides on the machine," he recalled. "I wanted to be making the decisions."

The truth was that Gerstner was also impatient. He had one minor setback, at least from his perspective. When the job running McKinsey's New York branch opened (called the Office Manager) he was one of the leading candidates. Thinking he was perhaps a bit too young, the company chose someone more experienced on the West Coast, and Gerstner decided it was a convenient time to leave.

An ex-McKinsey hand saw this first job change as a defining moment not only in Gerstner's career, but in his ambition and his personality. Climbing to the top of corporate America's premier dispenser of advice had limited prestige and compensation. You could not become a titan of American business if you remained at McKinsey.

When he arrived at American Express, he assumed he was going to be the number three man in the company. After a reorganization, Gerstner discovered he was only number five in the firm's hierarchy. At first, he wasn't even listed on the proxy statement, and that worried him.

He was always intently concerned about his standing. "If he wasn't going up, he became increasingly unhappy," a former colleague said. "That's why he finally left McKinsey. Lou had what I think of as a vertical vision of reality."

6

The Making of a CEO

Robinson's and Waters's initial instincts about Gerstner's inexperience being a hindrance were correct. He had never managed a large enterprise with hundreds of people under his command. In fact, there never were more than a handful of people in his reporting chain. Gerstner admitted this shortcoming in a Harvard Business School case study done in November 1987. He told an interviewer, "I remember going to early meetings at American Express where there were three or four levels of management present. Perhaps foolishly, I started behaving as I had at McKinsey. Somebody would ask a question or say something, and I would start probing around the table. Sometimes I would go to the third-level person and talk with him or her. Naïvely, I showed a disregard for the structural, inherent rigidity of the system. It seems that I shocked people some, and I had to back off a little bit. People would come to me and say, 'Why did you do that? Why are you questioning my subordinates?' And I started out with a distrust of formal bureaucracy and a positive attitude of 'let's have relatively informal problem solving.' But I wasn't sitting around consciously thinking about a management style. That was just the way I developed, so I was practicing the only behavior I knew." Considering Gerstner's unflagging self-confidence, his carefully crafted public remarks, this was an unusual confession, coming nearly a decade after he had arrived at the company in 1978.

Gerstner was an outsider, and he was steeped in the consultant's methodology. "I guess the best way to describe it was that he was a different kind of cat than anybody we'd ever seen," recalled Edwin Cooperman, who headed the U.S. consumer card group and was Gerstner's general counsel. The AmEx routine wasn't haphazard, but company managers had not spent a lot of time on strategy. Throughout the 1960s, the company had owned the marketplace. There were only three cards that mattered, American Express, Diner's Club, and Carte Blanche. AmEx dominated the domestic market. Those at AmEx who were successful in marketing the card did not see any reason to run the business differently, despite the fact that the products were beginning to mature. Corporate hubris had settled into the company culture. So here comes Gerstner, a fairly young guy, brash and brimming with confidence, explaining the need for a well-thought-out strategy, a means of adequately testing an idea or solution before they committed a large amount of money to a project.

Gerstner told Harvard Business School professor John Kao, ". . . one couldn't argue with our past success. The results had been good. On the one hand, if one looked back two or three years, it was becoming clear that growth was slowing down. The competitive environment was changing rapidly. The world was talking electronic fund transfer, cashless society. Because our current chairman, Jim Robinson, saw all these things, he brought me in to be a change agent. Hell, I was thirty-five years old. What else was I going to be? I was not going to preside over a status-quo approach to the business."

Gerstner tried to shake up AmEx managers at off-campus retreats where executives played War Games. Team building was becoming fashionable in business, and this was a concept that Gerstner thought was important. He divided his managers into small groups, told them they were members of a team, gave each group a problem to solve, and put them in a room for four hours.

They were not allowed to emerge without a battle plan that everyone on the team endorsed.

The idea was for everyone to own his part of the business. Under Gerstner, "ownership"—direct responsibility for a project's success or failure—became a term that would find its way into IBM management training as well. "Who's driving?" an initiative became a middle- and upper-management mantra for individual accountability within a team. A "deliverable" was a tangible short-term assignment with an inviolable deadline.

To soften his brusque image, Gerstner's communications executives also scheduled hour-long "walk arounds" on Friday afternoons. These were typically meant to be informal exchanges with American Express's lower echelons. But they were in fact highly structured, scripted, and well-planned events. He did not leave anything to chance. "He can ratchet up the charm as he moves down the organization," explained one senior executive who worked for Gerstner. "At high levels, his demeanor can be blunt and straightforward. He gets warmer as he goes down."

Gerstner's relationship with his old firm changed. McKinsey now worked for him; he was the client. Mac Stewart, his old mentor, reviewed McKinsey's work with Gerstner every six weeks or so. Sometimes they would meet at 6:30 A.M. at AmEx's offices and spend an hour or more together before the business day began. The other routine was for Stewart to travel to AmEx's tower at 5:30 P.M., ride down in the elevator with Gerstner, and travel uptown with him in his car. By then, Gerstner had a driver and had moved to Greenwich. In the evening rush-hour traffic on the East River Drive the two often caught up. Stewart then lived on East 72nd Street. Gerstner would drop him off at the 63rd Street exit. Stewart thought it curious that he was never driven the nine blocks to his door. All told, it was about a mile out of Gerstner's way. It would have taken too much time, Stewart eventually concluded. That he'd never had his driver drop Stewart at his apartment, even when it was raining, was typical of Gerstner's focus. Gerstner behaved this way because it was his management style. He had no spare time, even for an aging mentor.

Also, along with his success, his arrogant streak was growing. He began disinviting Jim Robinson to meetings, not even allowing Robinson the courtesy of attending as a nonparticipant, just to watch him "cook sausage." As one former AmEx board member put it, "He's that kind of a manager. He doesn't welcome his boss's input. In fact, he does not want to take advice from anyone who is older than he is because he thinks they're over the hill, and are therefore no longer useful."

Gerstner also had the enviable management knack of knowing when to disregard the logic and trust his instincts. He had no compunction about tossing out McKinsey's recommendations when he disagreed with them. When McKinsey did a study of AmEx's sputtering Vacation Packages division, it reported to Gerstner that it could not be fixed and ought to be closed. Roger Ballou, a junior executive who had been brought in to turn it around, disagreed. Gerstner decided to give him the chance. "You're sitting there, and the choice is close it or fix it in six months," Ballou said. "So Plan A and Plan B are a little scary here. Plan C was, oh shit, look for a new job. As it happened, we were right, we turned it around and made money with it. I was impressed that he just didn't take the knee-jerk advice of the business consultant."

Gerstner also knew when to trust his gut feelings when it came to his hires. After he left McKinsey, he asked Rick Thoman, an original member of his Finance Group, to join him at AmEx. Thoman, who would later work his way up to the presidency of the company's International Group, became an executive whom Gerstner would continue to rely on. He would soon garner a reputation for firmly attaching his career to Lou Gerstner's shirt-tails. This was particularly vexing to some at McKinsey, who thought of Thoman as a nice guy, well-mannered and impeccably dressed, who made a great presentation but had little else to offer. What did Gerstner know about Thoman that they didn't? Thoman was an intellectual who was short on business operational muscle, they felt. He had been known as an "unguided feather," a bon vivant who was often off at his home in the South of France or unreachable when an important client needed immediate attention. Returning phone calls was not a Thoman priority, at least early in his career.

Thoman was a useful aide to Gerstner, however. A former aide recalled a trip he took with Gerstner and Thoman with stops in London, Paris, and Frankfurt, among other places. On the AmEx jet, Gerstner had sifted through the briefing books and then asked Thoman to answer a slew of questions. Thoman had thoroughly done the advance work. He seemed to anticipate the details that would flag Gerstner's attention, especially esoteric business customs of small or obscure countries. For example, when AmEx's traditional blue color did not appear on an AmEx office awning in a foreign country, Thoman could explain the particular parochial local law that called for it to be green instead.

Gerstner followed no conventional formula or pattern for his hires. At AmEx, the addition of Jerry Welsh indicated he was adept at identifying a wide range of good people. Welsh's appointment contradicted any notion that every Gerstner hire was required to have a business background. Welsh had been a professor of Slavic languages, particularly Russian, and his avocation was ultra-marathon running. He was known around AmEx as "Wild Man Jerry," and his expertise was in his gut understanding of the consumer spending psyche. He was constantly pitching new ideas. "Welsh was a very smart guy," said Jim Calvano, a former AmEx executive to whom Welsh reported. "Of the ten ideas Welsh had, nine were insane. But the other one was genius." More than one AmEx executive credited Gerstner's tolerance for a certain number of misfits as the only reason Welsh wasn't drop-kicked out of the company. Welsh didn't dispute this: "When I was head of marketing—I had no particular qualifications—Lou and I were in Europe at that time, and I said, 'Lou, who are we putting in charge of the business in Europe?' When he told me, I said, 'What are his qualifications?' He said, 'About the same as yours.'"

One of Welsh's most successful campaigns was dubbed "cause-related" marketing. When the Statue of Liberty was undergoing a massive restoration in 1983, Welsh proposed that for a three-month period the company should donate a penny of every charge transaction—and a dollar for every new card issued—to the statue's capital improvement.

Gerstner knew it was one of Welsh's one terrific idea in ten and acted immediately. The playbook was jettisoned. No focus groups, no test marketing, no protracted meetings or consultants. "Gerstner said, 'I love it. Let's do it,'" recalled Welsh. "Not one piece of paper ever was exchanged. He approved it in ten minutes. He said to try to bring it in for under $12 million." The statue received $1.7 million from the program, and card usage spiked twenty-eight percent during the promotion period compared with the previous quarter.

The campaign worked so well, AmEx began supporting all kinds of causes worldwide; zoos, symphony orchestras, operas, and ballets. Gerstner created a "monomaniacal" atmosphere, demanding new ways to expand the reach of the card. Welsh responded by developing marketing and advertising campaigns specifically tailored toward professional women and recent college graduates. It was Welsh who plucked the line, "American Express is part of interesting lives," from a sheaf of advertising storyboards and decided to emphasize its subtlety—the company name and product weren't disclosed until the end of the commercial. AmEx's ads were so enlightened and sophisticated that even feminist Gloria Steinem lauded them. The "Do You Know Me?" campaign of not-quite-recognizable celebrities and the "Don't Leave Home Without It" series were created under Gerstner's watch. And they worked. Between 1980 and 1984, TRS revenues doubled, from about $6.5 billion to nearly $13 billion.

Shelly Lazarus, then a young executive at Ogilvy and Mather (she is now chairman and CEO), the agency that handled AmEx's advertising, met Gerstner at about this time. She had to fly to a meeting with a tape of a new "Do You Know Me?" spot featuring the Mills Brothers, a popular singing group from the 1940s and 1950s. She had just begun work on the account. She screened the commercial, and Gerstner said he didn't like it. The Mills Brothers were kind of dated, even for a campaign like this one. Lazarus responded that she "loved it." She refused to budge. "We sort of got into this whole thing," Lazarus said. "And Lou said, 'Look, you know, the campaign's terrific, if I don't like one, it doesn't really matter, more or less.' And I said, 'Well, I'm glad to hear you say that because I think it's terrific, and I think we just ought to run it.'" After additional debate, Gerstner ultimately relented, and she said, "I think we were friends after that."

One thing Lazarus discovered from her AmEx experience: Gerstner was an ad agency's preferred client. That he was willing to approve something he personally disliked showed that he trusted the agency. The plus was that he had a passion for the value of branding at a time when many top-level executives did not. "He was maniacal about protecting the American Express brand, absolutely maniacal," Lazarus recalled, using what would become a frequently repeated Gerstner adjective. "He would say things like, 'It is the most important equity we have, it is the most important thing in our business, we have to understand what it is and never violate it.'"

Meanwhile, CEO Jim Robinson had grand plans to expand AmEx's business through a merger with Shearson, a respected brokerage house. He believed that their combined forces could produce a full-service financial firm. Each company could benefit from the customers of the other. This was the 1980s, remember, and the cliché du jour was "synergy." "Jim, if you cut his arm open, he bled these American Express droplets," said Edwin Cooperman. "On the other hand, he had this grand vision of a giant company; he wanted to buy Disney. He always wanted to run something bigger."

Not everyone was sanguine about the merger. Howard Clark, the retired AmEx chairman, voiced his doubts. A brokerage firm's profits were unpredictable, a slave to the vagaries of the stock market. To Clark it meant committing a large amount of capital and putting the company's financial health at risk.

Gerstner, too, was conservative. He felt that there was still a lot of room for expansion among its core products. Also, he was aghast that Robinson wanted to call the new company Shearson American Express, and not the other way around. Robinson, firmly in command, reportedly told Gerstner that if he was paying a billion dollars for a company, he would call it anything he wanted.

Nonetheless, the Shearson American Express merger was approved in 1982. Not only did it bring together a phalanx of talented executives, it caused a massive turf war between the two cultures. Everyone involved assumed that a restructuring would mean more money, a bigger title, a larger playpen. Two executives defined the new company's image: Sanford "Sandy" Weill, Shearson's master deal maker (he later became the architect of Citigroup, the 1998 megamerger of the Traveler's Group with Citicorp), and Gerstner, whose group was churning out fifteen to twenty percent earnings growth a year for Robinson. Gerstner was AmEx's flag officer and biggest moneymaker; Weill was the newcomer who represented future growth. Both Weill and Gerstner began jockeying for position and power. Weill was named president of AmEx, theoretically the number two spot of the merged concern. Reportedly, Weill, who already had been a CEO, felt that he should have Robinson's job.

Robinson did nothing to stop the contentious atmosphere that prevailed. In fact, he openly encouraged it. His top two executives were high-powered and intensely competitive. For as long as possible, he would keep them separate but equal. Weill could concentrate on finance, mergers, and acquisitions. Gerstner would grow the intrinsic businesses that already constituted AmEx.

That Gerstner and Weill would clash, and eventually grow to dislike each other, was not an unexpected development. They were talented businessmen, but both had considerable egos and their styles clashed. Weill had grown up in Brooklyn's Bensonhurst section, the son of a Jewish garment manufacturer. He was a sloppy dresser who liked to go snowmobiling in the Adirondacks. Gerstner had nicer suits, they fit better, and he liked a good pair of cuff links. Gerstner understood that golf was AmEx's game, especially for serious businessmen.

Their business acumen came from different strains as well. Roger Ballou said, "Sandy is clearly a very analytical guy, but Sandy is more inductive, where Lou is more reductive. Sandy always had a logic to what he did, but a lot of stuff he did was based on an intuitive understanding of a situation [from] a lot of experience. Sandy projected an image of being more of a rough and tumble guy, whereas Lou was more methodical and purposeful in appearance and style." Gerstner was the consummate manager, unceasingly analytical, antiseptic, humorless, objective. Two executives who worked closely with Gerstner called him a "control freak."

Weill was the consummate networker. He was peerless when it came to working a room, and he frequently stayed until the end of business parties. Gerstner, on the other hand, did not enjoy this ritual. He stayed at office parties only as long as necessary, then it was off to do homework. Once, the Shearson contingent arranged for a stripper to celebrate the birthday of an executive. She arrived at a tax-planning meeting posing as an accountant. When she began disrobing, the Shearson side of the company thought it was hilarious. The gag backfired, however. Gerstner, according to a published account, was "horrified." This was certainly not proper behavior, for either a committed Catholic or an AmEx executive.

Clearly, there were two distinct cultures within the new Shearson American Express, the button-down conventional types in Gerstner's organization, and the more freewheeling guys in Weill's. "There was a nuclear war going on," Cooperman said. "It was like armed camps." Those in AmEx's TRS division were all but forbidden to speak to Sandy Weill and his protégé and number two exec, Peter Cohen, and anyone else of stature in Shearson. So much for Robinson's synergy.

It was obvious to everyone at the company that either Gerstner or Weill would be Robinson's successor. And Gerstner didn't need to commission McKinsey to do a study on who he thought it should be. At one point, a popular joke circulated throughout AmEx about Gerstner's outsized ambition: that he yearned for an office on the fifty-second floor. The AmEx building had only fifty-one floors. Roger Ballou summed up the space problem in the rarefied air high above the financial district: "Realistically, with a company as big as American Express, it wasn't going to work to have somebody as strong as Lou Gerstner, somebody as strong and accomplished as Sandy Weill, and Jim Robinson all up there. It just wasn't going to work." There just wasn't a conference room large enough to contain those three egos.

But this classic power struggle ended with Gerstner besting Weill. After AmEx's board turned down a deal he had concocted with Warren Buffet to buy an insurance company, Weill resigned in mid-1985. Gerstner was named president, now officially Robinson's number two.

In the late 1980s, AmEx flourished, but there were blemishes that appeared under Gerstner's watch. Visa and MasterCard drew a bead on AmEx's charge card, the company's lifeblood. AmEx had the premium brand, and for this customers were asked to pay $35 a year for the "privilege" of being a "cardmember." Gold card members paid more for a few more services. Visa and MasterCard offered revolving credit, had looser qualifying restrictions, and made deals with banks to give the cards away. As American consumers borrowed on their no-fee credit cards with high interest rates at a frenzied pace, it cut into the famed green card's market share. Those who couldn't qualify for an American Express card happily settled for one of the other brands. Also, more retail establishments began accepting Visa and Mastercard because they charged a lower transaction rate. Suddenly, every retailer accepted "all credit cards." The brand's elite image had eroded.

Still, Gerstner's team countered with both the Optima card, which issued revolving credit, and the Platinum card, for very high-end customers. Optima was a disaster at first. Crucial mistakes were made early and often. Ed Cooperman, who was responsible for the card's rollout, and who reported to Gerstner, distributed Optima cards to AmEx card customers. This was a questionable strategy because many of those cardholders were using corporate expense accounts that had large balances and paid on time. There was no way to immediately and accurately evaluate them as consumer credit risks. They were not especially good customers. AmEx did not have in place a reliable system to check creditworthiness. This mistake was compounded by collection agents who were given wide discretion to reschedule late payments and negotiate with defaulters. These agents were given incentives to "reset" the accounts, which led to greater defaults, and hence large losses. At least $150 million—and possibly much more—was lost the first year, an item that was not revealed on AmEx's annual report. One former AmEx communications executive said, "I don't know how we buried that kind of number." Another equivocated when it came to assigning responsibility. "Lou was, I think, a fence sitter on the Optima card," Cooperman said. "I'll take credit or discredit for Optima, but I remember a number of meetings where I was hoping that Lou would make the speech to make it happen. I won't say he left me out there to hang and dry, but I was the guy who honestly had to carry the ball. I'm not saying he didn't approve it. Yes, he was the one who gave us the money."

It was Gerstner, along with Jim Robinson, who also began implementing Project Genesis in 1988, a five-year $250 million global initiative to upgrade AmEx's technology infrastructure. Gerstner envisioned a computer network to integrate all of AmEx's products and services among all of its regions. At that time, there was a mixture of different computer systems depending on the country. Compatibility was a problem; it was impossible to quickly gather comparable data from any two foreign divisions.

AmEx also had been dreadfully slow in billing customers because thousands of international vendors had been using old technology. The ROCs, or records of charge receipts, often gave cardholders months of free float on their debt at company expense. Genesis would not only speed up AmEx's billing, saving the company tens of millions of dollars, but it would add greater efficiency to complaint resolution, lost cards, or airline tickets, and use sophisticated programming to make better use of customer buying habits and demographics. In sum, this investment would reestablish AmEx's position as the leader in customer service.

Though Genesis had a staff of twenty executives and more than three hundred people, it was far too complicated a project to manage. Technology outsourcing was not yet a sophisticated business. IBM had been a main hardware vendor, but it hadn't been awarded the contract to implement the entire project. Perhaps as a precaution, AmEx concluded that no one company should oversee the entire system. That was left in-house, and several systems integrators were involved. AmEx did not manage it well. In the end, it took AmEx eight or nine years to revamp its computing infrastructure. The countless delays produced huge cost overruns. Roger Ballou, the executive in charge of Genesis, said, "It never worked as soon as it could have, or should have. It got a ton of resistance, elements of it didn't work out."

Though the problems couldn't be traced to a single vendor, IBM was a large part of the problem. "In that era with IBM, whatever your issue was, their solution was hardware," Ballou said. "If you said, 'I'm having a problem getting the data I want,' they said, 'Oh, you need a new box.' That was the culture you dealt with then. I always found dealing with IBM more like dealing with the federal government rather than dealing with another business. They'd drive you friggin' nuts." Rick Thoman said of IBM, "What the customer wanted was irrelevant. It couldn't organize itself to accommodate the customers."

The AmEx relationship with IBM was definitely strained. Angela Russo, a former IBMer who worked on the AmEx account during that period, recalled there were several tense meetings between the two companies. Mike Armstrong, once a top candidate to succeed John Akers as CEO of IBM (and who is now CEO of AT&T), was IBM's "customer satisfaction" executive on the account. Armstrong was not the day-to-day account executive; he was called in only for special presentations or when there were pressing concerns about IBM's performance. But IBM had to know it was in very serious shape when its chairman and CEO was called in. Armstrong wasn't enough of a troubleshooter for Gerstner, who insisted on John Akers's attendance; and when Akers arrived, he would also meet privately with him. "Gerstner always wanted to deal with Akers," Russo said.

Though he would never say so publicly, Gerstner's complaints as a customer of the IT industry undoubtedly had much to do with his horrible experiences with IBM while he was AmEx's president.

Meanwhile, Gerstner had become disenchanted with his own career development. It was the vertical vision thing. He was impatient with Robinson, who had thought seriously about Gerstner succeeding him as chairman and CEO. Also, there were theories that Robinson had political ambitions. He was a staunch George Bush supporter and fund-raiser, and there was speculation that when a newly elected President assumed office in 1989, Robinson might be offered a cabinet post. Others eschewed this hypothesis, saying that while Robinson enjoyed hobnobbing with politicos and power brokers inside the Beltway, he was merely planning a leisurely exit from AmEx that would allow him to maintain his business and social rank—perhaps a lucrative consulting arrangement with AmEx, access to a company plane, retention of his board seat.

Privately, Robinson bristled at Gerstner's guileless attempts to hasten his retirement. He was not about to be elbowed out the door on Gerstner's schedule. A genteel Southerner, he thought Gerstner's behavior rather gauche. Robinson, along with George Waters, had begun second-guessing himself. Though Gerstner possessed all the right business tools—few doubted his executive skills—they wondered whether he was the right choice to lead American Express into the 1990s.

Robinson began cosseting Peter Cohen, now an M&A star in his own right, as a possible contender for the top position, pitting him against Gerstner. Gerstner sensed Robinson's hesitancy. When the United Airlines CEO slot opened, Gerstner advanced himself as a candidate. A former Gerstner associate actually overheard a conversation with a United board member confirming his desire for that job. When Pillsbury's board was looking for a CEO, Gerstner's name was floated. Word of Gerstner's attempt to find *any* high-profile CEO job eventually filtered back to Robinson, and this effectively ensured that an ever widening fissure would come between the two.

Now Gerstner felt the same way as Sandy Weill, who once felt like a perpetual copilot. But Gerstner's chance finally came in late 1988 when Henry Kravis's investment firm, Kohlberg Kravis Roberts and Company, stunned the business world by acquiring RJR Nabisco for $24.5 billion in junk bonds. KKR had defeated a bid by Shearson Lehman Hutton, then a subsidiary of AmEx, in a fierce takeover war. By January, it was prowling for a new CEO, someone who was skilled at identifying assets, selling off non-core companies, and reducing debt. One of Kravis's partners, Paul Raether, had known about Gerstner's availability. Raether and Kravis conducted one interview at Gerstner's home in Greenwich. "I was impressed with their questions," Gerstner said, recounting their meeting later for *Business Week*. "But I told them, 'If you're looking for a liquidator, I'm not your guy. I'm a builder.'" Gerstner had other reservations. He had no intentions of setting up shop in Atlanta, where Nabisco was based, or in Winston-Salem, where RJR had its headquarters. He wanted to remain in the New York area.

The more they talked, the more the two partners thought Gerstner was the right guy.

At the same time, Mac Stewart had done all he could to keep the Gerstner-Robinson relationship intact. He persuaded Robinson that it was in AmEx's best interests to let Gerstner know that he was his choice to be his successor. Robinson finally agreed, and asked Stewart to be the liaison and sound Gerstner out about Robinson's continuing role as chairman emeritus. That same morning, a Thursday in mid-March, Stewart left Robinson's corner office and walked around the building to Gerstner's corner office. Gerstner was on the telephone. Stewart told Gerstner's longtime secretary, Isabelle Cummins, that it was urgent, he had to see him right way. Cummins responded that Gerstner was absolutely booked all day and Friday, but that Stewart should return first thing on Monday. "I thought for sure this would keep for over the weekend," Stewart recalled. But he later found out that phone call represented inauspicious timing for AmEx; Gerstner had been talking with Kravis, finalizing his deal. So Stewart never got the chance to tell Gerstner that Robinson had finally agreed to let him have the top job. It had been implied, but never promised, and that had always bothered Gerstner.

KKR offered Gerstner roughly the same in salary and bonuses that he had made the previous year at AmEx, about $2.4 million. But as is traditional, KKR bought out and awarded him his considerable stock equity in AmEx. He also received a large block of RJR Nabisco stock options as a performance incentive, upward of one percent of the value of the new company. Though Gerstner had a huge personal upside—his five-year package was conservatively worth $25 million—he parried questions about his pay. "In no way do I feel financially secure," he said, in what was a bizarre and perplexing attempt at rationalization for his potential increase in personal net worth. Since his new options did not fully vest for five years, Gerstner said he felt like he went in the hole for $6.5 million.

The announcement on March 13, 1989, of Gerstner's resignation stunned Wall Street. AmEx director Henry Kissinger lamented the company's loss, saying that "Lou was irreplaceable." Robinson assumed Gerstner's title of president.

Now in only the third job of his career, Gerstner relished the challenge and revealed just how unhappy he had been at AmEx.

He told a reporter, "I said to my wife, 'I really can't wait to get to the office tomorrow.' It has been a long time since I wished for Monday morning to come." At RJR, Gerstner inherited a new shop that included dozens of well-known products on both the tobacco and food sides of the supermarket aisle. Though he had no experience in these businesses, he did understand respectable brands like Camel, Winston, Salem, Doral, Chips Ahoy!, Fig Newtons, Oreos, Ritz Crackers, Wheat Thins, Planter's Peanuts, and LifeSavers. Whatever joy and comfort he had with the public's loyalty with these cookies, crackers, candies, and cigarettes, however, was quickly overshadowed by two immediate problems.

First, the company had been saddled with a mountain of debt, about $26 billion. This figure was "more debt than most developing countries," Karl M. von der Heyden, Gerstner's new CFO, told *Business Week*. As a debtor, RJR would rank tenth, right behind the Philippines and just ahead of Morocco. Despite Gerstner's professed desire to be a builder and not a liquidator, he'd have to sell off a number of assets just to keep cash flowing and meet an annual loan payment of $3 billion. Bank notes of $6 billion were due in two years.

Second, all but a few of the two dozen members of the senior management team had deserted the company during the buyout struggle. "I came in to be CEO, but I was CEO, CFO, general counsel, head of tobacco operations, and at one point, there was no treasurer," he lamented. At that moment, Gerstner certainly did not have to worry about who was in control.

Though Kravis installed several directors on the board from his own buyout group, Gerstner had a say in bringing in others, including Vernon Jordan and John Medlin, the CEO of Wachovia Bank in North Carolina. Medlin had actually been asked by Kravis to be a director before he'd chosen a new CEO, but he politely stalled, saying that he had better wait until he knew who it was. He was relieved when Kravis later called and told him he'd hired Gerstner. Medlin had first worked with Gerstner back in the mid-1970s, when Wachovia used McKinsey's services to help it sell some small assets. Medlin had a lot of confidence in Gerstner, and had no concerns at all about his lack of experience in cigarettes and cookies.

Gerstner coped with his personnel problem by hiring three of his most loyal executives, David Kalis, Rick Thoman, and Larry Ricciardi, his general counsel. Kalis, who had been the media gatekeeper for him at AmEx, would methodically dole out to the press Gerstner's strategy for recovery. When Gerstner made a tour of a cookie factory or a supermarket, Kalis made sure a trustworthy journalist was on hand. There was the CEO wearing a hair net as he toured an assembly line, there he was in the food aisles making notes about housewives' shopping behavior. Business reporters and Wall Street, in general, needed to be mollified during Gerstner's first crisis year. Creditors were worried. A lot of nervous bondholders wondered whether RJR Nabsico would have enough cash flow to meet its interest obligations.

The company's previous management had left the company in disarray. Haunting the offices of RJR Nabisco were vestiges of the profligate spending habits of Gerstner's predecessor, F. Ross Johnson, a freewheeling CEO who had assembled a fleet of eleven corporate jets—it was dubbed the "RJR Air Force"—along with dozens of apartments and hundreds of cars for company use. About thirty athletes were on advertising and promotional retainers, and they apparently did little work for large fees. Everywhere Gerstner looked, he saw waste.

Gerstner calculated he could reduce operating costs by more than half a billion dollars a year, some twelve percent, by laying off three thousand employees. Most of the jets went on the block, along with the apartments and cars. Sweetheart contracts were allowed to expire. Excessive perks Johnson had lavished on his top managers suddenly disappeared. RJR's executives, accustomed to working in a fraternity-like atmosphere, soon realized that under Gerstner's rule the company would foster a more monkish existence.

Gerstner spent much of his first year in the air, logging some 250,000 miles visiting customers, plants, and employees. Beijing, where the Chinese are famous for their high rates of cigarette consumption, became one of his frequent stops. He canceled Premier, a "smokeless" cigarette, after his advisors told him that it tasted so bad, nobody would even steal it. He ended the company's practice of making excess shipments of cigarettes to wholesalers, which artificially inflated quarterly sales, only to see losses appear later when the stale tobacco was returned. Johnson had spent billions of dollars to modernize cigarette manufacturing facilities, and plans already were on the drawing board to invest $2.4 billion on new food factories, nicknamed "Cookieville." Gerstner knew he did not have the luxury to embark on such ambitious investments. He canceled two baking plants and decided instead to upgrade others. It was difficult to criticize Gerstner for myopic thinking. There would be no long term unless RJR survived the short term.

Gerstner held a veritable garage sale of assets. He sold the Del Monte canned food operations—except for its Canadian unit—for $1.5 billion. He sold a fresh food company, a candy business (which included Planter's, LifeSavers, Baby Ruth, and Butterfingers), Chun King canned goods, and a number of foreign subsidiaries. Also on the block was RJR's twenty percent interest in ESPN, the cable sports channel. He floated more high-yield junk bonds, but he managed to grow some of his core businesses. He was sensitive to any criticism that he was merely performing fix-it chores. He made it a point with employees and the press to emphasize investments in remaining businesses. For example, he authorized a $10 million capital spending project at a nut plant. As he told Kravis and Raether in his job interviews, he did not want to be pigeonholed as a CEO whose specialty was just as a turnaround artist. Not every move was brilliant, or even strategic. He enlisted his daughter, Elizabeth, then a fourteen-year-old junior high school student, as a one-girl focus group. Gerstner brought home samples of a new product called "LifeSaver Holes," which Elizabeth tasted and apparently thought her classmates would like. Gerstner approved an early launch, but it was a dud in candy stores.

The tobacco side of the company caused Gerstner great concern and not a little angst. Americans were in the midst of a health craze, and antismoking sentiment was beginning to rise. The market pie itself was shrinking. "They loved talking about cookies," said a speechwriter who worked with Gerstner and other senior RJR Nabisco executives during this period. "Triscuits, [there were] lots of jokes about that in their speeches; they didn't really love talking about tobacco. I never had the feeling that any of them were comfortable." When Gerstner did a speech at the Amos Tuck School at Dartmouth, he was well prepped for the Q&A from the business students. It all but copied the briefing books of the tobacco lobby. He had no moral objections to smoking, he said. He smoked cigars himself. It was legal and it involved personal choice. People who smoked understood the health risks. And, of course, he wouldn't encourage his kids or any others to smoke. Gerstner, of course, knew this was simply posturing and corporate blather.

Gerstner knew running a company that profited from smoking certainly did not enhance his curriculum vitae. When he took the RJR job, he was an active board member at Memorial Sloan-Kettering Cancer Center. Paul Marks, Memorial's CEO, said that in the early 1980s, Gerstner had helped Memorial rewrite a tenure program for its professors. He also was instrumental in guiding the hospital through a tricky physical plant issue, where Memorial razed a dormitory and replaced it with a new research center. Gerstner desperately wanted to serve on the board. But there was no way the head of a tobacco company could remain on a prestigious cancer center's board. He was asked to resign his seat, and would not regain it until five years after he took over IBM. It might have been sooner, but he had to wait until Jim Robinson, who was Memorial's chairman of the board of overseers, stepped down.

Gerstner had been a member of the National Cancer Advisory Board on Cancer Prevention and Early Detection, a position that he also was forced to give up. Mark Green, then the incoming Commissioner of New York City's Consumer Affairs, published an op-ed piece in the *New York Times* entitled, "Warning: RJR May Endanger Kids' Health." It was adapted from a letter he wrote to

Gerstner—and given in advance to the press—that began, "As the father of two young children, I am appalled at your 'Smooth Character' Camel advertising campaign, which risks addicting children to cigarettes." What particularly irked Green were RJR's Joe Camel pullout poster ads in *Rolling Stone* magazine that urged readers to tear off the perforated Surgeon General's health warning. This kind of public criticism couldn't have made the CEO's business any easier, considering that the number of Americans smoking was on the decline, and that Winston, his leading brand, had been steadily losing market share to Philip Morris's Marlboro.

It was clear that the combination of selling food and tobacco was not something that Gerstner was wholly comfortable doing. Also, with the way the company was structured financially, he probably had his fill of constantly dealing with anxious bankers. After only four years, the IBM opportunity presented itself, and Gerstner was poised to begin the most significant challenge of his career.

Overall, he probably left RJR in better shape than he found it. He navigated through the delicate shoals of a dying junk bond market. He had never missed an interest payment, and he had whittled the company's debt nearly in half. Gerstner has said that the restructuring of RJR Nabisco was a "traumatic" experience. He also said the task was "like crossing the Sahara. It just goes on and on."

The RJR experience prepared Gerstner to face an even larger bureaucracy and an even sicker enterprise. The troubles he faced in Winston-Salem and Atlanta were merely a prelude to those he would confront in Armonk.

It was either brilliant prescience or pure luck that Gerstner left RJR when he did to take the IBM job. He had just stabilized RJR's cigarette business after spending a few years developing low-priced brands and shoring up the quality of his mainstays, Winston, Camel, and Salem. A day after he arrived at IBM, Philip Morris announced a big price cut on Marlboro in order to regain lost market share. A price war ensued, and RJR was hurt worse than Philip Morris. The stock was hammered, and Kravis's once-masterful deal became one of the biggest mistakes in the annals of modern LBOs. In December 1993, in its annual year in review, the *New York Times* business section cited Gerstner for leaving his job at just the precise moment. He won the "Career Timing Award."

His judgment was further vindicated when the company's food and tobacco units were separated once again in early 1999. The $24.5 billion that Kravis had paid for the conglomerate was then worth about $9.5 billion.

Seismic Shakes in Big Blue's Culture

7

ARMONK, NY—Late 1993

By the fall of 1993, after only six months on the job, Gerstner had made the rounds of dozens of IBM sites, determined to inspire the troops. He was the consummate change agent. He preached a new gospel, a new corporate culture, where the company would be faster and more competitive. He promised employees that the journey through the long, dark night of IBM's nightmare would soon end. Big Blue would soon rediscover its soul. "From what I learned, there is a lot more right than wrong with this company; and I'm convinced our weaknesses can be overcome by our strengths," he wrote in a July 27, 1993, message to employees. Though he did not foresee a profit until at least the last quarter, he was upbeat in his internal meetings with employees.

The corporate spinmeisters labeled his visits "town meetings," and the formats were simple. Typically, Gerstner walked into a small auditorium on a bare stage. He'd speak without any prepared remarks for just a few minutes, and then he'd field questions from IBMers for about an hour. His opening message was this: *I hope you understand what I'm trying to do with this company.* He was the IBM evangelist, and it was important for everyone throughout the organization to understand the need to revamp and simplify the system. "Leveraging" the company's size and its assets became a byword in every pitch. Managers were encouraged to "empower" their direct reports. Work "out of the box," step up and take charge when nobody else on your team wants to. I'm not going to stop talking about the need to change the way you think, the need to focus on the customer and not internal issues. Some managers still don't get it. *Now, I'll take your questions.*

Though Gerstner was known for his curt, aloof style in small meetings and one-on-one situations, he showed he could be masterful in front of a crowd. David Harrah, a former communications manager, remembered one particularly impressive town meeting. Gerstner took off his suit jacket, sat on the edge of the stage, his feet hanging down. Harrah recalled, "He said something like, 'We're making $64 billion a year. By far, the most money in the information technology business is being spent with us. This is such an endorsement, this is an order of magnitude over anybody else. The problem is that it's costing us $69 billion to do it. So, how do we deal with this?' He put things in such simple, logical perspective." When Gerstner wrapped up, Harrah and his colleagues were nearly bowled over. Akers had never attempted to identify IBM's problems with such candor, let alone sit on the edge of a stage.

Despite the pressure of trying to coax IBM into profitablity again, Gerstner was relaxed on his employee tour. He even revealed his normally reserved sense of humor on a trip to a chip factory in Burlington, Vermont. The IBM Gulfstream IV had Gerstner and an entourage on board, and when they landed in Vermont, limousines shuttled them to the plant. On the way, there was a roadside shack that sold golf equipment. Gerstner's limo pulled over, and out popped the CEO. The motorcade stopped. He disappeared for a few minutes, and then returned to his car. On the return flight to Armonk, everyone on the plane was unwinding, drinking cocktails. Someone finally asked Gerstner about his foray into the golf outlet. He was shopping for a new putter called the "Fat Lady," and a left-handed model was difficult to find. Once inside, he found a rather large woman standing on a ladder checking the inventory. Gerstner asked, "Do you know where I can find a left-handed Fat Lady?" Before he realized the double entendre, the woman shot him a look and told him he could check out the bar down the road—a fat lady worked there. "It was the first and only time I'd ever seen Gerstner laugh," said a former IBM manager who has known him for many years.

That might have been one of the few laughs Gerstner allowed himself during that first difficult year. Town meetings would only do so much, he knew. He had to wrestle the old guard, the remaining senior managers, from the grip of IBM's bureaucracy.

Gerstner attacked the high echelon with particular disregard for IBM's traditions. He demanded that business reports be kept to ten pages. If you can't say it in less than ten pages, Gerstner put it bluntly, then you probably can't explain your business. This was no small thing to many senior executives who struggled for brevity. They were accustomed to using acetate foils where the graphs and charts were projected on screens while the lights in the room were turned down. Foils were legendary at IBM, perhaps more so than at any other American company. Some managers literally could not make a presentation without them. Gerstner decided IBMers had to walk without the crutches. In Armonk, he ordered the foil projectors removed, though they are still little-used fixtures in conference rooms at other IBM sites.

Next, he began to tinker with his own high command. On September 13, 1993, Gerstner announced that he was creating a special advisory group consisting of himself and ten other senior executives called the CEC, or Corporate Executive Committee. Gerstner's directive said the committee would serve three purposes: first, it would make IBM's businesses "cohesive and responsive" to customers; second, it would implement "corporate-wide integration initiatives"; and third, it would "advise me on broad issues of corporate strategy."

To some it seemed that Gerstner was adding a new level of bureaucracy. In fact, he was consolidating his brain trust. The CEC was an antidote, almost a replacement, to IBM's long-standing WMC, or Worldwide Management Council.

The WMC had about thirty-five members, and it included the general managers of the foreign subsidiaries. In the past, it had considerable clout in determining IBM's strategies, even more decision-making power than the board of directors. Nothing important—no large capital expenditure or commitment to a course of action—could happen without the sanction of the WMC.

The WMC operated like the old Soviet Union. Everyone had to be in absolute agreement. The company once had an infamous policy where a lone WMC member could derail a project or a product by claiming he "nonconcurred." The remnants of Politburo rule still existed everywhere. CFO Jerry York said, "From what I was told, one stinking person out of twenty-eight that had equity in a decision could block it. If the vote was twenty-seven to one, the thing still didn't go. John Akers had abolished the nonconcur process officially around 1990, but the culture still carried on, even though whatever forms they used had long since disappeared."

Nonconcur had evolved into pushback, yet another IBM coinage that strangled the company's ability to make timely decisions. When Gerstner first heard the term "pushback," he was told that it meant that an executive or team was resisting an initiative, or worse, there was so much pushback the project was simply stalled somewhere in IBM's netherworld. Gerstner was sardonic: He thought "pushback" referred to customers who no longer wanted IBM computers. They "pushed them back" to vendors.

Under Gerstner, management by committee would change. The WMC still held meetings every three months or so, but it was an unwieldy body. According to York, it "was one [committee] that Lou never really came to grips with how he wanted to use it . . . but his general view came to be one of, well, the most important aspect of the WMC may be to help move along the culture change in the company." Jack Welch was invited to address the WMC, and he gave a short course in his management philosophy. Condensed, it went something like this: If you can't be number one or two in your business, then you should fix it, sell it, or close it. And he talked about corporate culture, becoming agile, the need for absolute candor, seeing an industry as it really is, not how you would like to to be. Welch made an impression on everyone.

The CEC would meet far more frequently, once a month, from around 8:30 A.M. until midafternoon. Also, the new committee would allow Gerstner to more closely evaluate the senior management team he had inherited from Akers. All but two (Gerry Czarnecki and Jerry York) on the CEC had carved out long careers at IBM prior to Gerstner's arrival. He had to find out who would buy into the new culture, and who were the holdouts. Six of the ten original CEC members would not survive the cut. It took two and a half years before these six would leave IBM. York said Gerstner put it this way: "Even if you make your numbers, if you do not become part of the solution—meaning the new way of business rather than the old way—your position is at risk." Basically, the new way meant that decision-making was a top-down exercise, and executives who didn't implement or act swiftly had no excuses. In other words, failure to execute resulted in your execution.

Bob LaBant was one of the first executives on the CEC who failed to adapt. He had begun his career as a sales trainee in 1967, and he worked his way through the traditional line of sales and marketing jobs at the firm. He was executive assistant in the chairman's suite during the transition from John Opel to Akers. LaBant's rise at IBM had gotten mixed reviews. Some observers felt that his movement upward was blessed. On the other hand, the soft-spoken forty-seven-year-old Midwesterner was a well-liked executive who always made his numbers. His break into senior management occurred in 1992, when he was appointed to head the U.S. sales force, one of the biggest such jobs in the technology industry, let alone at IBM.

But it was obvious to many in the company, even among those in lower management, that LaBant's future with Gerstner was in doubt. He had just too much invested with the old guard, the old culture. One only had to recall one of LaBant's large customer meetings at a conference center in Chantilly, Virginia. LaBant was entertaining the chief information officers of its two hundred largest accounts. The CIOs were the ones who made the decisions on the major technology investments for America's biggest corporations. To wit: They bought mainframe computers, and that part of the technology business had been slumping for the past few years.

Gerstner was invited to the meeting, and right away the tension was brewing. When Gerstner slipped out of his suit jacket, LaBant did likewise. Somehow, it didn't have the same effect. It looked like he was mimicking his boss. Gerstner used his pitch to vent about IBM's past sins, its ignorance of customer problems and requirements. He was emphatic about one thing: A customer was now in charge at IBM. When he told the audience that he couldn't believe a company with $64 billion in revenues was so hard to deal with, the CIOs cheered loudly. It was apparent that LaBant's meeting had become Gerstner's meeting.

During the Q&A, LaBant was at the podium answering a question about IBM's client-server strategy. Client-server is a method of combining large and small computers in a network so data is readily available when and where it's needed. Gerstner apparently felt that LaBant was not getting to the salient point. He rose and interrupted him, saying simply and succinctly, "We will do several different implementations of client-server, depending on specific user requirements. We would be foolish at this point to say there's only one way to do things." Those who witnessed the scene were surprised. Executives, especially those in sales, rambled forever, eventually wrestling the exasperated questioner into submission; but IBMers, even Akers, were always too polite to interrupt.

The coup de grace against LaBant at Chantilly occurred after a CIO asked a question that particularly rankled Gerstner. The CIO wanted to know, "If I buy a PS/2 from IBM in the U.S., but I'm using it in Canada, why can't I get this machine serviced or fixed in Canada? Why do I have to send it back to the U.S.?"

Gerstner was dumbfounded. He replied that he didn't know why, but by the end of the day Bob LaBant would have an answer. At that moment, LaBant quietly scurried out of the front of the meeting room.

LaBant would barely survive for another year, finally quitting after Gerstner merged the U.S. sales force with the international unit. "Bob LaBant was a good salesman," a corporate vice president said. "But he protected too many old-time IBMers who worked for him. He couldn't clean house because he went to sales school with them. That was his weakness, much the way Akers protected people who worked for him. He carried too much baggage." Those businessmen at IBM who evaluated executives first by their bottom-line performance were stoic about LaBant's departure after twenty-eight years with the company. One former executive said, "You look at his numbers, he was doing a superb job. But, you know, Lou didn't feel that he was participating in the cultural change that was needed."

Ellen Hancock, the lone woman CEC member, was another high-ranking IBMer who fell out of favor with the Gerstner regime. Hancock had begun her career at IBM as a programmer in 1965, and she was one of the few tech-heads to rise alongside the men in marketing. During the 1970s and 1980s, when IBM barely had a bad day let alone a disappointing quarter, she was continually promoted. Soon Hancock became Big Blue's systems software guru—meaning she was the executive in charge of the company's DB/2 programming for mainframes. Eventually she had responsibility for software that was developed by six different IBM divisions. She also ran the Networking Systems division, which in the pre-Internet era meant both hardware and software for data transmission and communications. She had a large sandbox, by anyone's measure.

Demure, almost grandmotherly in appearance, Hancock lived in an ordinary middle-class home in Ridgefield, Connecticut, nothing manorial. But as Hancock's power and station within the company rose, she began to emulate the least enviable characteristics of the WASP old boys' network that she joined.

During presentations, she was given to making lengthy, sometimes muddled speeches that rivaled the best (or worst) of
IBMers. More than once, she was attacked and embarrassed by
John Landry, the Lotus technology guru, who basically said she
didn't know what she was talking about. Nobody defended her.
Hancock became somewhat intoxicated with the perks of the
office, including access to company planes and helicopters. She
thought nothing of making some managers wait for weeks to get
on her calendar. During one trip to Heathrow Airport, she tried
to use her rank when she couldn't locate her passport. When a
customs official detained her, she elevated the incident to an
embarrassing level. To her executive assistant's amazement, she
berated the inspector, citing her high title at IBM—"Do you
know who I am? Do you realize who you're talking to?"

She suggested to Akers that because IBM was a worldwide
concern, her networking group should be relocated in someplace
more global—England, for instance—than one of the Westchester
locales. So Hancock relocated the entire group, some four hundred people, to Staines, England, outside London.

Hancock was a force in the technology industry, no doubt.
But she had more of an affinity for software engineering than for
management and the marketplace. And her often quixotic
behavior normally would have been overlooked if she had consistently delivered results.

She had a large blind spot in networking, however, one that
eventually would cause IBM to miss a market worth many hundreds of millions of dollars.

Hancock had been part of IBM's high-flying early days of networking. In the 1970s, Big Blue had developed a programming
language called System Network Architecture, or SNA, which
allowed mainframes to share data with other computers
throughout a company. A decade later, the division produced the
Token Ring adapter, which enhanced the linkage of all kinds of
computers. With SNA and Token Rings, IBM appeared to have
an invincible hold on the market. Local Area Networks, or LANs,
the internal data links that corporate America was increasingly

relying on, were in her domain. But two new notions in networking soon appeared: Ethernet and TCP/IP, for Transmission Control Protocol/Internet Protocol. Ethernet was designed to link PCs, and is now a commonly used corporate network; and the TCP/IP, the Internet Protocol communications language, was destined to become the language that would begin building the Internet.

Hancock, however, clung to all of IBM's original technology, which was quickly bypassed by the industry. This was a shock to many because IBM had done some of the early backbone development work for the federal government during the nascent days of networking. These backbone components, like switches, hubs, and routers, were back-office products that the public was generally unaware of. But they were critical to a connected universe. Without them there is no e-mail. A router, for example, is a device that acts as a traffic signal to shuttle data among different networks, redirecting it depending on loads.

Hancock stood by and watched as other companies jumped to an advantage. Cisco Systems stepped in and dominated the next wave of hardware accessories, which today is a multibillion-dollar market and still expanding. "When people would walk in to talk about this thing called Cisco or the router, or whatever, Ellen wouldn't hear of it," said former Wall Street analyst Dan Mandresh. A software marketing manager who worked at Lotus added that Hancock "drank from the Token Ring Kool-Aid and thought that that was going to be the end-all, be-all, and Ethernet and IP jumped up from behind and bit her in the ass." If she hadn't been focused on selling $99 Token Rings, an IBM manager said, Big Blue wouldn't have conceded an entire industry to Cisco and others.

By any calculation, IBM's market neglect did much to help Cisco become the dominant market player it is today. Of the thousand or so people who work for Cisco in its Interworks Business Unit in Raleigh, about half or more once worked at IBM. Even after Gerstner took over, Selby Wellman, the senior vice president of this Cisco division (and himself an ex-IBMer who spent fifteen years there), had taken the lead to forge an alliance with IBM that from any vantage point would have benefited Big Blue. Wellman says he made "countless attempts . . . with no success." He even sent a team up to the Watson Research Labs to jointly devise new technology that could replace the outdated mainframe SNA that IBM then used. He pleaded with IBM to look toward the Internet Protocol, which Cisco believed was the future, at least for the short run.

Wellman's team wanted to create a channel-attached router that went straight into a mainframe at channel speeds that could be compatible with any number of different transfer protocols. "Fundamentally what this means is, let's create a fat pipe into the mainframe and a fat pipe out," Wellman said of this joint proposal. The Watson researchers were enthusiastic with what Cisco cooked up; it worked fine.

But then they had to sell the idea to the appropriate product group, and that meant Ellen Hancock. "Ellen said no way," Wellman recalled. She was afraid that " 'this will eat into our FEP [Front End Protocol] revenue. That's a cash cow, that's where we're making all of our money, we just won't do it.' She violated or did not understand the Silicon Valley rule, which is that if you do not replace your technology, somebody else will."

Cisco's promotional literature brazenly plays right into the hearts of IBM's legacy customers. "CiscoBlue—the Safe Solution for IBM Internetworking," reads one pitch. Today, Cisco has captured eighty percent of the IBM networking market with more than 300,000 routers and switches that compete with Big Blue's once dominant SNA. Could IBM have manufactured those products? Certainly, either by itself, or in partnership with Cisco.

Missing markets was never fatal to IBM senior executives. When Gerstner began tweaking his organization at the highest level, he ordered Hancock's staff back to the United States. An IBM manager said, "It cost us millions to move the people there, and millions more to bring them home."

Still, Gerstner was going to give her a chance. Hancock was

promoted to senior vice president, reporting directly to the CEO. She was by then the highest-ranking woman line executive in the history of IBM, the only woman on both the WMC and the CEC. Hancock's kingdom comprised $9 billion to $11 billion of the company's annual revenues. Despite her spotty record, she was one of the most visible executives in the technology industry. Hancock's most recent distinction: She was one of the latest senior officials to be anointed with the midlevel managers' elite IBM acronym: FUMU—"Fuck Up, Move Up."

Ellen Hancock could not emerge from the culture that had nurtured her for so many years. She was still stuck in the Akers mold, white papers, meetings, and an entourage that bewildered her colleagues, many of whom were still lopping headcount with dispatch. After the Staines, England, debacle, she assembled a large support staff in one of IBM's North Carolina sites, some one hundred and twenty, who drafted strategy and policy for Hancock's various businesses. She analyzed and conducted her internal debates until "everything was studied to death," according to a former senior financial officer. Hancock did not sense Gerstner's urgency.

It took Gerstner about a year to conclude that her track record was not likely to improve. Finally, Gerstner and York consolidated the software business to cut administrative costs, and they handed her portfolio of businesses to John M. Thompson. Hancock, a lifer who had been at IBM for twenty-nine years, left shortly thereafter with a generous severance package. In return she agreed to a noncompete clause that allowed IBM to veto a number of job openings at software outfits like Novell. When Gil Amelio, then running National Semiconductor and later Apple, called Gerstner and expressed interest in hiring her as chief technical officer, he approved without hesitation.

Hancock, however, got the last smirk. After working with Gil Amelio for a couple of years (she was ousted by Steve Jobs along with Amelio), she took over Exodus Communications, a small Silicon Valley company that builds and manages corporate Web sites. When the company went public, Hancock's stock options reached about $30 million.

. . .

Gerstner had given both LaBant and Hancock plenty of time to adapt, and then he showed no remorse when he shunted them aside. This sent a tough, unambiguous message to others. "IBM executives traditionally never had to worry about their next job. Now, all of a sudden, it's gotten more competitive," Sam Albert, the former IBM veteran, said.

Executive paralysis permeated IBM's divisions everywhere. Big Blue's company culture—even one site located in Silicon Valley, a few thousand miles from company headquarters—was still hopelessly mired in its past.

The sad story of IBM's collapse in large-scale storage systems was somewhat embarrassing, and almost unbelievable. It was similar to its networking hardware misadventures.

Ed Zschau was the main character in this story, and his brief stewardship of one of the company's most important business units indicated how Gerstner operated. He was another senior executive inherited by Gerstner, different from most of them in at least one respect. He hadn't had a long, distinguished career with IBM. This was probably a plus in Gerstner's book. No excess baggage, no loyalties to a stream of managers who should have been long retired.

Zschau was first hired by Jack Kuehler, Akers's technology guru, to run IBM's AdStar storage systems division in San Jose. This was an odd choice, given Kuehler's admiration for those managers who came up through the engineering ranks. Zschau wasn't one of those guys. He had been a Congressman in California, and he had once lost a close bid for the Senate. Beyond politics, he had been the catalyst for a couple of small Silicon Valley start-ups, and a strong technology advocate, though his experience as a businessman was described as somewhere near "questionable to terrible," according to a technology consultant. He had never run a large enterprise, and storage was anything but small at IBM. Maybe Kuehler felt that he could personally cover the R&D end of storage for Zschau, or that it wasn't absolutely essential anyway.

To be fair, Zschau inherited a division that already was in disarray. Just as it did with networking hardware, IBM had practically invented the storage business. It introduced the first disk drive in 1956 and had made several advances since then. The tape drives that archived the mission-critical data for hundreds of large corporations, governments, and scientific research facilities were once entrusted almost exclusively to Big Blue. At the beginning of the 1990s, even when IBM was convulsing in its near-death throes, it had nearly eighty percent market share of large systems storage.

Well before Zschau arrived, IBM had steadily lost market share. Generally, IBM was weak in three critical areas. Its products were too expensive, they performed too slowly, and they took up too much floor space. Seagate had taken over the high-end disk drive business when IBM had difficulty ramping up competitive products. Along came another fierce competitor, EMC of Hopkinton, Massachusetts, which now dominates worldwide mainframe storage with more than half the market share. EMC took advantage of new technology known as "RAID," for Redundant Array of Independent Disks. RAID technology had everything that IBM's clunky ancestors did not have. It was smaller, faster, more reliable, more powerful, and thousands of dollars cheaper. It did not take long for the CIOs to discover the bargain. The reversal in dominance between IBM and EMC was so profound and so fast that many in the industry still cannot understand how it happened. EMC even had a poster made with its CEO displaying blue-stained knuckles with the caption, "Had Enough, Big Blue?"

With Ed Zschau as the new general manager of the storage division, IBM expected to bring in new business and help it recover. This did not occur, however. Ed Zschau was a good meeting-and-greeting guy who, as a former politician, understood the value of social networking but little else. He was a nice guy in the old sense of an IBM senior executive, but his expertise was not in management or line operations. Kuehler had hired him because he embodied the traits of the salesmen who had first built IBM into the powerhouse it became. Unfortunately, some thought Zschau spent too much time decorating his office with expensive wood paneling and nineteenth century antiques, and too little time worrying about IBM's eroding market share.

A consulting firm focused on the high-technology industry had a ten-month contract with IBM to help Zschau's division produce a competitive high-end disk drive. The firm, a small but highly respected outfit, has helped companies like Hewlett-Packard and Compaq improve their manufacturing operations. At one time or another, some division in almost all of the major technology players goes there seeking advice on process reengineering.

The consulting director assigned to storage was first asked to study Zschau's plan to design and build a competitive product. He immediately noticed, however, that Zschau's manufacturing unit was woefully understaffed. In fact, it was understaffed by a factor of four. The director, a highly experienced consultant who had worked successfully with several other IBM divisions for many years, said that he had typically seen fifty to seventy percent miscalculations, or even one hundred percent in a "really screwed up" high-tech company. But IBM storage, in his view, was in far worse shape. There was no way Zschau could meet production deadlines at his current pace. "We rolled all that up for Ed and his management team," he recalled. "And we said, 'Look, here's the facts. You need to hire X hundred more people by tomorrow morning to make your commitments for the year. You need to make this decision.'"

Zschau did not make the decision, and he kept scheduling meetings with the consulting team to continue not making the decision. For anyone involved, Zschau was running storage like the old IBM, and not the new one Gerstner had been building. Finally, only four months into the job, the exasperated consultant realized he had no alternative other than to resign the account. "To keep us around any longer is going to hurt our reputation," he recalled telling IBM. "We're pulling our people out of here today. We said, 'This is dumb, you just don't want to change, you don't want to make any tough calls, we can't help you, we're done.'" This shook him a bit. He had never before resigned an IBM account.

Few people outside of storage knew about this. One can understand why. It was the kind of revelation that was not unlike a psychiatrist telling the patient he could no longer help him because he refused to change.

When IBM's disk drive came off the production lines a year late, Gerstner had seen enough. Jim Vanderslice, a Ph.D. with a sound track record as a senior manager at IBM, was brought in to restructure the division. Known as "Slice," he is tall and lean and has the soft-spoken, confident demeanor of a Texas poker player. One of the first things he did when he moved out to San Jose was rip out Zschau's office and move all the executives down to the basement.

It was a statement about the new corporate culture, one that Gerstner certainly would have endorsed.

The issues concerning Big Blue's corporate culture usually referred to the numerous layers of management and the white-collar workforce. Understandably, the blue-collar employees, wage earners, had a different view of the new IBM.

So it wasn't much of a revelation to learn that during Gerstner's town meeting tour there was a site that did not make it on the schedule. Less than an hour's plane ride from Armonk, in the southern tier of New York, many of IBM's blue-collar employees were demoralized. Even with the mandatory layoffs in 1993 and 1994, they understood the need for restructuring. They tried to remain optimistic. They had agreed with the argument that IBM might not have survived under Akers. After Gerstner downsized IBM, he also began the task of trying to "rightsize" his business units. So even as layoffs were continuing in some areas, IBM was running classified ads looking to hire in others. But when the rank and file realized that Gerstner planned to continue layoffs even after business improved, they felt only shareholders would benefit at their expense (including the CEO's elite managers, all of whom had sizable stock option grants).

To be sure, this is not an original view, endemic to IBM. For many years, all across America, labor has long held corporate management—and not simply the vagaries of the economy— accountable when layoffs occur. What was so painful was that IBM was now becoming like any ordinary corporate conglomerate. It was not a special place to work anymore, and never again would be, even with someone other than Gerstner at the helm.

When the CEO reported that company morale was rising, the blue-collar IBMers wondered whom Gerstner was talking about.

In Endicott, where the company was founded, Lee Conrad, a twenty-two-year veteran who worked in the check-sorting division, had been trying to organize IBMers for many years, well before Gerstner's era, only to be thwarted by management at every turn. He was trying to achieve the highly improbable. In eighty years, there had never been a union within IBM.

When would be a better time? reasoned Conrad.

In less than a year, York and Gerstner had stabilized IBM's bottom line. Business was considerably better by the first quarter of 1994. "Revenue grew in all major regions of the world," Gerstner reported to analysts on April 21, 1994. "We've improved in many areas, but we still have a long way to go." IBM's first-quarter earnings were $392 million, a modest 64 cents per share. The following quarter, earnings reached $689 million, a $1.14 per share return to stockholders. By the third quarter, earnings per share inched up to $1.18. IBM's stock had rebounded to about $75, almost double the price when Gerstner took command.

Lee Conrad and his coworkers read the financial results.

Despite past setbacks, Conrad hoped to realize his dream. The full-bearded, affable, enthusiastic union organizer often was seen outside one of the dozen IBM factories, bullhorn in hand, rallying fellow workers. He carefully followed the rules that required union organizing activities to take place off company premises and on his own time. Conrad refused to believe he was losing the war, relying on his own money and small donations for his newsletter.

A section of Conrad's newsletter, the *Resistor*, referred to the "IBM Body Count." The November 1994 issue reported that temporary workers were replacing permanent employees, and more manufacturing layoffs were expected in the Endicott, Poughkeepsie, and Burlington plants. When Gerstner first took over IBM, the rank and file called him the "cookie monster," a reference to his widespread layoffs at RJR. Now they were using that sobriquet once again. The *Resistor* had its own translation for IBM's layoff plan. ETOP, or the Endicott Transition Opportunity Program, was called by the rank and file "Eliminate The Old People."

Working-class perks disappeared, including the company picnics and the Quarter Century Day celebrations commemorating long-term service. (Perks for white-collar employees were cut as well. The traditional Golden Circle awards junkets for salespeople who exceed their quotas were cut from eleven events to four, and the resorts and destinations were downgraded.)

Endicott workers were shocked to hear that nobody was immune to IBM's cutbacks. Gerstner's human resources team had discovered that some 120 executive secretaries in Westchester were earning six-figure salaries, including overtime. In the spring of 1995, he slashed their top pay to about $40,000 a year, what IBM called the competitive range in the region. The story was leaked to the *Wall Street Journal* after one distraught secretary called an IBM consultant who sympathized with their plight. Another angry secretary wrote in Conrad's newsletter, "If there are . . . secretaries whose salaries are off the grid, we should cut the salaries of the executives and the office managers who approved those increases over the years. I think they call it accountability." It did little for company morale anywhere when it was reported that Gerstner's personal chef had a base pay of $120,000 a year. Also, Gerstner was not making any sacrifices in his pay, Conrad noted.

IBM's management was careful and cautious with Conrad; there were no overt attempts to curtail his efforts other than a letter IBM distributed that cautioned workers to "seriously consider the costs and obligations of union membership." Conrad was never harrassed by management. But he noted he was one of the many workers who had not received a raise in several years. When he attended shareholder meetings, the security detail knew who he was. At the 1994 annual meeting, security rummaged through his briefcase before letting him in. He laughed and wondered what they possibly hoped to find. Management already had read his organizing literature.

"Electronic workers had management very nervous, very paranoid," Conrad said. "They weren't so worried when I was organizing within; they felt they could withstand that. When I went to the electrical workers [International Union of Electrical Workers, an AFL/CIO affiliate], that's when they were really worried, when we took it outside. They got in a tizzy, because it was outside the family."

IBM's response to Conrad's organizing initiative was fairly consistent. It maintained that the majority of the workforce was content without a union, wages were competitive, and that workers might have to "accept less" if they joined one. After several years, Conrad finally gave up.

Despite the rumblings from the rank and file, Gerstner was determined to bring accountability and standards to everyone who received an IBM paycheck. A new personnel evaluation system was adopted, one that was designed for greater equity participation in the company's success. The grading would be tougher, but the rewards were better. Still, this concerned many longtime IBMers who had been told so many times in the past that IBM's human resources program was among the most progressive in America. Perhaps the best.

The new system was called the PBCs, for Personal Business Commitments. Not only would your manager make a year-end performance evaluation, a half dozen peers of your own choice would be asked to fill out confidential electronic forms that asked two or three boilerplate questions. This was known as "360-degree feedback," and it was entirely anonymous (except for your manager). So while you could choose only those colleagues who you thought might respond favorably to your work, you could never be certain what they would say, or who said what. At the end of the year, each employee had to write a plan that described his or her goals—or business commitments—for the following year in three distinct areas: "win," "execute," and "team."

Those who knew how Gerstner operated realized this was not a plan he ordered pell-mell from a human resources consultant. The theme words were those he had used to motivate employees for his entire career. "Execute" worked its way into almost every one of his internal speeches, and had since become a favorite among turnaround specialists in many other firms. "Team" was important to Gerstner because he understood IBM's fiefdom-like society and the propensity for certain managers to demand divisional autonomy. "Win" was a concept he assumed everyone could buy into. It meant that every day IBM was up against its competitors, scrambling for new business. When Gerstner announced the new evaluation system, he made a wry comment, noting the company's insatiable affinity for acronyms. He hoped that "WET" would not catch on. One speechwriter, frustrated at a meeting where a project seemed endlessly stalled by executive indecision—too many people, too many meetings—deadpanned, "The only way to win is to execute the team."

The evaluation system worked in concert with the reform of IBM's performance ratings. Once consisting of four tiers, it was reduced to three. If you received a "3" ranking, it meant that you fell short of your business commitments. You needed work, and an exceptionally poor report, a low 3, could result in a six-month probation. A 2 indicated that you achieved your goals, you were a good soldier. Those who earned a 1 were known throughout IBM as "water walkers." You were a high achiever who exceeded your goals and could do no wrong.

The ratings were critical in two respects. First, managers knew it was almost impossible to fire a "1" or a "2." They had to dish out a series of 3's before they could rid themselves of a nonper-former. At IBM, it was easy to fire tens of thousands of employees at a time; canning a single incompetent might take years. The usual routine is to transfer such an employee so he or she becomes the problem of some other manager in some other division. The ratings were also used to determine "variable pay," or the year-end bonuses, which are paid out annually to every IBMer during March of the following year.

Variable pay is based on a formula so complex that few in the company understand how it works. It still goes over the heads of most department finance gurus. The short explanation is that bonuses are calculated by three components: personal performance rating, division performance, and IBM's overall performance. The algorithm that weights these three items is unknown to most.

Just around Thanksgiving, the white-collar workforce in various offices would begin praying to the computer gods for the senior vice president of their division to make his or her numbers. Depending on the year, PC Company employees were invariably nervous—the bulk of those sales occurred in the fourth quarter, while those in software (where profit margins were highest) were fantasizing where to spend their fat checks. In a good year, a 2 performer received a ten to fifteen percent bonus. A 1, of course, naturally received more—as much as eighteen to twenty-three percent. A 3 was awarded the least amount.

The 1 performer was difficult to find, and this was intentional. Too many might show that IBM was soft. They were so rare in some departments that when someone received a 1 rating, it became the stuff of cafeteria gossip. Gerstner was anything but soft, and IBM's recovery period was no time for grade inflation. Also, too many 1's would upset the formula and bankrupt the bonus pool. The system was designed along a bell curve, so the vast majority of IBMers received 2's. There was a quota system for 3's, however, and this angered many competent managers who had to dole them out, as well as those who felt they did not deserve to receive them. Questions were immediately raised. If a complete department was performing in an exemplary fashion— cruising past its sales goals, for example—wasn't it possible there were no nonperformers? Suppose everyone achieved his personal goals? Conversely, why not stick an entire department of incompetents—a woefully underperforming unit—with 3's?

Dave McGovern, an IBM director who was in marketing and communications for the Personal Systems Group, is among those who agree these are legitimate questions, and he describes the flaw in real terms. A vice president to whom he once reported told him that a certain number of 3's had to be "in the system." It was mandated by executive fiat: "We all have to deliver some 3's," he was told. It turned out that half of McGovern's managers had already completed evaluations of their subordinates. McGovern didn't feel comfortable asking them to redo the appraisals, especially since virtually overnight, a number of IBMers—all competent people—would be suddenly told they were downgraded to accommodate a bell curve. "I had thirty-five people, and half of them had already been appraised," McGovern said. "I was going to issue an extraordinary number of 3's to get close to the percentage. That didn't feel right. So I offered to take a 3 myself. I felt I was doing right as a manager. Keep the team motivated and do good work." His boss gladly accepted the offer.

"When they came down with this edict that you're going to have a certain number of 3's, I do have a fundamental problem with that," McGovern continued. "The system should award the very best people, and also identify those who are the weak links. You're going to have a broad distribution in the middle of that bell curve. We should be basically grading people not on the curve but on their own performance."

The specter of a lower bonus based on a quota of nonachievers did not appeal to anyone. Still, it was Gerstner's way of getting an across-the-board buy-in to the new regime, now a supposedly less-encumbered culture. The PBC system was meant to increase accountability but also foster a modicum of discomfiture. Perform and you have nothing to worry about. But it promulgated fear because of the inherent inequities. As one IBMer put it, "If IBM is once again becoming a player, if this is now a company that our competitors will respect, then shouldn't by definition we be the kind of company that would hire only 1's or 2's?"

As one moved up in the management ranks, the bonus system had its distinct quirks. Not every division or senior manager used the same metrics to determine performance. So there was a dichotomy. Some managers and unit heads were held to one standard, and others to another. It was difficult to compare two managers if their PBCs had different measurement standards and different stated goals. Some were held to volume standards, and others to profit standards. How can you reconcile that?" asked one former IBM middle manager. "Those two things don't jibe." So it was not surprising to hear some high-level IBM product managers saying, especially in the fourth quarter, "I don't care if I have to sell it for $16.99, I will."

Nothing was perfect; there would never be total harmony at IBM, just as there can never be total harmony at any large enterprise. But the company was solidly into its reform movement, and while many internal changes were difficult to digest, most IBMers understood that they were inevitable and probably for the better.

IBM now had to show the outside world it was a different company.

8

Two Camels in Front of a Pizza Hut

When Lou Gerstner installed Abby Kohnstamm in June 1993 as his senior vice president to head worldwide advertising, she was first charged with a single priority: restore IBM's once revered image. In corporate-speak, the brand was "severely eroded." And in Gerstner-speak, brand erosion was nothing less than the eighth deadly sin. IBM's tracking studies probed customer attitudes, and they weren't pretty. Negative responses were high in four descriptions: "arrogant," "bureaucratic," "inflexible/rigid," and "provides poor service."

Probably nothing bothered Gerstner more than knowing that IBM, once the go-to company for American office products, computing, and overall technological know-how, even after showing signs of life in late 1993 and early 1994, was still viewed with derision. Could this be the same company whose computers helped man land safely on the moon? The same company whose computers traveled aboard the Space Shuttles? The digital cognoscenti, the early adopters, thought of IBM as a has-been. They didn't care that Gerstner was lifting the company's earnings per share. Worse, the most important customers, the "end users"—the large market who bought the products that the early adopters test-drove—didn't think of IBM at all anymore. They already owned the clones.

By early 1994, IBM was spending some $400 million to $500 million in advertising that appeared in 144 countries. The account was spread among forty separate ad agencies, and even as many as sixty at times.

IBM was about to make a bold statement to the IT industry and the world at large that it was preparing for an offensive. Timing was crucial. Gerstner and Kohnstamm knew that such a move during the first year of recovery would have been premature, but now they didn't want to wait much longer. The two concluded that it might be more efficient to unify their message—and that message was that IBM was back. What if a single agency had the responsibility of handling all the print, TV, and radio spots, rather than the current cluster of shops that were flogging individual products in narrow markets?

To handle IBM's entire business, an agency had to have substantial global reach and also a good track record with technology accounts. Madison Avenue sensed a change was in the works, and word of IBM's plans traveled quickly. When Kohnstamm was scheduled to visit the offices of Ammirati Puris Lintas, the agency's top executives anxiously awaited her arrival, checking the lobby area every few minutes to greet her personally. They did not notice her sitting patiently in a corner of the reception area. They had mistaken her for a secretary waiting for a job interview. Her low profile was invariably an advantage in the showy world of advertising, where no opportunity to impress a potential client is overlooked.

Kohnstamm quietly began sounding out the consolidation approach to other shops as well: McCann-Erickson Worldwide, BBDO Worldwide, and Ogilvy and Mather Worldwide. BBDO was a possibility because it had the Apple account, and Ogilvy was currently handling Microsoft's advertising.

BBDO was attractive in another respect. It had Steve Hayden, who was arguably the single most well-known, widely respected technology expert in the industry. He was a shrewd strategist, a topflight manager, and as a creative director, a nurturer of talent. He followed the tech industry with a passion; he actually used the gadgets he pitched. He wore jeans and black shirts, and he usually contemplated the marketing universe with a cigarette. He had earned his bones as the copywriter who cooked up the memorable "1984" commercial that introduced Apple's Macintosh computer during the Super Bowl. Then working for Chiat/Day, Hayden and film director Ridley Scott had shown footage of a parade of lemmings marching in lockstep off a cliff. The startling ad was a direct salvo at IBM, its PC business, its workforce, its very soul. It was beyond edgy, the industry's word for chancy, groundbreaking advertising. To anyone in Silicon Valley—and many outside the business—that single minute was more arresting than anything that happened during the football game.

At Ogilvy, Kohnstamm's contact was Shelly Lazarus, then the president of the agency's North American division. Lazarus, Kohnstamm, and Gerstner had all worked together at American Express, and they'd developed a strong mutual trust. Lazarus was in line to assume the rule of agency CEO (and eventually chairman) when her boss Charlotte Beers stepped down. She needed the business. Lazarus had been summarily fired by Compaq U.S. eight months earlier, and she had spent three years trying to convince Microsoft that its logo alone would not cut it in the years to come. Gates's company needed an international brand campaign. Ads heralding the introduction of the latest shrink-wrapped software weren't enough. Steve Ballmer, the number two Microsoft executive, finally had come around. Ogilvy was right, he conceded. But then Microsoft decided to put the account in review. Lazarus was as close to livid as the normally taciturn executive could be when she learned that Microsoft wanted to interview other agencies. "This was just preposterous," she exclaimed, recounting her reaction in an interview. She thought of herself as one of the most loyal people on Madison Avenue; Microsoft's behavior was anything but that.

Sensing Microsoft's possible defection, Lazarus now desperately wanted the IBM account. She had one compelling argument for Kohnstamm and Gerstner. She was convinced IBM was getting woefully shortchanged with its current arrangement. "Are you sure you're spending $500 million?" she asked Kohnstamm. "If you spend $500 million, a million dollars at a time, on five hundred different things, then I'm not surprised, because you get no impact from it." Also, she knew that Gerstner would be receptive to a fresh, even radical approach. Few CEOs she knew were as "brand-sensitive" as he was. Gerstner, she said, was an ideal client. He trusted advertising people. He bought into chancy campaigns.

In May 1994, IBM reached a decision. Without listening to a pitch, looking at a single storyboard, or perusing any particular ideas for a campaign, it awarded Ogilvy the entire account. David Kalis, IBM's chief flack, assured Lazarus the news would make the front page of the *New York Times*, unless war broke out or there was an Elvis sighting. When she questioned his news judgment, Kalis assured her that IBM was under so much press scrutiny that if they changed the color of the wallpaper in the ladies' room in Armonk, it made the papers. Kalis was right; the *Times* called the move "the largest shift in advertising history."

The news rocked the ad industry, as several small firms had been relying on substantial chunks of IBM's billings. For some, it amounted to losing half their work. Comments from pundits on Madison Avenue ranged from "absolutely unbelievable" to "very surprised" to "amazing." A few years later, a profile of Lazarus appeared in *People* magazine implying that the deal had been sealed while Kohnstamm and Lazarus were together having their nails done. Lazarus laughs at this characterization. Gerstner was not in the habit of casually committing half a billion dollars of his company's capital without serious review.

Snaring the IBM account was a coup for Lazarus, not only because it reversed her recent run of bad luck on technology accounts, but because she was viewed as a savior by Charlotte Beers, her boss, and Martin Sorrell, the ad magnate who headed the WPP P.L.C. Group of London, the holding company that owned both Ogilvy and Mather and J. Walter Thompson. Sorrell had been overextended through acquisitions, and his business was rocky. He needed a big win. Robert Chandler, the former executive creative director of Ogilvy's Los Angeles office put it this way: "When [Sorrell] landed the IBM account, his fortunes reversed. So you could say that Shelly Lazarus probably saved his cookies. He could have lost the company if it weren't for that account."

IBM hammered out favorable terms. Nobody paid retail on Madison Avenue anymore. Instead of the usual agency commission of fifteen percent of billings, that number had been whittled down to ten percent or so, depending on the deal. Kohnstamm and Gerstner, by giving all their business to Ogilvy, would be charged far less than ten percent. Howard Anderson, president of The Yankee Group, a consulting firm, said that Sorrell told him it was closer to five percent. Ogilvy might earn considerably less than the $50 million it could normally expect from a client the size of IBM, but it would more than compensate for the discount if it provided a great campaign. Marquee clients attracted new business.

By winning the IBM account, Ogilvy was obliged to resign Microsoft because of a conflict of interest. Lazarus was bound by a ninety-day notice clause in the standard agreement. That meant it had to complete any work in progress for Microsoft and couldn't begin crafting IBM advertising for three months.

Lazarus, ever polite and tactful, wanted to inform Microsoft immediately, and she carefully planned it as if it were a D-Day invasion. Jerry McGee, who was running the L.A. office and in charge of the account, and another Ogilvy executive were dispatched to Tokyo to track down Steven Ballmer to deliver the news. Ogilvy also wanted to get the word to Bill Gates, but he was more difficult to reach. Gates heard about it, according to Lazarus, while standing on a pay phone line at the Atlanta COMDEX show. A trade reporter wanted to know how a billionaire felt after being dropped by an ad agency. A former Ogilvy executive said, "When Bill Gates was apprised of this, and we said, 'It looks like we'll have to resign the account,' he said,

'Why? There's no conflict.' As far as he was concerned, IBM was sort of irrelevant."

Now the pressure was on Ogilvy. In was May 1994, and Lazarus had less than six months to create a dazzling rebranding campaign for IBM, ready for delivery well before the year-end holidays. The only ads anyone remembered from IBM were the Charlie Chaplin "Little Tramp" spots done a decade earlier for the PC. They were effective at the time, but in retrospect, too cute by half. Anyway, IBM PCs walked out the door at that time. Lousy advertising might have worked just as well.

The first thing she did was to roll out the focus groups. Lazarus hired a first-rate data gatherer to conduct 104 separate question-and-answer sessions. When respondents were asked whether they thought IBM was good in technology, whether they had smart people, forward-thinking products—were these goods of high quality?—the reactions were mainly neutral or positive. The superficial questions were not very revealing. To get to the heart of a damaged brand required more penetrating questions using "projective psychology techniques." This included asking respondents to leaf through magazines and cut out pictures of things—other than computers—that reminded them of IBM. In short, Ogilvy had to probe the deeper emotions of computer professionals—customers, ex-customers, and potential customers.

After only the second focus group, the research maven called Lazarus to confess that he couldn't finish the job. Lazarus, taken aback, recalled, "I mean, this was going to be really significant focus group testing. And he said the feelings people have about IBM are so significant, he doesn't know if he can do this another 102 times. The level of emotion was so strong."

The MIS people—Managers of Information Systems, key department heads of IBM's largest corporate customers, "buyers"—already were well aware of the mainstream spin about IBM. They knew Big Blue had four Nobel prizewinners working there, that it was the year-in, year-out leader in patents awarded, it had some of the smartest people in the industry, incredible raw technology. They had heard all the polite things about the company.

Lazarus continued, "Then this focus group leader would say, 'I guess you do a lot of business with IBM.' And these guys would say, 'No, we can't stand those guys.' And all this stuff would come pouring out about they had trusted IBM, they had believed in IBM, they had supported IBM, and then IBM had let them down, let down the whole world of IT, let down America, actually; stopped caring, stopped worrying about their customers, became too arrogant."

Lazarus, who had been in the ad business for a quarter of a century and thought she understood all there was to know about focus groups, learned a great deal from the IBM experience. The objective questions weren't worth a damn. When they went Freudian and tried to find out how people really *felt* about IBM, then they got a torrent of spiteful replies.

Shelly Lazarus discovered what Lou Gerstner had just spent a year learning: great technology alone didn't mean a thing.

With such a dauntingly negative image, the agency turned to one of its more experienced hands to take up the challenge. Robyn Putter, the creative director based in South Africa, was assigned to handle the branding campaign. Working in Johannesburg, Putter and his partner had founded their own agency and sold it to Ogilvy. They had good client relationships, and Ogilvy execs wisely had decided to retain them. They had an outstanding creative reputation—"a nice reel," as they say in the trade—and they had prior experience handling IBM in South Africa. They had done some award-winning spots for IBM, well before Ogilvy won the worldwide account, so Putter's shop seemed a logical place to begin.

At the same time, Charlotte Beers and Shelly Lazarus also enlisted Bill Hamilton, a creative director and all-around point man in Ogilvy's New York office. Hamilton, who was smart and highly regarded, did not know or love technology per se, but he possessed a particular genius in sneaking through the offices of the creative types and sniffing out unusual ideas. Frequently, they turned into wonderful ads. Hamilton was not known in the business for total thought clarity. Robert Chandler said, "His creative directing style is rather mysterious. He is mumbly and inarticulate. He kind of waves his arms around. He communicates very well, but not like regular people do, with words. But like insects do, with their antennae. But, who cares?" Hamilton might be a bit flaky, something of a nutcase genius, but he was adroit in unleashing talent and had a canny understanding of image and brand.

At first he was assigned to come up with something brilliant that might revive IBM's PC business. Ogilvy knew that the PC was the main face to the consumer, and that would be instrumental in creating the buzz that IBM was a changed company. Maybe Hamilton could come up with something that had the impact of Chaplin's tramp in the 1980s. He spent several weeks on the PC problem, hunkered in the trenches on the twelfth floor of Ogilvy's worldwide headquarters on Manhattan's west side.

Meanwhile, Putter's South African team worked up a campaign, and they flew to New York to present it to Abby Kohnstamm and several other IBM executives. Essentially, in keeping with Gerstner's grand mandate, Putter had been asked to play off the equities and the bigness of the brand. The theme centered on a "whiter shade of blue," and "whales towing icebergs," recalled Bill Hamilton, a little hazily. It was difficult to explain, and harder to remember. That in itself was a bad sign. It was very high concept and so off the mark, however, that it wasn't even met with polite nods. It was back to the South African drafting table.

One problem was that Putter's group was half a globe away, and it wasn't near the pulse of all the meetings with IBM in Armonk and Somers, the central headquarters complex where most divisions were located. Hamilton felt strongly that creativity required proximity. IBM is in Armonk. You can't be in South Africa, or Barcelona, or Frankfurt. You have to be ensconced, everyone locked in the same room, eating the same pizza, pounding away on it every day. It was a certain gestalt that didn't always work. But then again, it might. Disparate offices? A good, noble idea that wouldn't pan out.

Lazarus and Beers sent down word to "activate the assets," Hamilton said. That meant a full-court press, a convocation of Ogilvy immortals, a blanket request for input, an open call for ideas, from the top creative offices, not just in Atlanta, New York, and Houston, but in Germany, France, South Africa, Spain. This was not a highly unusual occurrence; mass efforts sometimes produced something memorable. Just as often, however, they resulted in chaotic, useless output. Senior ad executives referred to this exercise as an "intramural competition," while a couple of rungs down, the creative types called it a "gang bang."

No long "briefs" were sent to Ogilvy's outposts. The marching orders were simple. It had to be fantastic, and it had to play anywhere in the world. In short, Gerstner and Kohnstamm had to embrace it.

Who knew what talent was lurking out there in Ogilvyland?

Six weeks after Putter's group pitched IBM's ad execs, a team from Ogilvy's London office came up with a presentation. Hamilton said, "The guy from the UK comes in, and he's got a cocktail napkin, and he holds it up, and he unfolds it. And it's another one of those . . . they ain't buyin'." Actually, the English group had a campaign planned along the lines of British Airways. Plenty of smiling faces, long shots of majestic scenery with corresponding choral or classical music. The theme was built broadly on "bringing the world together." It was another major presentation at an IBM conference table—one executive said the meetings resembled UN Security Council sessions—with a number of befuddled executives wondering what the message was. It was too obtuse for Big Blue.

"We were still not there," Lazarus said. Kohnstamm was worried.

Lazarus, of course, was aware they were at square zero. There wasn't yet a sense of dread, or a feeling of panic within the agency. But it was clear that all the intellectual might of Ogilvy was stuck. Call it the pre-panic stage.

Robert Chandler likened the period to a typical situation in rebranding. False starts are common, almost necessary, because you're trying to "crack the code." He said, "IBM was this great company, certainly recognition was not the problem. We didn't need any awareness. The problem was to convey the sense that this company was changing in a good way. We needed to take their size and their globalness and make that an asset as opposed to making them look like big, dumb dinosaurs."

"You had to bring IBM back down to earth," Bill Hamilton said. "My philosophy is, when you're a big company you act little, and when you're arrogant, you act humble. You had to work your way back to credibility. You really pissed off the IT category so much. You were the big, bad, dumb, lugubrious, slow-witted company. People loved to hate IBM at that point."

Hamilton had the notion that IBM needed something really edgy. Like pornography, he would know it when he saw it.

The big ideas weren't working. Maybe it was time to think small, Hamilton thought. Charlotte Beers strolled into Hamilton's office one morning. "Billy, would you mind working on the brand campaign?" drawled Beers, the regal, Texas-born CEO. One Ogilvy hand described Beers as a cross between former Texas Governor Ann Richards and Queen Elizabeth. Regal, yet down-home. Hamilton said yes, of course. How could he deny Charlotte Beers? Beers saw that Hamilton was lit up at the prospect of taking on the agency's latest challenge, and she wondered why he was so enthusiastic. "I just wanted to prove it could be done," Hamilton said. He was assigned to coordinate the worldwide effort.

Ogilvy and Mather had its own bureaucratic issues and internecine battles to contend with during the ramp-up for the IBM account. While the brand campaign had assumed almost every Ogilvy honcho's maximum attention, there were still product ads—software, the PC Company, even routine trade magazine ads for large systems—that had to be prepared.

The Los Angeles office had been working for months on the upcoming Windows 95 launch for Microsoft, when Ogilvy suddenly had picked up the IBM acount. Robert Chandler, for one, was informed, never mind, just move your team onto IBM's

OS/2 Warp campaign. There was a certain amount of jockeying with executives and creative types calling in favors to work on the sexier, more prestigious parts of IBM. Chandler said that Ogilvy was a "peculiarly dysfunctional ad agency" at the time, and some of this was wrought by political infighting generated by the Big Blue branding challenge.

The people who actually create advertising typically work in two-man teams, a copywriter and art director. "Ideas always come down to two guys in a room, or three guys," Chandler says. "You can have all the worldwide stuff, and that's good, but ultimately it comes down to a couple of guys in a room." Chandler had a talented team, one that recently had been reassigned from Microsoft to IBM software. The copywriter, Charlie Tercek, was thirty-three, and his partner, art director Bruce Bousman, was a couple of years younger. There were two executives senior to Chandler in the L.A. office, and when word of the gang bang filtered west, Chandler suggested that Bousman and Tercek be shifted to the brand problem. One executive approved it, and the other resisted, but Chandler, after a considerable amount of interoffice hip-checking—it took "muscle, guile, and stealth," was how he put it—finagled the Tercek/Bousman team onto the assignment.

Back in New York, Bill Hamilton didn't even know who these two guys were. He was waiting for lightning to strike.

Charlie Tercek was vaguely aware that Ogilvy had fallen behind on the branding campaign, but he didn't feel any particular pressure to come up with something spectacular. Gang bangs were de rigueur. The creative director needs a lot of ideas fast, so he asks anyone he runs into in the elevator to take a whack at it. The grunts know it's a contest, and if you're fortunate enough to win, terrific. You'll get a bonus, or at the very least something "bookable"—a résumé grabber—that will ensure a raise on your next job. If you don't, it's back to your mundane hair color ads, just like the other hundred or so copywriters and art directors who were staring out the windows of Ogilvy offices around the world, hoping a brilliant idea would waft its way into their offices.

Bousman and Tercek settled into one or the other's cave on Wilshire Boulevard, browsing through all their previously aborted sketches and scripts. They also began sifting through travel guidebooks, looking at pictures, thinking they might find some inspiration within some exotic locale, preferably a place neither of them had visited. Tercek said, "The thing for us was that we wanted to travel on the company dime. The old joke is that every script begins with 'Open on palm trees.'"

Bousman recalled that they both began thinking that they could do a script that was either dubbed or with subtitles, so it could run in any country. They had four or five ideas, but the first one they wrote was about two ordinary Frenchmen walking by the Seine in Paris. One guy's talking about how his hard drive is all backed up, it's going to crash, he's got to get some help, and then the other guy suggests IBM—they have a new way to store stuff. Tercek's idea was to do the dialogue in French with English subtitles. They both felt a clever punch line wasn't necessary, a grace note would do. The script ended with the other Frenchman saying "cool." The juxtaposition of computer-speak babbled by nontechnical types in a foreign tongue was simple, elegant, amusing, and wholly original. Also, it was distinctly global, which was what Gerstner and Kohnstamm demanded. Tercek and Bousman next wondered what it might be like if a couple of Czechoslovakian nuns were bantering while walking through a church in Prague. What if a subtitle read, "I can't wait to surf the Net"?

The two decided not to mock up the ads on a storyboard; the scripts themselves would have to be strong enough to carry the idea. Their boss, Robert Chandler, had been in London and had stopped back in New York. They decided to fax three scripts to both Chandler and Bill Hamilton.

At about 7 P.M. that evening, Hamilton was fretting over some pedestrian ideas that had been suggested for IBM branding, and when he read the scripts from Chandler's guys, he connected in an instant. Lightning. He called Shelly Lazarus's office. With a mock flair for the melodramatic, Hamilton asked softly, "Are you alone?" Lazarus said she was. Containing his excitement, he said, "I've gotta show you something." He rushed into her office, opened a manila envelope, and gave her the three Tercek/Bousman subtitle scripts. Like Hamilton, she had no idea who these guys were.

A few minutes later, Hamilton asked, "What do you think?"

"I think it's brilliant advertising," Lazarus replied. "I think it's absolutely brilliant. But I don't know if they're ready for that."

"I don't know either," Hamilton said. "What do you think we ought to do?"

This was a typical but critical exchange among advertising executives. They know they have a showstopper, something edgy, and they're not quite sure the best way to present it to the client. Sometimes your best stuff is relegated to the trash icon at the bottom of your screen. How would Abby Kohnstamm and Lou Gerstner react to the description of nuns speaking in Czech about OS/2 Warp? This was still IBM, after all, and not a Silicon Valley company with a weird name that nobody ever heard of. These would be funny ads. Could IBM actually acquire a sense of humor?

Lazarus understood that the only way Ogilvy could get IBM to buy this campaign was if they didn't try to sell it. If they had to explain it, then it wasn't right for Big Blue. She called Kohnstamm to tell her that Hamilton was heading to Armonk the following morning, and that he was going to present two "very strong, solid, and responsible campaigns" to her and the IBM team. In his briefcase, she told Kohnstamm, there will be a third campaign. She wanted Kohnstamm to see it alone, and if she liked it, she could take it from there. "We're happy to show it to everyone, but I don't want to sort of shock IBM," Lazarus said.

The next day at the IBM presentation, Hamilton pitched as planned. Nobody was wowed by the two "responsible" campaigns. When he asked Kohnstamm to step out of the conference room to show her the subtitles campaign, she said, "This is the advertising. It's fantastic. It's exactly what we need." The two returned to the meeting, just as the other advertising and marketing execs were closing their briefcases. Hamilton passed the scripts around. There weren't any objections or confused looks this time.

When Kohnstamm and Lazarus first showed the subtitles campaign to Gerstner, Lazarus felt that he immediately grasped it as good work, but she knew it wasn't enough. She had known Gerstner too long to expect instant approval. It was nothing personal. Of course, she thought, it never was with Lou. She still had to defend the Ogilvy and Mather Ph.D. thesis with oral arguments. He was thinking academically now, looking for the holes in the concept. He would assume the role of the customer. Lazarus was prepared when Gerstner said, "Okay, so I'm sitting here. You want me to run this advertising. So, is anyone ever going to look at subtitles? I watch television, I never *just* watch television. I have the TV on, I'm doing the crossword puzzle, I'm eating something. There's something going on in another part of the house. I'm going to read subtitles?"

Lazarus said, "Okay, Lou. Now try this. You're sitting, the television is on, you're doing the crossword puzzle, it's all been English. All of a sudden, this funny language comes on. It happens to be Czech, but you don't know what it is. A language you'd never recognize. You look up. There are nuns walking down these stairs, speaking Czech, and then you start to read subtitles that go, 'I can't wait to get my hands on OS/2.' Don't you think you're going be intrigued? Don't you think it's going to capture your attention, and you're going to spend a little time with it, as opposed to all those commercials that are really easy to take in, and you don't have to look at them? This insists that you engage. It's our responsibility to make them interesting, but you must engage, because you've got to figure it out."

That was enough. "I think it's a great idea. Let's just do it," Gerstner said. And $250 million was committed to the campaign for the first year.

Tercek and Bousman dug in for several months of writing, rewriting, and polishing scripts, commuting to Ogilvy and IBM meetings in New York. Leslie Dektor, a highly respected director on the West Coast, was chosen to film the ads. They never even bothered with a storyboard. A test commercial with the Frenchmen (who were brothers) was shot in Bryant Park in midtown Manhattan. Tercek and Bousman's travel fantasies were eventually fulfilled, as they wrote scripts that took them to such far-flung places as the Amazon jungle and Morocco. In fact, filming a subtitle commercial in Marrakech, Bousman was inspired by the sight of two camels tied up on a dirt road in front of a Pizza Hut. It was an eye-opening, unforgettable juxtaposition. It had the humor and flavor of what he and his partner tried to do with their commercials, which was to show that IBM could make technology accessible anywhere.

A lot of nervous tension, some luck, and hard work went into the development of the brand campaign. But there was still an element lacking, and again, the god of creativity shined his tiny beam on Ogilvy and Mather.

There wasn't any grand debate on whether the subtitle campaign should contain a slogan or tagline. Bill Hamilton was one who did not favor them. How many were memorable? How long would it last? "Bill Hamilton is actually very anti-lines," Shelly Lazarus said. "I don't know, he finds them confining." Despite Hamilton's view, divine intervention was percolating halfway around the world. A number of focus groups had been held in the Far East, and the results were collated in Ogilvy's Paris office. Apparently, there was one respondent in Singapore who had been fairly articulate about IBM's challenges and what he thought the company should do to meet them. He thought that technology was making the world smaller, and that people who used technology wanted nothing less than to have a computer company solve their problems.

When Bill Hamilton got hold of the research, he began scribbling ideas for a tagline, against his better judgment. He "paraphrased the sentiment" of the man in the Singapore focus group. Hamilton drafted three or four phrases, including "Solutions for a Small World." Hamilton liked the notion of a "solutions company"—while working on the Microsoft account, he had suggested it to Steve Ballmer. Ballmer had been intrigued, but it never went anywhere.

Now that the phrase "Solutions for a Small Planet" has been attached to much of IBM's advertising, the question of who actually coined it is murky. Ogilvy prefers the romantic notion of the anonymous man in the Far East. Hamilton put together the rough cut, no doubt, but he's reluctant to make anything of it, given his admittedly shaky recall and low regard for slogans. He said, "I just thought we'd hang this set of words, and then the IBM eight-bar logo, and see if the dogs eat the dog food. We might have changed 'world' to 'planet.' It's more of a fifties word, it sounded better. It was that fast."

In one of the early brand campaign presentations to Gerstner, Hamilton didn't even bother reading the tag line aloud. It was just there, and when Gerstner saw it on a repromatic or a story-board or a print ad—nobody quite remembers—he asked, "What was that line at the end?" And Hamilton said, "Oh, it's something we're fooling around with as the summary line." Gerstner said, "I really like that. I think that could be the idea. Let's really think about this." Ogilvy credits Gerstner with pushing it along, but in the end, there was no "Eureka!" Nobody thought it was a line that had legs, one that would be adopted as a company slogan. Least of all the guy in the Singapore focus group.

The slogan is more appropriate than anyone thought. Not because it emphasizes problem-solving rather than technology, which it does. One Ogilvy executive said it reflected "humble stature." It is smart and cocky with a dash of humility. It's a line that largely reflects the essential elements of Lou Gerstner's personality.

The subtitles campaign lasted for about a year and a half, and some thirty to thirty-five commercials were filmed. Probably the edgiest was the one with the band Spinal Tap shown in concert. Amid a loud, heavy-metal riff, the subtitles translated the band's rock vernacular, and then ended by one of the band members saying, "Let's call IBM." Ogilvy felt the commercial would make the case that IBM could be hip, young, and relevant to a group of twenty-five- to thirty-five-year-olds. These were the future CIOs and MIS types who, if they hadn't already, would soon make the major technology buying decisions for corporate accounts. Bill Hamilton pushed Lazarus hard to convince IBM to run this spot. "If you talk to young people," Lazarus said, "it's a bit of a cult thing. My twenty-five-year-old son has seen Spinal Tap, I bet forty times at least. So it actually wasn't hard getting it by them."

While the subtitles campaign was a huge success, Lazarus knew that Bill Hamilton did not have the technological breadth or organizational desire to command the entire worldwide account. So in November 1994, she successfully lured Steve Hayden from BBDO. Hayden had been working on the Apple account for twelve years, and he had faithfully served a trio of disparate CEOs—John Sculley, Mike Spindler, and Gil Amelio. Apple's market share had dissipated, and its identity crisis had been enervating for him. He was ready for a new challenge, a fresh identity crisis.

Hayden stepped into Ogilvy during the middle of the subtitle campaign, which was propitious for IBM, but he had to contend with myriad problems. For one, Martin Sorrell had visited him, ostensibly to tell him he was "very concerned" with revenues on the IBM account. Hayden had to convince the chairman of Ogilvy's holding company that they might have to struggle for a year or two with low profits. Ogilvy needed to make large investments in its own infrastructure if the agency was going to succeed on the account in the long run. "There were a lot of Ogilvy offices that didn't even have computers," said Hayden, enumerating a number of issues to Sorrell. "We had like two hundred people in an office and one phone line." Ogilvy had to know what every one of its shops was doing at any given time. Some outposts were running ads on IBM products that had been discontinued. Hayden refurbished Ogilvy's infrastructure to handle IBM's advertising, from the brand all the way down to the smallest divisions.

This wasn't as routine as it seemed. Hayden was well acquainted with the paranoia that still permeated Big Blue. "IBM still has that feeling of secrecy; maybe it comes from its being in the defense business," Hayden said. "We had to buy shredders for every executive office because IBM wants us to shred everything that we throw out that has IBM on it. It's like there's going to be the KGB going through our trash, and they might find out that we bought two full pages in the *Financial Times* next week. Who knows what someone could do with that information?"

Of course, IBM, like many other companies, has important trade secrets to guard. Even two years into Gerstner's tenure, Big Blue's fixation on secrecy was akin to the Pentagon's. There were five layers of security; Unclassified, Internal, Confidential, Confidential-Restricted, and Registered. Three were eliminated. Limiting the choice to "IBM Confidential" and "Non-Confidential" was a gallant attempt to simplify what the company deemed public or private among the thousands of reams of documents it created every day. The impact has not been felt. If there's any doubt in any IBMer's mind, the tag line "IBM Confidential—Do Not Copy" is immediately attached to every document he or she produces. Today, most IBMers find the copy decree laughable. It is not unusual to receive a third-generation photocopy of a document that was verboten to copy and distribute. Sometimes they're even sent into the company intranet via Lotus Notes. The fact is, there will always be locked rooms with communal printers at IBM. And there will be plenty of shredders screeching from offices, destroying benign documents that have people like Steve Hayden scratching their heads.

Hayden needed an all-hands enclave to cope with the long-term challenge of the IBM account. So he scheduled a worldwide Ogilvy meeting in Montreal in May 1995 to persuade the account teams that a kind of cultural shift was required to deal with IBM. Because half of IBM's budget went to the brand (meaning "corporate"), and the other half went to the product guys (meaning the divisions), he anticipated a divisiveness within Big Blue that would spill into Ogilvy. He expected IBMers would fight among themselves for ad dollars. He was right. Marketing managers in Raleigh who sold PCs, for example, wondered whether Kohnstamm's office would free up ad money when business was roughest.

During his Montreal presentation, Hayden told Ogilvy account people they could expect infighting, delays, and abrupt change orders from IBM. There will be many times, he said, when you can correctly asssume the client doesn't know what it's doing. He was brutally honest, and he spelled out the three requirements he felt were necessary for Ogilvy's success with IBM:

1. You need a high tolerance for ambiguity.
2. You need an (almost) superhuman resilience.
3. You need a sincere and almost pitiable sense of optimism.

These tenets would have been appropriate for any giant corporation, not just Ogilvy. They might have been appropriate, too, for IBMers to cope with its own bureaucracy. Beyond his advertising expertise, Hayden well understood the organic nature of large enterprises, both his own and his client's. He knew Gerstner could not possibly reengineer the brains of every middle manager, no matter how much he tried. At IBM, as with almost every company he had worked for in the past, some things never changed. And not all of them were good.

Still, he would press hard to develop bold advertising for IBM.

Ogilvy wanted Gerstner to appear in a TV spot where the CEO faced off against Deep Blue, IBM's chess-playing computer. But there was no way Gerstner would agree. He had trouble loosening his tie. IBM couldn't relax itself to sneak a sexual innuendo in its advertising either. Ken Segall, a forty-eight-year-old copywriter who has written for both Apple and IBM, recalls producing a Lotus ad that emphasized the power of replication—reproducing icons and files in other locations, even around the world, from your desktop. At the end, a woman in the ad cooed, "I think I'm replicating right now." Segall said, "It was funny and racy and edgy; it was very creative, but as soon as Abby and her staff saw it, they said, 'No way, much too risky.'" For Segall, who had written some of the original Chaplin ads, IBM was the same old place. It will never go all the way.

By 1996, the third year of the Ogilvy-IBM relationship, Hayden had to mastermind a follow-up to the subtitles campaign that had at least as much impact. Ogilvy developed the "letterbox" series, which had two IBM blue bars painted at the top and bottom of the screen. Originally created for Lotus Notes, Ogilvy adapted it to run as part of the worldwide brand campaign. Mostly, the commercials pushed "e-business," IBM's thrust to gain mindshare on the World Wide Web, with a series of contemporary office skits accompanied by bouncy music. The e-business logo was clever and simple, a takeoff on the @ sign used in Internet addresses. Hayden dreamed up the idea and substituted the *e* for the *a*. When he sketched it out, nobody liked it. When his art director redrew it, it looked a lot better than Hayden's scrawl, and it was subsequently approved.

Hayden continued to test the boundaries. One e-business ad caused IBM to muster more courage than it thought it had. An ad that addressed the networking security issue used fear tactics. Years ago, Gerstner once used fear. Actor Karl Malden warned families their vacations could be wrecked if wallets were lost or stolen. The message was that life itself could not possibly go on without your American Express card.

The IBM spot played for much higher stakes. Two late-night hackers break into their company's confidential personnel files. They're clicking the keyboard in front of the computer screen. Wow! One mentions that a senior vice president earns only half what another earns. The other says it doesn't matter if the guy earning less doesn't know. The first one says the guy will soon find out, because he just e-mailed the salaries to everyone in the company.

This was definitely putting the fear issue in your face.

Shelly Lazarus recalls, "They didn't want to do that initially. That made them very nervous. Lou actually said, 'That's every CEO's nightmare. I don't know that IBM should put it in front of them, because it's the thing that's so scary about technology. Do you want to raise the fear?'"

Lazarus knew this was an important question for a CEO to ponder. She knew the ad would increase the threshold of acceptability for IBM. Gerstner approved it. Big Blue had traveled a long way from its old Chaplin ads.

That Strange, Elusive PC Company

Beginning in mid-1993 and lasting through most of 1994, CFO Jerry York managed to spread the wrath of Armonk's cost-cutting campaign to almost every venue, every division. As he darted into IBM outposts, he did not underestimate the value of even the most basic belt-tightening. Amid a stream of four-letter words, he exhorted managers to spend less money. Nothing eluded his scrutiny, even packaging and envelopes. In a way, Gerstner and York were a good-cop, bad-cop routine. Where the CEO made noble and arduous efforts to imbue a new feeling of worth within his remaining workforce, the CFO went on a tear about the company's obscene inefficiencies. If York asked an IBMer, "Why are we doing it this way?" the one wrong answer was, "Because that's the way we always do it."

So it had to be one of the defining moments in IBM's recent history when in the winter of 1994, York donned an all-white space suit and, viewing the IBM world from a plastic window in its hood, entered a factory that manufactured circuit boards in Austin. Nobody could remember if any CFO of Big Blue had ever deigned to visit Austin, let alone tour a clean room. York, though, was not uncomfortable in factories, and he enjoyed dissecting the manufacturing process. He had done it for Chrysler many times. This was far less grimy, and the assembly line was shorter.

Bill Amelio, a trim, prematurely balding plant manager who headed the tour, was a guy in his mid-thirties who had graduated from the engineering school at Lehigh University and gone right to work for IBM. He'd been with the company for fourteen years. Amelio dutifully answered York's probing questions about glass fiber circuit board production. York wanted to know about every process, how much material was used, what was waste. Where can we save money? When they finished the tour, Amelio told York that they had been making ten thousand boards a day over the past five years, and they hadn't had a single one returned because it was defective. This astonished York, who could not conjure a zero-defect factory. If defects were so few, why were his warranty costs soaring? Also, it did not square with the mail that his boss, Lou Gerstner, received from users who complained that the once-vaunted IBM quality was now more myth than reality. IBM machines broke down not infrequently.

"It's the best plant in the world," Amelio said.

"I don't believe you," York said.

Despite this exchange, there began a relationship of mutual respect between the two men. York quickly discovered that Amelio was one of the young guys who understood how to fix something that was broken. Amelio knew that IBM had both manufactured and procured thousands of parts, and had strong suspicions about where the waste was being buried. A vice president on board the company jet on the trip back to Armonk with York talked about how he was impressed with Amelio's enthusiasm for manufacturing. In fact, he thought it was funny how anyone could be so passionate about something as mundane as circuit boards. York didn't see the humor in his comment and "just stared . . . as if I had thrown up on him." York liked manufacturing guys who were obsessed. The best lived and breathed process-efficiency.

It did not take an advanced degree in quantum mechanics to understand the main flaw in IBM's production cycle, and nowhere was this more evident than within the PC Company.

Every class of product was designed by a unique group, and each group "qualified" the parts they wanted to be in their product. Qualifying a part meant that each team listed the specifications that were required for its particular product. This was done independently of other product managers. So, for example, a circuit board designed for a given computer didn't necessarily fit on another computer's chassis, even though they performed roughly the same functions. Or, you could have five different vendors supplying you with a one-gigabyte hard drive. And those five vendors' products, although functionally equivalent, were unique to different models.

It is extremely difficult to accurately forecast demand on a specific model number. What would happen was, for example, product A might be a raging success, and sell out. The PC Company couldn't produce any more. Why? Because it was short of one-gig drives. There was product B, there were a hundred thousand of them sitting in the warehouse unsold. Why didn't IBM use the drive from product B on product A? Well, they couldn't because when the products were designed in the first place, nobody thought about interchangeable parts—or in manufacturing jargon, there was no "commonality of supply."

Here was one basic explanation for unacceptable inventories and shortages. Such a problem could take years to fix. Worse, it gave IBM's competitors insurmountable leads in all kinds of PCs.

This was an enlightening discovery for Jerry York. At Chrysler, where he had spent so much of his professional life, parts were infinitely interchangeable among given cars. Such flexibility saved millions of dollars when markets for certain vehicles were misread or when models were discontinued.

What York at first didn't understand was how to value—or more accurately, devalue—the parts inventories of computers. Automobile parts, especially standard parts, had long shelf lives, often many years. And replacement parts constituted a multibillion-dollar business. Some parts did not depreciate. Conversely, computer parts were notorious commodities, subject to the next wave of newer, cheaper, and more sophisticated replacements, which flooded out of the R&D labs and into product cycles at mind-bending speed.

Moore's Law, named for Intel cofounder Gordon Moore, maintained in the mid-1960s that the size of each transistor on an integrated circuit would be reduced by half every two years. Moore's Law has been quoted so often, and the microelectronics industry has accelerated its upgrades at such a spectacular pace, this once-bold pronouncement seems outdated. Thanks to fierce competition and shrinking profit margins on hardware, prices dropped faster than anyone predicted in the boom years—the 1980s and early 1990s—of the PC business. It is estimated that a computer parts inventory loses value at a rate of two to five percent per *month*. The goal in IBM's PC business was a gross margin of twenty percent, but to attain that it had to strive for a thirty percent margin the day a given product was launched. Two months later, gross margins are reduced to twenty percent, and two months after that, it's down to ten percent. Over a six-month period, a twenty percent margin average is respectable.

The bottom line: If you are late to market by two or three months, you lose a great deal of your profit. If you're late by six months or a year, you might as well not bother building the product. Market timing mistakes in the computer business are deadly.

The key to a successful PC business is not in manufacturing per se, but in the logistics of the supply chain. How carefully you procure parts, when you consume them, what level of inventory you keep, how common the parts usage is across all of the designs. This last crucial element goes back to the basic engineering of the product, R&D, and where exactly those R&D efforts are aimed.

IBM was doing it all wrong.

Midway through 1993, Bob Corrigan, who ran the PC Company, and his CFO, Eddie Rogers, told York and Gerstner that sales were growing faster than they had predicted. They said they thought they could sell a half million more units—three and a half million instead of three million—than they had originally planned. Corrigan wanted extra cash to buy parts. "A nice fat payback in the fourth quarter" was promised, recalled one former IBM senior official. He and Gerstner authorized the expenditure.

If Bob Corrigan had one discernible weakness, it was his intrinsic love for pure technology. He was a disciple of the technology-rules school of Jack Kuehler and Jim Cannavino, IBM's self-taught mainframe whiz who marveled at record-breaking memory capacity and processor speed. Corrigan was championed by designers because he loved to engage colleagues in sophisticated dialogues on circuit board design, chip architecture, processor speed, and all those things that had little to do with solving customer problems.

York would have found out earlier that so much had gone awry, one can speculate, if IBM's complex transfer-pricing agreements had not masked fiscal reality for so long. One could surmise that when the CFO learned how the bookkeeping really worked, he realized the PC Company was losing money and was not in the black, as had been reported originally.

It took only four months for Corrigan's 1993 plan for a nice fat payback to crumble. There were three reasons. First, the PC Company as a whole, but particularly in the United States, had been chasing what they thought was very strong demand. This was true—but for products made by IBM's competitors. Compaq absolutely vanquished IBM in that selling season. Nothing magic about it. Compaq had an equivalent or better computer and simply sold it for less. Second, IBM's logistics and supply systems were so outdated and inadequate that it couldn't cut off the parts coming in. Third, a new version of the PS/2, IBM's commercial desktop computer, had huge technical problems, and they weren't discovered until a few weeks before it was introduced. The PS/2 was delayed six months, and the parts already were on the shelves, so there was an unmitigated surplus in IBM warehouses.

When the technical glitches were finally solved and the computers were assembled, there was a seven-month inventory, depreciating every day. To clear the warehouses, prices were discounted heavily. In sum, the PC Company was about to miss its forecast by "several hundred million dollars," according to one former IBM executive. IBM's corporate management was unhappy, of course, but Corrigan promised that he would reduce inventories to about $2 billion by year's end. "Well, when the end of the year came, their actual inventories were $3 billion and the whole thing was just a fucking fiasco," said York. According to two IBM sources, net loss was $1 billion. The news from Somers was always worse than they anticipated.

By the new year of 1994, Gerstner and York had seen enough.

Gerstner felt the problems in IBM's desktop units were so intractable that only someone from outside the company could solve them. He also surmised that once the manufacturing and supply chain was straightened out, the remaining hurdle would be marketing.

He decided on his fourth significant hire, Rick Thoman, forty-nine, perhaps the most loyal executive who had ever worked for him. Thoman had been linked with Gerstner for more than two decades, following him from job to job. Other than the titles, his résumé looked remarkably like Gerstner's. He also had an affinity for finance, working in Gerstner's group at McKinsey. He had three masters degrees and a Ph.D. in economics. He had held a number of divisional CFO jobs. Thoman had made a great effort to shake the "lightweight" label that had followed him since his McKinsey days. He had run the international operations for Travel Related Services at AmEx, and for the past eighteen months he had headed Nabisco's international food business. Like Gerstner, he had no experience in the computer industry before arriving at IBM, other than being an unsatisfied customer. Gerstner, nevertheless, felt that Thoman's marketing zeal would jolt the company. Some who knew Thoman, however, were completely perplexed. They considered him more of a finance guy than a marketer.

Thoman's arrival in the PC Company was viewed by the technology community with the same jaundice that Gerstner had faced. What was a cookie salesman doing in this business? Some felt he was probably too soft, and not enough of an operations person to succeed in such a fast-paced, cutthroat industry. Thoman's reputation was not in the day-to-day details. And in PCs, details were everything.

Gerstner brought Thoman in at the group executive level with responsibilities not just for the PC Company, but also for Prodigy, IBM's flagging joint effort with Sears, Roebuck and Company in competition with America Online; the PowerPC; the RS/6000 line; and the printing division. As head of the Personal Systems Group, he was one of the six or seven most powerful executives at IBM. Thoman did not yet know it, but his problems would be far deeper and more complex than he had ever suspected. As one former senior executive who reported to him put it, "We were in deep yogurt."

By far, Thoman's most significant initial move was the removal of Bob Corrigan and Eddie Rogers from the PC Company. These changes were fomented by Gerstner and York. By opting to not replace Corrigan, Thoman became the de facto head of the PC Company.

Although Thoman had virtually no clue about how the computer business really worked, he had a broad notion of how much redundancy existed within his units. He decided to consolidate the PC Company's numerous sites. There were a half dozen labs all struggling to come up with new products, and the duplication of effort consumed millions of dollars. Thoman shut down facilities in Boca Raton, in Lexington, Kentucky, and others around the world, and placed the entire development operation under one roof in Raleigh. This staved off some of the bleeding.

Thoman's next move was to kill all the PC Company brands except for ThinkPad. He asked Bruce Claflin, the executive who had spearheaded the development of the ThinkPad, to become the general manager of product and brand management. "The brands didn't make any sense," recalled Claflin. "PS/1 was a worthless brand. It meant nothing to a consumer, and its name was chosen because we already had a PS/2. So we gave it a number less than 2, not more, that was the logic. We didn't want any name to go on the consumer version that would in any way give the appearance that it was more powerful, or superior to the commercial machine. We had to give it a brand that made it less than the brand that existed." It was the typical result of the twisted logic that came from the collective input of too many special interests within IBM.

PS/1, PS/2, Value Point, and Ambra were all shelved. The new lines were called the PC 300 and the PC 700. "We took a page out of BMW's playbook," Claflin said.

Value Point was a low-end PC, and Ambra was a "direct," no-middleman machine that attempted to compete with Dell and Gateway. Ambra represented a halfhearted attempt to create distance from IBM's name, which in the PC market was synonymous with "too expensive." IBM was armed with a sheaf of surveys that revealed staunch consumer resistance. Some would not buy any product labeled "IBM" merely because they sensed it was unaffordable. The advertising contained small print that noted Ambra was a subsidiary of IBM. Ambra and Value Point simply didn't sell.

Arguably, ThinkPad was the only sub-brand that had any respect within the industry, though Toshiba's and Compaq's laptops were more popular. The sleek, matte black IBM laptops had knocked down rave reviews and produced excellent sales. Not surprisingly, Claflin had endured infighting and resistance when IBM was about to introduce the ThinkPad line. When he took over the mobile group, the ThinkPad name already had been appropriated by another IBM team that was developing an electronic writing tablet, a high-tech version of the kind typically given out to conference attendees. It was a formidable idea. You made notes on a legal pad, and the results were then digitized with an inexpensive chip embedded in the tablet, and the information—including sketches—were uploaded to your PC. (This product subsequently became known internally as ThinkScribe and was ultimately manufactured in 1998 in a joint venture with the Cross Pen Computing Group. It is called CrossPad.) At the time, it was in the prototype stage; researchers were still refining the software.

This group, however, felt ThinkPad was too good a name to give up. There was a heated debate. The tablet group felt IBM's reputation in PCs and laptops was so bad that when the new line bombed, critics would call it the "StinkPad." They fought it because they thought the name would be perverted by the marketplace. Claflin finally asked his team if anyone could improve on the name "ThinkPad." He glanced around the room, and when nobody spoke, he commandeered it. It took only two years for ThinkPad to become IBM's most well-known sub-brand.

Thoman continued to concentrate on marketing new PC brands, but he knew virtually nothing about manufacturing. And the more that Jerry York examined the results, the more he realized IBM wasn't getting the computers into the pipeline cheaply enough. The problems were still in development. So York summoned Bill Amelio from Austin and asked him to assume leadership of a massive reengineering effort.

Shortly after Amelio arrived in Raleigh, the heart of IBM's PC development effort, he plowed through the fine print of the PC Company's product descriptions. It was like reading Proust; you didn't think you'd ever finish. There were thousands of Stock Keeping Units, or SKUs, upward of 3,500. It was a classic case of the shoemaker not being able to make shoes for his own family. IBM's mainframes had an impeccable reputation for managing parts inventories for Fortune 500 companies. Yet it couldn't do the same for its own PC Company. "The world's premier computer company had a horrible backbone inside all of the facilities," Amelio said. The mentality in the past had been that IBM had to stock almost anything they thought it could sell. And since there was no commonality in the product spectrum, SKUs had become a problem that had spiraled out of control, like a virus that kept replicating, each time a product team wrote a new specification for a design change. This was the legacy of Bob Corrigan and Jim Cannavino. They had been lured to the corner of computing that appealed to those who must

169

have the latest technology, even if the market turned out to be minuscule. When Cannavino was once asked by an IBMer why the PC Company catalogued hundreds of different models and configurations, he replied, "It's customer choice, kid. Customers want all these different configurations, and it's our job to provide them."

So Amelio spent a lot of time reducing the number of SKUs that were available. It would take more than a year to identify parts and products that IBM manufactured, stocked, and sold at a loss simply to accommodate a dwindling market.

Amelio lamented the atmosphere of indecision in Raleigh. The PC Company wasted millions on products that were never finished. "IBM is great at being able to analyze shit, but the market moved before we got our analysis done," he said. Paul Mugge, a manager in Raleigh who was intimately involved in the reengineering project, summed up much of the problem when he learned how incredibly deficient IBM was in one respect: It kept tabling decisions in the middle of product development. Mugge repeated a colleague's sage analysis when he said, "We don't kill products at IBM, we wound them."

Despite these inefficiencies, Jerry York hoped the PC Company was headed for a turnaround. The major cost reductions in SG&A and R&D were similar to those being implemented throughout IBM, and Thoman had absorbed most of the write-offs of Corrigan's disastrous 1993. The PC Company actually turned a small profit of about $75 million during the first half of 1994. But that upward move quickly proved illusory. It was apparent when the staffs in Armonk—finance and manufacturing—began to analyze the third-quarter forecasts. "It initially appeared that Thoman was making very substantial progress," a former senior executive said. "Then things just didn't seem to be getting much better. IBM, because of the problems in R&D, was always late, so it never got the thirty percent margin. Its margins were depressed."

Put succinctly, IBM was at a huge disadvantage with its desktop products because neither Gerstner nor Thoman had ever worked in such an R&D-intensive business. While Gerstner greatly respected technology, he and Thoman were lost when it came to understanding how critical it was to reinvent a product line on a regular basis. You had to consistently and correctly predict what would sell in eighteen months or less. The PC industry's innovation occurred in a blur that was alien to these executives.

One of Gerstner's glaring weaknesses, however, was his apparent blind spot in PC pricing, especially in the consumer market. Margins were so slim and IBM was such a huge enterprise that it could never hope to sell the equivalent for less. It couldn't compete with smaller PC firms. The PC Company continued to limp along, hoping to offer value-added features that might justify spending more to buy the Big Blue name plate. IBM had regained respectability, but it didn't matter much in the PC business.

IBM's innovative technology continued to seduce Gerstner. ThinkPad engineers had come up with the "butterfly" keyboard, which fanned open to a larger typing space, and the space-saving TrackPoint, an orange device—the "pencil eraser"—in the middle of the keyboard that replaced the mouse or trackball. TrackPoint was welcomed with enthusiasm by customers; despite good reviews, however, the butterfly keyboard made little impact beyond being a clever gimmick. It was discontinued. While ThinkPads were a success with business users who bought them on their company's expense budgets, they were not popular among home users who prowled the aisles of CompUSA, Circuit City, and Best Buy. Other laptop brands—just as good, if not better—continually underpriced IBM.

Gerstner was frustrated and unhappy with his PC business.

In early January 1995, after Thoman had been at IBM a year, Gerstner called York in to talk about the PC Company. It wasn't coming together quickly enough, according to sources at IBM who knew about the meeting. A former IBM executive who worked for Thoman could not understand how Gerstner could have relied on Thoman to untangle the perpetual mess. "He [Thoman] took notes of everything," this executive said. "Now, what the hell happened to the notes, I have no idea." The implication was that Thoman was good at taking notes, but less than good at taking action.

Gerstner ordered York to immediately investigate what was happening in Raleigh. It could not wait until Monday. There was nothing discreet about the directive. Gerstner mentioned that he had already explained to Thoman that York's involvement was essential. On a Sunday morning, York, Bruce Claflin, Bill MacCracken, who was the PC Company marketing and sales head, and Joe Formichelli, another executive, boarded an IBM jet in Westchester and flew to North Carolina. They began meeting that afternoon with several Raleigh managers, finance people, purchasing people, and everyone who managed the PC Company. The meetings continued through Monday and Tuesday.

York began to delve into the details of product development, now acutely aware that IBM's problems were aggravated by the short product cycle. IBMers were not doing a good job of product definition. In fact, they were awful at it. For example, traditionally the marketing team does the research to find out what features customers want in their new products. Then marketing asks engineering to design the computers with the features, and finance runs the numbers. The questions that come up are ones like, Should there be a CD-ROM drive built in? If so, what speed? How fast should the modem run? How many serial or parallel ports should there be for add-ons?

Because IBM's designers were never quite sure what customers wanted, they left too many specifications open. So engineering began sketching, and marketing then changed the configuration, and it slowed the development cycle. This, in turn, delayed testing and compromised quality control. The PC Company, desperate to meet ship deadlines, took shortcuts in testing. When the product finally went from engineering to manufacturing and purchasing for assembly, a technical flaw suddenly would be discovered. They then would write engineering changes, do additional development, and waste more time. Finally, to compensate for the chain of mistakes, the PCs were priced higher and were less competitive. It was a vicious cycle.

"It doesn't matter what kind of widget you are making—cars, PCs, or whatever—if you have a fuzzy handoff from marketing to engineering, bad things are going to happen," York explained. "Your product will either be late to market, or you will run development risks that can lead to higher costs." For example, if the initial spec on a PC did not include a CD-ROM drive and then months into development you decide to add one, it either delays the program or it makes it much more risky. York implored the marketing people to clearly define the next generation of products. He knew that with automobiles, product planners decided on horsepower, which features would be put in which model, and so on. With PCs, the questions were similar: how much RAM, hard drive capacity, microprocessor speed, whether or not it will have a built-in CD-ROM drive, what peripherals it will support, a modem, and so on.

Though few knew it, beginning in 1995, Jerry York became the de facto head of the PC Company, according to several executives and managers. For the next nine months, he all but ran the PC Company on weekends. York initiated a daily reporting system. He told Thoman's executive team that he wanted to know what was going on in every plant around the world, and every product line in that plant. When York was at Hertz he got a daily business report from every rental location in the nation. At Chrysler he knew what every assembly plant was shipping on any given day. When the same theory was applied to the PC Company, it galvanized the organization to address problems more quickly. "When something is going on in the business, or going wrong in the business, nothing could be swept under the rug," York said. "They either had to ship the unit, or they had to tell senior management they weren't shipping and why."

York got Thoman to focus his team on the fact that they couldn't hope to compete in the PC business on a nine-to-five basis. Every Saturday from 8:30 A.M. until 10:30 A.M.—often until noon— Thoman held a worldwide conference call of his senior management team to review their weekly progress. Thoman had been able to track cartons of Fig Newtons at Nabisco at any time with apparent ease. So it was reasonable to assume it was less of a challenge to find out what happened to ten thousand missing PCs.

The PC business, however, had no real strategy to compete with its more nimble rivals in the marketplace. Other than pure profit, one of the other scorecards was inventory turns. Compaq, Dell, Hewlett-Packard, Gateway, and others were able to sell and replenish their warehouses at rates far faster than IBM. Not only were they more efficient, they understood that in a low-margin business, volume was king. They continually undersold one another while IBM was still cautious about lowering prices. It took years before IBM ads would quote prices on new products, unless they were being severely reduced to deplete an inventory.

Every instance of the competition drubbing IBM's PC Company added to its lack of confidence. After a while, it became a self-fulfilling prophecy, and the PC Company's ability to judge market demand was stifled. One reason was that it was gun-shy from costly mistakes of overproduction. IBM was afraid to take risks in a business that rewarded those who did. Its decision makers felt it was better to underproduce and lose sales on a hit product rather than overproduce and be left with unsold computers.

Bruce Claflin explains this with a nautical metaphor: "It's a little like trying to navigate your ship out into the open sea. You've got to go between two islands. Your job is to sail between them to get out to sea. Now, one island is sandy, and one island is rocky. But it's never clear sailing in this industry. It's stormy and there's fog and your electronics are out. That's the reality of the PC business. You don't have exact data, so you're estimating. If you hit the sandy island that's not good, but you can float off and sail away later. If you hit the rocky island, you sink. The sandy island is not having enough supply. It's bad, you're missing some demand, but it won't kill you. The rocky island is too much supply. Too much supply, you are out of business. You're sunk. So the trick is, you're trying to sail between them, but you'd better sort of overcorrect, and if you're wrong, hit the sand."

Either way, IBM continually ran aground.

One manager who worked in the PC Company's strategy unit in Raleigh echoed Claflin's sentiment. They were conditioned to failure, he said. They had a history of building machines that didn't sell. So when he suggested a big production run for what looked like a hit product, they balked. The manager recalls, "They'd say to me, 'Well, you weren't here four years ago when we had warehouses full of inventory.' And I said, 'Yeah, you're right, I wasn't. I'm sorry you didn't know how to forecast then.'"

IBMers still haven't learned how to forecast, even though their rivals face the same challenge and do it better. When the PS/1 was discontinued and the Aptiva replaced it in the fall of 1994, the manufacturing run was typically cautious. The Aptiva was a sellout, and IBM could not ramp up enough to refresh the supply chain during the lush fourth quarter, when the biggest number of the year's PC sales are generated. The company lost millions of dollars in potential sales.

In a draft of an IBM internal white paper, staffers in the Market Intelligence unit voiced their concerns: "The historical perspective of IBM's PC share position is very disturbing. In the U.S., for example, we've experienced a steady decline from a high of 22 percent in 1985 to our current share of eight percent. Competitors have been very successful in taking market share from IBM in the education and government channel. Compaq has dedicated systems for K-12 educational use. Compaq has set up a special marketing force. . . . Dell and other competitors have unseated IBM as the notebook of choice at the university level. Dell is rapidly becoming a major player with the GSA [General Services Administration, a federal agency]."

This was hardly an epiphany. Some IBMers in the PC Company wondered what took Market Intelligence so long to figure this out. Market share erosion also was not a revelation to those in Armonk who controlled the budgets. The executive in charge of Market Intelligence, Bob Corbisiero, was an amiable enough guy, and he had put in more than twenty years with the company. He sort of fell into the job by accident. After he left management jobs in the sales force, he carved a small niche doing research.

For years the Market Intelligence unit was located in IBM's North American headquarters in White Plains. Then it was transferred to a floor in Somers. The logic at the time, said an IBM vice president, was "with Compaq and Dell just chewing us up, if we needed market intelligence somewhere in this company, it's in the PC business."

Market Intelligence was one of the small pockets of bureaucracy that still exist within IBM. Corbisiero's unit ultimately grew into a small fiefdom of two hundred in support staff. It produced reports, statistics, analyses, and more of the same during every quarter. It tracked market share within decimal points worldwide, but it was primarily after-the-fact data. Corbisiero's group of intelligence gatherers really did nothing much more than compile and regurgitate volumes of data already gleaned by dozens of expensive technology consultants. Some in the corporate staff in Armonk often wondered if any of Corbisiero's staff had ever seen the inside of a Radio Shack, Best Buy, or CompUSA. They also wondered if "Market Intelligence" was like the military oxymoron, "Army Intelligence."

The charts and graphs rendered by Market Intelligence often quote The Gartner Group, or Jupiter Communications, or Forrester, or IDC, or some other respectable high-tech research firm. And, of course, many of these firms are clients of IBM and its competitors. They have a vested interest in a bull market for technology products. They extrapolate business forecasts from the sales and marketing data often supplied by—guess who?— their own clients!

Thus, there is a circular flow of research that is questionable to begin with because there is no way of knowing where it originated or how reliable it is. If a research group projects that a market for a given product will grow to X billion by the year 2002, who can argue? How can you debate the reliability of a prediction in this business?

IBM's lagging in the PC business couldn't be blamed on the lack of real intelligence in the Market Intelligence unit, of course. Market research in the PC business is an inexact science, to be sure, and the inherent flaws in data gathering contribute to its often specious predictions. The problem with Corbisiero's group was that it did little more than reveal what the PC Company did or was doing. It was not much help in suggesting what it needed to do.

Gerstner came to quickly understand that IBM had become a minor player on the desktop. He realized that the small computers were a black hole at IBM, and he'd continue to lose large sums even though revenues were continuing to grow. Also, whenever IBM was criticized by the press or analysts, the first thing they began with was the PC Company. He needed to do something proactive, and soon. A merger or acquisition was one alternative. And Apple Computer was a likely candidate. Apple's recent strategy to shift its market focus from consumers to business customers had largely backfired except in some small pockets like desktop publishing. It, too, had ceded market share to its competitors. Its stock was depressed, and it was an attractive takeover target.

IBM's senior executives did not have to look very deep in studying the figures. IBM had ten percent of the business PC market, Apple had about six and a half percent, while Compaq was leading with fourteen points. They realized that a combination would immediately double its market share and leapfrog Compaq. Also, Apple dominated the education space, and it was second only to Packard Bell in the overall home market. IBM-Apple leverage could be formidable in every area—R&D, parts procurement, distribution, sales. Not to mention that crucial Madison Avenue word, "mindshare."

An outright friendly takeover of Apple was not a new idea. It wasn't new in 1993 when John Sculley had suggested it during his job interview with IBM's board. In fact, Jim Cannavino had mulled over this idea with his boss, Jack Kuehler, as far back as 1990, when he was running IBM's PC Company. Probably no other senior executive at IBM knew as much about Apple's attributes and technology potential than Cannavino. He liked the Apple techies, he spoke their particular dialect. Apple officials also knew Cannavino was not your typical IBMer.

Cannavino was the epitome of the Watsons' "wild duck" theory. According to this belief, it was important to have a few brilliant, unconventional, nonlinear characters in their management ranks. Cannavino had spent much of his time flying outside IBM's formation, from his early days when he talked his way into a job as an eighteen-year-old technician repairing and maintaining mainframe computers. He'd risen to a wide variety of senior positions in the company, and he was one of the few executives among the old guard who had run business units in both large- and small-scale computing. He wasn't hindered by divisional snobbery and infighting. He bled blue. He understood IBM's politics and bureaucracy perhaps better than anyone at his level, and he knew how to circumvent it for his own interests. Legend had it that Cannavino once commandeered—in the middle of the night—a mainframe. When management discovered who was behind the disappearance, the indiscretion was shrugged off. He held that much sway.

Cannavino's vision for the melding of the assets of two of the most influential technology companies, Apple and IBM, could have been the capstone of his long career at Big Blue.

Acquiring Apple also would raise the profiles of both companies in the consumer market. It would give Gerstner two alternatives. One, he could shut down the IBM PC Company. This would mean a considerable write-down, including additional layoffs, and a loss in terms of IBM's prestige. But he could then use the Macintosh as the company's primary desktop brand, both in the office and in the home, and build new products using it as a base.

His other choice would be to continue with IBM as the primary commercial desktop brand and target the Mac strictly to consumers. Apple could continue to exploit its own strength—selling computers that ended up in living rooms and classrooms rather than offices. He could reconfigure IBM's face to the home user through an already accepted brand.

Either approach was fine with Cannavino. He had his eyes on just one prize: the Mac OS and its superior graphical user interface. It was the quickest and most painless way to loosen IBM's reliance on Microsoft.

It was a brash idea, given the intrinsic forces that seemed to pull against it. Inside Apple, IBM's intrusion was highly controversial because Apple had always been a go-it-alone company. Its early slogan, "the computer for the rest of us," went even further. Those who worked there felt it was the corporation for the rest of us. People who worked at Apple did so precisely because it was founded on principles that were antithetical to IBM. Given IBM's past failed partnerships, the common wisdom circulating in Cupertino had always been, "What do you get when you combine IBM and Apple?" The answer was, "IBM." Their cultures were of such diverse roots as to form a gulf that many felt would be impossible to bridge.

Despite the fact that it would be a difficult match, IBM began to proceed early in 1994. IBM's mergers and acquisition team began poring over Apple's financials, the SEC filings, every 10-Q and 10-K report.

In the spring of 1994, an IBM delegation was dispatched to Dallas to meet with Apple principals, including CEO Michael Spindler. The two sides were out of sync from the start. In the opposite of what might have been expected, Cannavino and his team went casual and the Apple contingent wore suits. Preliminary discussions centered on the benefits to both companies, the possibilities of meshing operating systems, and the cash and marketing muscle a revitalized IBM could provide for Apple. A lot of time was devoted to the desktop operating system, either IBM's OS/2 or Apple's System 7. Both were problematic and tended to freeze or crash, and to a greater extent than either company wanted to admit. IBM had installed a microkernel in OS/2 that had greatly improved performance over earlier iterations (most recently OS/1.3). It gave the OS/2 a degree of robustness when running multiple applications. According to a source close to these negotiations, IBM raised questions about System 7: "Can it work in the big leagues? Can it work with the 390 [IBM's mainframe OS], can it work with the networked world? Is it strong enough as a piece of technology?"

Cannavino felt that integrating the better characteristics of both companies' operating systems would be a technical hurdle. But more important, he thought that Apple had to make a transition from a hardware company to a software supplier. This would be almost as difficult. He thought the deal could work if IBM could get Apple at a relatively cheap price. They'd have to lower the cost of building Macs—which commanded a premium at the retail level—to stay competitive.

Despite the open questions, the meeting went well. When he returned to Armonk, Cannavino reported to Thoman and Gerstner that a friendly takeover was viable. Gerstner then called Mike Markkula, an official who had been at Apple during its nascent years and was now chairman, to confirm his interest. An IBM source said that Gerstner was gearing up to make an offer. "We were very serious about Apple," he said. "It wasn't just, 'Let's go out there and kick the tires.'"

Several high-level meetings between IBM and Apple executives were held during the summer of 1994. At least two took place in Silicon Valley, in a stifling conference room in a hotel a short drive from the San Francisco International Airport. If both sides could agree on terms and a price, they were on the verge of a history-making deal in the high-tech industry.

Apple's contingent, however, balked at one particular item. IBM's technical people—meaning Lee Reiswig, who headed up OS/2, and John M. Thompson, the company's senior executive in software—wanted to ensure getting early and adequate access to the source code inside the Mac. A big concern on both sides was the time it might take to gain Justice Department approval of the deal. A federal review could take a year or more, and IBM did not want to waste any time waiting for critical specifications.

Two final meetings were held in Chicago, at the Westin Hotel in Rosemont, near O'Hare. Entourages from both companies, a dozen people in all, sat around a table in the Premier Gold room, a dozen stories above the traffic, amid a backdrop of jets roaring through the takeoff and landing pattern. At the first meeting, IBM's Jerry York, Jim Cannavino, Rick Thoman, and John M.

Thompson were confident and optimistic. The Apple contingent busied themselves doodling on whiteboards about various product lines, and where the Mac OS would fit in.

The IBMers were ready to negotiate. Apple had retained Goldman Sachs as investment bankers, while IBM had hired Morgan Stanley's mergers and acquisitions unit. When it appeared that a deal was imminent, Gerstner joined the second meeting in November. While Gerstner's Gulfstream IV flew to Chicago in the early morning, David Kalis remained behind in Armonk, readying his staff to take a flurry of press calls. With Gerstner showing up, Spindler and Markkula expected that IBM would not leave until an initial offer was on the table.

The meeting began at 8:30 A.M., and only an hour after the executives sat down, someone from the IBM contingent said, "This is a tremendous opportunity for these two companies to work together, and you guys at Apple, you know, will really get rich as a result of this." Spindler was somewhat taken aback by the reference to how much money they would make on the deal. His reply was icy: "Well, we're already rich enough. If we like working for IBM, we'll stay around, and if we don't like working for IBM, we'll leave."

Gerstner then asked to be excused with Spindler and Markkula so the three could talk privately. Gerstner right away asked Spindler how much of a premium he wanted for the company. The Apple CEO said he was hoping for something in the range of double the share price. Apple had been stuck for some time in the mid-$30s, and since it was at about $37 a share, Spindler said the board probably would approve something in the $60-plus range. Gerstner said he felt it was way too high. He had been prepared to offer only a few dollars a share more than the stock's current trading price. He was bottom-fishing.

Though they were a long way from a realistic figure, in this kind of negotiation price is usually not the deal breaker. Spindler said that while there was a wide gap in both boards' expectations, he assumed there was a figure in the middle that both IBM and Apple would feel was fair. According to a former IBM senior executive who attended the meeting, when Gerstner and Markkula met privately,

Markkula gave Gerstner a document that included a pay package for the Apple executives. "It was apparent that they had done more work on their compensation than they had done, for example, on figuring out how Apple and IBM would jointly sell computers," this executive said. "And so Lou concluded that was the end of any deal right there." Another IBM source in Armonk confirmed this. "The Apple guys were interested in only one thing, golden parachutes for their guys," he said.

Gerstner returned to the conference room, stuffed his papers into his briefcase, and announced to his colleagues, "We're leaving."

Personal compensation is always touchy, even though Spindler had said that Apple executives weren't in it for the money. It's like saying job titles aren't important, even though who reports to whom is critical. After all, Spindler knew Gerstner wouldn't be answering to the Apple board. Apple was by far the smaller company. Spindler would have to report to IBM, and if it didn't work out, he'd be leaving, not Gerstner.

On balance, it's almost preposterous to believe that the deal was scotched because Gerstner felt the Apple executives' priorities were unrealistic. In the past, Gerstner himself had been accused many times of demanding excessive compensation. So it's reasonable to assume that Gerstner's executives were merely posturing and making a bigger issue out of one that is commonly discussed during any M&A, and early on as well.

The Apple side claims that at least the initial figures were tossed out. IBM says it never made an offer. The one fact nobody disputes is that IBM withdrew. So one might reasonably conclude that almost as soon as he walked in, Gerstner smelled a bad deal in every corner of the Westin Hotel meeting room. He used the pay package as an excuse to bail out, thinking they might never reach an agreement on price.

Spindler, perhaps sensing he made a faux pas that eventually could be forgiven, later made overtures to IBM to revitalize talks, but Gerstner was no longer interested.

When Gerstner was asked about the Apple deal, he said it was apparent that the corporate cultures were just too different.

Though it was a long way from explaining what really occurred in that last meeting at the Westin, few executives—either from Apple or IBM—could disagree with his explanation.

Despite the failure to acquire Apple, IBM ended 1994 with a flourish of courage, and once again the PC Company was at the forefront. Bruce Claflin remembers it well. It was a Wednesday and IBM was getting ready to shut down for the long Thanksgiving weekend. He received a call from Paul Otellini, a senior vice president at Intel. Otellini wanted to give Claflin a heads-up about an article being published the next day saying there was a flaw with Intel's new Pentium chip. IBM was one of its three biggest customers for the Pentium. Getting right to the point, Otellini said it was nothing to worry about. Intel had done the homework. The problem did exist, but it was very small, and it might affect one out of a million customers. Otellini had explained there was a problem with some esoteric math, where a floating decimal point apparently danced the wrong way during some calculations. "I didn't want you to be alarmed," Otellini said. Claflin was reassured and thanked Otellini for the call, and didn't think much about it. But later in the day, preparing to pack up, he thought, why did Otellini call me? This is odd, his showing me this courtesy, especially during Thanksgiving week. Claflin suspected there must be something more.

When the story broke, there was a flurry of negative publicity, and Intel's board was faced with a problem that would cost it $475 million to fix. Worse, there was the company's image. "The result was pandemonium as Intel's customer-support lines were flooded with anxious callers," wrote Tim Jackson in his book *Inside Intel.*

Intel's response was to say the problem was minimal, and if a customer could demonstrate they had a problem, the company would pay for the replacement. And Intel wanted all of their customers, their OEMs, the computer companies, to follow their lead. Basically, IBM was being asked to ship its Pentium-based

PCs, with the chip flaws, during the busiest selling season of the year.

After the Thanksgiving holiday, Claflin got another phone call from an IBM research manager. More bad news. The manager said that one of his mathematicians had been testing the Pentium chips, and he had concluded the problem was a lot worse than Intel was letting on. Claflin told him to bring the guy over. The IBM technical guy said the risk was highly variable, depending on what kind of computing the user did. He demonstrated scenarios where the flaw could disrupt "typical" computing tasks. Right there, Claflin decided to get the IBMer on the phone with his equivalent at Intel, and listen to their conversation. "Without knowing anything, I thought, these guys at Intel are in deep denial," Claflin recalls. "There's something wrong. And we had this terrible dilemma. We can unilaterally go to the market and say the flaw is fundamentally bigger than Intel is saying. And if we do that, we have an obligation for total recall, which can cost us huge amounts of money. Or, we can let Intel take the lead? What should we do?"

It was time to escalate the problem to the CEO. Claflin alerted Thoman, and a meeting with Gerstner was called late on a Friday in early December. Gerstner, York, Kalis, Thoman, Claflin, a lawyer, and Jim McGroddy, IBM's chief of research, began the debate.

Gerstner began, saying it was imperative that IBM make an immediate decision. What is the right thing to do? he asked. Someone first proposed a response that would allow IBM to assume slightly higher moral ground than Intel. Its customers wouldn't have to demonstrate a problem; Big Blue pledged to take back any PCs with the chip, no questions asked. But, bottom line, IBM should ship its Pentium-based machines. The risk of liability was less than the risk of a disastrous sales result.

Gerstner turned to Jim McGroddy and asked him to explain precisely what his researchers had discovered. One of McGroddy's great strengths is that he can take complex technical issues and translate them for a lay audience. He concluded by saying his faith was in IBM's analysis and not Intel's. The problem was real, worse than Intel CEO Andy Grove was willing to admit.

When McGroddy was through, Gerstner said, "Jim, would you bet your job on this?"

"I already have by bringing it to you," McGroddy replied evenly. "You must take decisive action and declare publicly that we're stopping product shipment, do a recall." Gerstner then continued around the table, and everyone else weighed in. Claflin also favored a total recall. When Gerstner asked him how much it would cost, he said as high as several hundred million dollars. The PC Company might not survive, but IBM would. It was an IBM decision, not a PC Company decision, he said. David Kalis warned, "We may not win the PR war on this one. We may do the right thing and not get credit."

IBM was not on the best of terms with Intel at the time because one of Andy Grove's objectives was to get into the mainframe business. IBM did not welcome more competition in this space. So there was some concern that Gerstner would be accused of deliberately trying to hurt Intel. Bruce Claflin admitted, "To be honest, a part of it was, what a great way to poke Intel in the eye and create strategic doubt as to whether they truly are enterprise-class suppliers. But it wasn't the whole thing."

In the course of a single meeting, IBM had decided it could get tough with the world's biggest chip maker. It would exhibit the kind of resolve it was never able to muster with Microsoft.

More important, in a single shining hour, Gerstner did the right thing. IBM announced to Intel, its customers, and the industry that it was recalling all its Pentium-based PCs. IBM's PR department sent out a press release saying it would not ship another box until the problem was fixed. When Big Blue's position was made public, Andy Grove heard it on the news. He was so angry that he had not been notified in advance, he called Rick Thoman, who was Claflin's boss at the time, to complain. The IBM action forced Intel to capitulate. Here was the world's largest chip maker that had developed the kind of customer arrogance that only a company like IBM could understand. But IBM's message was clear. Intel changed the way it did business. It set up an 800-number hot line, and anyone who already had bought a flawed machine and wanted a chip replaced, in IBM's or any other vendor's computer, would be immediately accommodated at no charge.

At War with the Evil Empire

I t is 8 A.M. on a bright Friday morning in Manhattan and in a small meeting room at the Sheraton Hotel, Doug Elix, the general manager of IBM Global Services for North America, is onstage with three other executives. It is an informal gathering of 150 IBMers, mostly salespeople, from several business units. The meeting is going well; there are several congratulatory cheers as large customer wins are announced.

During the Q&A, one cheerfully long-winded IBMer eventually ends up asking about the still-delicate issue of customer preferences for competitors' software offerings rather than IBM's. Elix, a genial, ever gracious Australian, squirms a bit, pauses, then smiles. He says, "First, here's what I think of the Evil Empire." He then makes an obscene gesture. Everyone in the room laughs uproariously; they know instantly that he is referring to Microsoft.

The CEO would have loved the sentiment, if not the gesture. During his own internal presentations, Gerstner sometimes projected an image of Bill Gates. "This man wakes up hating you," he said. Forget the fact it was a hackneyed motivational device. The IBMers who saw it knew that Gerstner felt the same way about Gates. Though IBM was still the largest software maker in the world, Microsoft was far more profitable, and closing the revenue gap every year. Gerstner's feeling that Gates woke up hating IBM showed, in fact, that Big Blue had taken a big step up. During IBM's great slide, the company hadn't even been on Microsoft's radar.

IBM's preoccupation with Microsoft had begun many years before Gerstner arrived. IBM had a long and controversial partnership with Microsoft, and the sages in the industry knew that Gates had become a billionaire only partly because he was a tenacious businessman with a vision. Beyond the hard work there was luck. The other reason was because of IBM's bluster and past blunders. It is often repeated that if IBM had been smarter, Bill Gates would be a nobody today.

Together, the companies were the prime architects of the PC revolution. Back in 1981, when IBM manufactured its first PCs, Bill Gates's fledgling company provided the MS-DOS innards that controlled the software. The Microsoft Disk Operating System was licensed to IBM as PC-DOS. At one point, during his company's tenuous early days, Gates offered to sell it outright to IBM for a pittance, but IBM declined.

In 1984, three years after IBM introduced its PC, Microsoft and IBM joined forces to develop OS/2. Neither company knew it at that time, but it was a partnership that was doomed in processing purgatory for nearly a decade. And in tech years, that is a very long time.

Various explanations of this torturous relationship have been recounted in books and magazine articles over the years. The short summary is this: IBM wanted the system to support a group of business applications called OfficeVision, hoping to challenge both Lotus and Novell on the desktop. But as was typical with IBM at the time, every division wanted OS/2 to do something different (or more), and Microsoft complained that the result would be slow and kludgy. Microsoft became continually frustrated in dealing with IBM's endless change orders and bureaucratic demands. Bill Gates could not countenance the fact that one version took three minutes to start up. Gates, sensing that this was a partnership with no future, simultaneously began developing Windows.

IBM, of course, quickly discovered Gates was hedging, and during Microsoft's dramatic growth spurt, accused the budding

Redmond billionaire of at least undermining, if not intentionally sabotaging, the joint effort. The best systems engineers were
taken off OS/2 to work on Windows. Gates probably was not far
off when he wrote in his book *The Road Ahead*, "OS/2 was not
just an operating system, it was part of a corporate crusade."
Over the course of the many glitches and delays in the product,
accusations flew from Redmond to Armonk and back. To this
day, Gates denies ever giving less than his company's complete
effort during the OS/2 partnership with IBM. In his view, he
simply decided to back two horses. In the end, it did not matter
where the truth lay.

What ultimately became the IBM-Microsoft "divorce" was
negotiated in a secret meeting in a trailer outside the Las Vegas
Convention Center during the 1989 COMDEX show. IBM
sources have admitted that in this single encounter, the des-
tinies of both companies dramatically shifted. From the IBM
side, Jim Cannavino, Lee Reiswig, and a group of other executives were present. Microsoft had Bill Gates and Steve Ballmer,
and others as well. An IBM vice president who attended the
meeting recalls, "Ballmer and Gates were just licking their
chops. Cannavino was doing the negotiating, but he didn't do
anything without first calling [Jack] Kuehler in Armonk."
Kuehler made all the technical calls for IBM and his judgment
was implicitly trusted by CEO John Akers.

The two companies discussed all the myraid platforms IBM was
involved in, and where OS/2 and Windows would be appropriate.
When the two companies arrived at a verbal agreement, they cobbled together a joint press release. The five-page statement was
headlined, "IBM and Microsoft Expand Partnership; Set Future
DOS and OS/2 Directions." Limned with technical specifications,
the release attempts to divide the operating system turf between the
two companies among desktop and larger systems. When you
sorted through the dense jargon, it was clear that Ballmer and Gates
had been crafty bargainers. IBM was basically conceding the small
machine market to Microsoft, while Gates would continue to support IBM's OS/2 on larger midrange computers.

Word about the deal immediately spread throughout the convention center's attendees. The following morning the two camps decided to hold an impromptu press conference in a small meeting room at the Las Vegas Convention Center. Hundreds of trade journalists and onlookers tried to pack themselves into a room that held only 140 people. The body language was telling. Gates and Cannavino stood up at the lectern, and Gates kept edging himself closer to Cannavino, while Cannavino tried to sort of drift away from his adversary/business partner. The first question went to Cannavino. A journalist wanted to know if IBM was now endorsing Windows. Cannavino hedged and stuttered. Already, he might have had some second thoughts. Perhaps he was letting Microsoft get a foothold in a market that should be controlled by IBM. After all, at the time OS/2 was far more reliable than the first couple of versions of Windows.

The IBM vice president continues, "What we did in essence, was let a Trojan horse into the IBM camp. I couldn't believe it. We could see it was a bad deal. We were keeping the current technology, which would be outdated right away. Microsoft was getting the future of technology."

Even back then, the computer world was moving toward a Windows environment. IBM, of course, knew this when they sealed the agreement in the trailer during that fateful meeting, but they thought they could somehow stem the flow with better technology. Cannavino and Kuehler wrongly predicted that their software architects could produce a better, more widely accepted operating system down the road than Microsoft's designers could. IBM's arrogance was worn on its sleeve.

IBM had never been known for its software, and now it was putting itself to the test. IBM didn't yet know it, but it was left to go it alone with OS/2, while Ballmer and Gates flew back to Redmond, ecstatic that Microsoft could continue to place its main effort on Windows. Gates continued to yes IBM, cheerfully "accommodating" every IBM computer unit's vision of OS/2. At that point, Gates knew he could compete with Big Blue.

By 1993, four years after the historic agreement, Gerstner had inherited the dregs of this infamous business deal. Some $2 billion of IBM's cash already had been invested in OS/2, and more was being appropriated every quarter for upgrades and marketing. When OS/2 was first released, it was an advance over Microsoft's DOS. But it was too little, too late. Microsoft already was well into its next iteration. When Windows 3.0 came out, it signaled the beginning of the end for OS/2. The IBM operating system was an Edsel, but senior officials at IBM still didn't believe it.

What IBM did not count on was Gates's brazen commandeering of Apple's groundbreaking graphical user interface, or GUI. The Macintosh operating system was light-years ahead of the C-prompt system, where users had to type in precisely correct numbers and characters to get a computer to do anything. The old DOS was impossibly difficult compared with the Mac. It was almost like typing hieroglyphics; without a manual or a tutor, it could take forever to locate a file. With the Mac, users easily navigated their desktops by pointing and clicking icons.

With Windows 3.0, Gates shrewdly copied enough of the Mac design (which Apple's Steve Jobs had first seen demonstrated at the Xerox Palo Alto Research Center) to placate its huge customer base of business users. Some features he did not adopt, either because Microsoft's developers weren't capable or because he was afraid of a lawsuit. Apple eventually did haul Microsoft into civil court, claiming huge damages for patent infringements. It couldn't prove its case, however.

By 1994, IBM had less than five or six percent of the operating system business, the Mac owned a slighty bigger piece, about ten percent, and Microsoft had the rest—eighty percent of the market. The industry was beginning to question whether IBM would stay the course. Microsoft's Windows 3.0 had won the hearts and minds of PC users and controlled the market much the way IBM had dominated mainframes in the 1960s.

Gerstner did not yet understand that IBM's OS/2 operating system was at a critical juncture. He hadn't yet looked deeply into the question, Should he concede the OS war to Microsoft, or continue to compete, which would take an investment of hundreds of millions more?

For months, the trade press speculated whether or not
Gerstner was going to discontinue OS/2. Gerstner did not yet
know what course of action he'd pursue because he hadn't thoroughly studied the issue. He had visited many large customers,
however, who had made substantial investments in the system.
How would it look when he traveled to Germany and told the
CEO of Deutsche Bank that IBM would no longer supply programming and services for OS/2? Or another large user, like
Royal Bank of Canada? For business systems, at least, Gerstner
could not afford to drop his largest accounts. He had to continue to support OS/2.

For smaller systems on the desktop, the issue was dicier.
Internally at IBM, the issue festered when the OS/2 development
team wrote Lou a memo that said the rampant speculation was
basically killing their business. The team had a point. If rumors
begin flying and you do nothing to stop them, they might as well be
true. They pleaded, in essence, If you don't publicly and forcefully
support OS/2, we've lost any chance of gaining any market share.

Gerstner expended a great deal of energy actively trying to resurrect it. When asked about OS/2 by reporters, he said IBM had
no intention of shelving it. He wrote an internal memo about
how critical OS/2 was to IBM's strategy. Bruce Claflin, a former
IBM senior executive, said, "You know he didn't want to send
that memo. He didn't want to get committed like that personally
to anything. He needed a chance to get the lay of the land, but he
got forced into it." The memo was partly a result of Gates calling
on Gerstner in Armonk. Though it was merely a twenty-minute
courtesy stop shortly after Gerstner had been appointed—no
business deals were discussed—the meeting was highly publicized. Many at IBM felt that the memo showed that Gerstner
refused to be backed into a corner by Microsoft. The meeting
with Gates may have showed weakness; perhaps Gerstner was
losing faith in OS/2, but he wouldn't want that to be known.

Privately, Gerstner thought OS/2 was a lost cause, at least
within the PC Company. Jerry York had thoroughly reviewed the
financials. He complained that OS/2 was a perennial black hole,

and there was no discernible end in sight. A manager in corporate headquarters recalls that just the mention of OS/2 made York absolutely livid. According to one IBM vice president, York said, "It wasn't sustainable, it's a loser, the fucking thing sucks. Those were almost his exact words. He could not believe we would continue to pump, six, seven, eight hundred million dollars a year into it. And, of course, he was right."

Gerstner decided that IBM would make one last effort to resurrect OS/2. He would attempt to build OS/2 into a sub-brand in the home market. This played to the CEO's strengths, and it was arguable that no other senior executive at IBM better understood the consumer psyche. When IBM's PC marketing team was assembled, Gerstner did not just keep a close eye on the project. His reputation for wanting to take total control oozed from the OS/2 consumer meetings. The code name for the consumer product was "Warp" because its designers hoped it would run faster and more efficiently than Windows. Gerstner liked the code name so much, he thought it should be on the product packaging. Why not just use the name "Warp"? When someone questioned whether the Star Trek TV production company likely owned the copyright, Gerstner picked up the phone and asked IBM's legal team to get it approved. As it turned out, "Warp" was available. The CEO personally reviewed all the packaging and the advertising. Ogilvy tried its best to make Warp appear edgy and cool, even though its savvier executives strongly suspected that the dog was not going to eat the dog food. IBM was backing a loser, one senior executive at Ogilvy and Mather said. But he gave Gerstner high marks for trying. Ogilvy's Robert Chandler called OS/2 a "suicide mission" that had "no chance to overtake Microsoft's immense PC OS lead, no matter how good Warp might be nor how much was put behind it."

Warp had one characteristic that, although not fatal, did not particularly endear it to users. Gates was absolutely right. It took a long time to load when you booted the system, mainly because it had an inexhaustible number of features. Perhaps because of his enthusiasm for the sub-brand campaign, Gerstner did not realize that Warp probably would become the most misnomered product in IBM's history. Still, he was willing to commit a truck-load of cash to a product because he thought he could still make a dent in Microsoft's domain.

There remained staunch opposition to OS/2 among some IBM executives, and they tried to discourage Gerstner. Bruce Claflin's research suggested that the PC Company would be bet-ter served if it just gave up on OS/2 and installed Windows on its PCs. "One of the things they did to try and prop up OS/2 was to tell the PC business, you must load OS/2 on every product you ship, whether the customer wanted it or not," Claflin said. "We had ample data that said customers were going to rip it [out]." He felt strongly IBM's strategy was a folly.

Also, for several months in 1994, Microsoft's public relations juggernaut had been rattling the trade press about its upcoming Windows 95. It promised to finally provide PC users with a much better GUI than the 3.0, even closer to the Mac's gold standard in ease of use. When Claflin showed his research to his boss, Rick Thoman, Thoman decided Gerstner should see it. The first ver-sion of OS/2 had been pummeled by Windows 3.0. Was there any reason to believe that IBM's Warp upgrade would gain any ground on Microsoft?

Jerry York had long since weighed in on this subject, more than once, in fact. Lee Reiswig headed the OS/2 group, and York did not have a great deal of confidence in Reiswig's projections. It was nothing personal with Reiswig. Reiswig had been spend-ing money, and next to nothing in revenues was coming in. He had been claiming for years that victory was at hand with OS/2. He was beginning to sound like General William Westmoreland in the war in Vietnam; few believed his forecasts anymore. In one of his more hopeful poses, he referred to himself as a "Blue Ninja." If anything, he was just another blue suit, hoping the winds of the market would shift in his favor.

York, by then exasperated, said, "The guys were just absolutely convinced they could increase their four percent share. [It was often reported to be two or three percent higher, but this was likely because IBM tried to build share by giving away tens of thousands of diskettes bound in computer magazines.] I racked my brain for months and couldn't think of any other case in any industry where someone had started from such a small market share and made major inroads against a well-entrenched competitor like Microsoft." Nobody else at IBM was able to come up with an example either.

Still, there was an unwillingness to face reality. But IBM forged ahead anyway. In the end, OS/2 either wasn't marketed right, or it didn't have mindshare, or the product just didn't have enough appeal. It's a surprise to some that York's bulldog opinion—and usually astute analysis—was not more carefully considered by Gerstner. "Jerry knew that the OS/2 strategy was fundamentally flawed," Bruce Claflin says. "Yes, he did bring that to Lou's attention. But he certainly didn't show his tigerlike instincts upward the same way he did downward."

Reiswig's group, aware its very existence depended on strong companywide support, especially from the PC Company, moaned that the customer had the right to make the choice *after* the point of sale. His latest scheme was, why not ship OS/2 and Windows together? He was willing to submit to a taste test in the marketplace, and this alone could best determine customer preference. IBM's naysayers correctly predicted that customers would immediately delete OS/2 and use Gates's Windows.

The whole experiment was flawed to begin with. This "dual-boot" solution imposed a unique software configuration that added cost and complexity to IBM's design. More work was necessary in device drivers, part compatibility, and in other areas, not to mention the additional testing required on every piece of software that could possibly run on either system.

It was a developer's nightmare. Shipping the PCs with two systems would greatly reduce the number of usable applications because so much disk drive space was already in use. The product design of IBM's PCs, as a whole, would suffer. IBM had been struggling for more than a year to produce PCs quickly and more cheaply. Claflin tried to get Thoman and Gerstner to focus on the time and cost constraints the two systems would pose, problems that Compaq, Hewlett-Packard, Packard Bell, and Dell did not have. If this was the IBM's idea of simplicity, then it was hopelessly regressing. It was the antithesis of Gerstner's mandate, and nobody—least of all Gerstner himself—did anything to stop it.

Nobody has come up with a reasonable explanation why Gerstner could not be convinced to give up on Warp. In a final, impassioned plea, Claflin explained to him that the dual-boot system would increase Microsoft's revenue by thirty-five percent. Before any discussion of the dual-boot, Microsoft was earning about sixty-five percent market share in new licensing fees, and now it was poised to gain the remainder. By doing nothing except watching IBM execute its plan, Microsoft was, in effect, double dipping.

When IBM insisted on selling its computers with OS/2, customers were cleansing their screens of OS/2 and installing Windows in its place. IBM's business partners—resellers and the channel—were doing it, too. Everyone seemed to want the standard Microsoft image. Microsoft was making hundreds of millions of dollars more than if IBM had not shipped its PCs with OS/2 on them in the first place. Had it simply caved in early, IBM could have received licensing fees from Microsoft by simply shipping PCs with Gates's operating system.

All this for effectively zero growth in user acceptance, Claflin argued. And, if you took the argument a step further, the dual-boot idea actually alienated more people from IBM. Who wanted to buy a computer having to fuss with such a mess on the screen, and then be forced to delete one system?

Still, Gerstner capitulated to the forces in Reiswig's group who insisted every one of IBM PCs would have both Microsoft's and IBM's operating systems.

"Well, it was a disaster," recalled Claflin, who in retrospect feels this was one of the CEO's biggest errors. "We told [Gerstner] it'd be a disaster, but he didn't care. There was ample information that said, Lou, you are about to step into a huge morass. And he just wouldn't listen to us. And he completely disregarded it in the most forceful way you can imagine."

There was a point when IBM executives sensed the risk of repercussion was too great to continue banging their fists on the conference table. Senior executives did not want to be labeled malcontents when it came to company strategy. Gerstner demanded their fundamental buy-in to every major decision. Executives were afraid he would dredge up one of his normally accurate assessments about old-line IBMers: You're parochial about your piece of the business. You're not helping the whole company.

Resellers and consumers deleted OS/2 in favor of Windows 3.0 in droves. Eventually, IBM stopped shipping the dual-boot systems.

Inside IBM, OS/2 dragged on much longer. A good deal of the workforce was perplexed by the company's internal strategy. Under Gerstner, the in-house IT staff had a clear mandate to ensure that IBMers "eat their own cooking." So OS/2 was the system of choice because of corporate mandate, even though it tasted like dreck to many. Some IBMers half joked that perhaps IBM's plan of "selling the product to ourselves" might be the only way to pick up a point or two of market share. Many technical managers and their staffs at the Watson Research Center junked OS/2 for Windows on their PCs. They weren't even sneaky about it. They didn't care what company policy was.

It wasn't until three years later, midway through 1997, that tech support in IBM's own PC Company would begin installing Windows 95 on employee desktops. Most IBMers did not notice any difference; perhaps there were fewer freezes and crashes. There was one improvement, however. Windows had a big start-up advantage in speed. You didn't have to go out for your morning cup of coffee while waiting for the OS/2 Warp logo to appear on your screen.

Publicly, IBM continued its support of OS/2, though it finally ended the millions of dollars in marketing expenses. The effort was now halfhearted. The disks were discounted heavily, in the hope for a sudden jump in market share. IBM claimed millions of copies were "distributed," an industry code word meaning that the company was willing to all but give them away. Accommodating headlines appeared. "IBM Refuses to 'Roll Over and Die' in OS/2 Battle," *Computerworld* reported. "OS/2 Hangs Tough," read another.

After this final blitz of optimism, the grim truth finally reached the powers in Armonk. Warp actually was a tired old dog that just wanted to roll over and die. Late versions had glitches, or at least gremlins. Peter Lewis, a *New York Times* technology columnist, tried to install an updated version of OS/2 on his Pentium-based computer and was stymied. He even called an IBM technical wizard, who spent more than an hour trying to make it work. "Let's put it this way," the IBM representative finally conceded to Lewis. "I'm going to put Windows 95 on the machines in my house." It did not help IBM when it was discovered that the new and improved version of OS/2 often did not work on its own Aptivas or PowerPCs. Shipping delays were inevitable until the problems were fixed.

There were delays on Windows 95 as well, and critics took aim at Gates when they suggested that perhaps Microsoft should rename its product "Windows 96." Still, despite Microsoft missing its initial ship deadline, IBM was never able to secure any substantial foothold in the desktop operating system game. If Microsoft stumbled, it could count on IBM to trip and collapse to the pavement.

Gerstner himself finally announced Warp's defeat as a consumer product, albeit reluctantly. When financial analysts asked him about it at a quarterly meeting in July 1995, he admitted that obsessing about operating systems was "fighting the last war." He said it was "too late to go after the desktop. We have to go on to the next thing." Calling the consumer and desktop markets "secondary" was the CEO's way of waving the white flag.

There is still a small OS/2 team working in Austin, upgrading the product. In an internal meeting as recently as 1998, Gerstner insisted that he saw corporate customers who relied on IBM to service and support OS/2.

Today, IBM is still stymied by Microsoft's desktop dominance.

Revenge for losing the operating system wars will not likely add to its revenues, but Gerstner is a CEO with a long memory. IBM's policy is to avoid public confrontation with any company whenever possible. Yet it did not hesitate to join other technology firms when the Justice Department gathered witnesses in its antitrust assault on Microsoft. In fact, the *Wall Street Journal* asserted that Big Blue was leading the government charge. When John Soyring, the IBM executive who headed network computing software, testified, he claimed that Microsoft did not provide standard development tools for programmers to adapt software for OS/2. The implication was that Gates's tactics with independent software vendors or programmers bordered on extortion and weren't always subtle. We like what you're doing for Microsoft, Gates seemed to be saying. But if you write applications for a competing system, you do so at your own risk. In other words, the veiled threat was, develop applications for competitors and your work with Microsoft might suddenly dry up.

Soyring complained that an OS/2 programmer would have to "re-create much of the application from scratch." If that was the case, who would bother? Thus, he concluded, OS/2 was at a distinct competitive disadvantage with Windows. Microsoft's response to his testimony was typically obtuse. "IBM made decisions with its OS/2 operating system that were not well received by consumers and did not make it easy for developers to make great applications for their platforms." This was true, but it did not answer the charge. (More will likely emerge on this. In May and June of 1999, Garry Norris, director of software strategy and strategic relations for IBM's PC Company, testified as a government witness for the Justice Department's suit against Microsoft. Some of his accusations were startling. Norris said that Microsoft executives charged higher prices for IBM's Windows licenses because it shipped its computers with Lotus's software rather than Microsoft's. In 1996, IBM was paying $47 per copy of Windows, higher than Microsoft charged Compaq. "I was told that as long as you compete against

Microsoft," Norris testified, "you will suffer in terms of pricing and support." The message was clear. Norris said that unless IBM agreed to "reduce, drop or eliminate" shipments of OS/2, Microsoft would continue to penalize Big Blue in pricing.)

Yes, there never was a killer application developed for OS/2 that would make customers demand they install the operating system. But then, what were the odds a killer app could have been written?

There have been vigorous debates as to whether the ultimate version of OS/2 Warp was superior to Windows 95. Though the marketplace has voted overwhelmingly for Windows, there are still staunch advocates of the IBM effort. Many are in-house. A few still cling to the belief that OS/2, now with a scant six percent of the desktop market, is a good product. They also realize that the better product doesn't always win the market. They are like VCR users who still yammer about how Sony's Betamax format dwarfed VHS in picture quality. (Betamax failed largely because the cassettes did not have the capacity to record feature-length films.) An ex-IBMer commenting in *Sm@rt Reseller*, a trade magazine, wrote, "OS/2 Warp was a pretty great product—honest. But it was just too darn difficult for the average person to grasp." A reader rationalized it as well, writing, "Having been an OS/2 user and fan, I'd say IBM never put an honest effort into promoting OS/2 to the user community—and perhaps more importantly the developer community. The PC division did a great job sabotaging OS/2 installations. It more or less slapped the OS on hard drives without attempting to optimize it for the hardware." This was an astute comment. Computer experts largely agreed.

Bob Balaban, a former programmer for Lotus Development Corporation, made a cogent observation about the two operating systems. "The developers hated OS/2," he said. "It was very hard to do development on OS/2, a pain in the butt. The tools aren't that good. It's just cumbersome, complicated, very slow, painfully slow. Hard to start, hard to use, it lacked half the features of Microsoft's debugging tools. Microsoft really goes out of its way to make things easy for the developer, maybe at times at the expense of the end user. I'm not saying that's the way it should be, but it is. The real market, to a large extent, is the developer community. And IBM never really understood that, as far as I could tell."

Put simply, even if you develop a first-rate operating system, if programmers do not want to write applications for it, it is headed for oblivion.

Gerstner had lost his war with Microsoft, spending more than $1 billion on OS/2, with little return. And he continued to hedge his bet, investing large sums in other operating systems that also had been in development before he took over. A few years earlier, IBM had begun a massive companywide software initiative that would finally, once and forever, make IBM's computing innards compatible throughout its diverse technology universe. The commitment was at least $500 million a year in development costs, and some sources say it was a lot higher. It was already a typical IBM development project, running behind schedule. This wasn't a shock to anyone, given that in any IBM-wide endeavor, every honcho had his opinion, every department had to "study" the plan. And naturally, every general manager and product chief wondered what was in it for him.

A single operating system appealed to Gerstner's instincts as an integrator. It also had fiscal appeal. A universal operating system might save billions of dollars in the future. The nature of the software-operating system beast is easy to understand: Every time you upgrade a line of code for a given application, an equal amount of labor must be expended for it to run properly on another system. Necessary duplication of effort ran IBM about $1 billion a year. He had mentioned several times that the old IBM had excellent ideas, well-thought-out strategies. Its problem was in the execution.

IBM's biggest advocate for a universal operating system was Jim Cannavino. Simplifying IBM's many platforms had been a dream of senior IBM executives over the years, and Cannavino was the one who was carrying this dream into the 1990s. Once Gerstner had appointed him to head corporate strategy, he could officially be called IBM's in-house dreamer. He was promoted to the job on the same day that Rick Thoman was brought into IBM. And if his dreams of building IBM's desktop hardware business had dissipated when the Apple deal went south, they were still alive in software.

But Gerstner had done enough homework to remain skeptical. He was not going to commit any more money to a Cannavino project on his say alone. To sell his idea, Cannavino needed a top-level line manager as a sponsor. So he enlisted the support of John M. Thompson, a senior vice president and group executive who began his IBM career as a systems engineer in 1966. He worked his way through the ranks to become general manager of IBM Canada, and he was known as a traditionally bred Big Blue executive. Well-mannered, likable, a little paunchy-looking in his ill-fitting suits, he meticulously rehearsed his presentations and was always well prepared for meetings. An avid outdoorsman, he spent his free time fly-fishing in Argentina or sailing his thirty-two-foot boat on a Canadian lake. He maintained homes in Toronto and Connecticut.

Thompson, however, did not pass muster with Jerry York. York felt Thompson was an insular type, a leftover from the Akers regime who needed months to make crucial decisions that might immediately affect IBM's business. "That guy never made a tough decision in his business career without having somebody hold a gun to his head," recalled one former senior IBM official.

Thompson was one of the few executives Gerstner and York disagreed over. Gerstner apparently felt that Thompson was a more talented businessman than did York. It's difficult to imagine how this was so, given the immense abilities the top two IBM executives had in judging talent. Sources speculate that Thompson was one of the few people throughout the organization who could adequately explain software to the chairman. Also, software was a high-margin business. Thompson's group accounted for a large piece of IBM's gross profits. It could cover for a lot of flawed strategies and executive mistakes. Thompson also protected other executives in his group, like Steve Mills, the general manager of the software solutions division, who didn't particularly welcome anyone meddling with his business. Mills might have been able to get by Thompson, or even Gerstner, but not York. When the software was examined closely, for example, one could see that the DB/2 was a huge winner in the mainframe business. On the desktop, however, it was a constant money drain, a total loser. York, of course, characterized Mills as a parochial IBM executive. Mills, on his part, did not take the CFO's scrutiny very well. York would remind him that not every part of his business was profitable—why not concentrate on fixing what's broken?—but Mills paid no heed. Overall, he delivered black ink, and that was what he saw as important. An outside consultant concurred with York. He said, "Steve Mills never accepted our diagnostic report and, in fact, shredded it right after we presented it! He collected all copies and immediately trashed them. What was strange was that his organization was actually performing very well in comparison to other software businesses."

So it came down, in part, to Canadian luck. Those IBM managers who were unimpressed with Thompson believed he had always had a charmed career at the company, and software was the capstone.

Thompson had bought into Cannavino's software dream under Akers's regime, and a number of other senior IBM executives continued to endorse it as well. So Gerstner committed funding for another year. The operating system was code-named "Workplace," and the development team was located in Austin. A fresh team of developers—from mainframes to small systems—descended in droves as the effort was stepped up. Old-line IBM managers were already shaking their heads in disbelief. This was another rerun of an IBM B-movie, throwing fresh money on yet another doomed idea. In the past, the company had tried similar systems integration of certain platforms, all of which had less-ambitious goals than this one. They had failed, not so much because IBM wasn't qualified technically as because of internal bureaucracy, infighting, and inertia.

Workplace was the "Grand Canal, the operating system that would work everywhere and do it all," said one IBM manager from the Server Group. This latest scheme would combine MVS, VM, AIX, and AS/400. Workplace would also work on the desktop. It could revolutionize the PowerPC. The main thrust was to develop a microkernel, the heart of the operating system that could become cross-platform compatible. Cynics in Armonk called Cannavino's universal operating system a "moon shot."

"Many of us knew it would never work because customers had bought these different products and had different requirements," said the Server Group manager. After IBM had blown more than $1 billion on Workplace, the project was shelved. The need for such an operating system became less urgent after Sun Microsystems released Java. It became clear that the Internet would function as a natural clearinghouse for disparate platforms.

Cannavino and his project had trouble coexisting in the new Gerstner-York environment. Gerstner had made it plain that IBM's investments had to have a clear, sharply delineated plan. Risk had to be tightly managed, and potential payback had to be more short-term. There had to be a high probability of profitability. "He [Cannavino] would give birth to these huge complicated projects that didn't have a snowball's chance in hell of ever getting done," a former IBM finance official said.

The Workplace fiasco finally convinced Gerstner that Cannavino had to go. IBM did not want to fund any more moon shots.

When Jim Cannavino's patchy career drew to a conclusion, few IBM executives and managers were surprised. He was only fifty years old, but he'd put in thirty-two years at Big Blue and succeeded and failed in several different arenas. He achieved the highest-ranking position at IBM for anyone without a college degree. Few had his breadth of experience.

He'd been rewarded for his loyalty and technical brilliance by Gerstner when he was promoted to IBM's chief strategist. But some company executives had viewed the bump upstairs with skepticism. One source in Armonk put it this way: "Gerstner figured out Cannavino pretty early. He wanted to take him out of the PC Company. He wanted to sort of assess, does this guy really have any technology moxie or not? He talks a good game. He's always talking technology, let's do this, let's do that. He's a very engaging personality. I'll bring him in as head of strategy and see if there's anything beneath all the talk."

Cannavino had to sense that Gerstner had lost confidence in him. He joked about his new title, saying, "Am I the V guy?" a not-too-subtle reference to the criticism Gerstner had taken for his lack of vision. It was, in the end, a hollow promotion. Cannavino was no longer a line manager with billions in revenue under his command, but a staffer with no direct power over any of the business. (Cannavino's predecessor as chief strategist, Bernard Puckett, also had been promoted by Gerstner. It was Gerstner's method of easing a longtime senior executive out the door. Puckett was a nice guy who had clung to the old Watson principles; he didn't adopt the new regime's management style and thus couldn't survive.)

In March 1995, Cannavino decided to take early retirement, spend more time horseback riding at his rural home in upstate New York, and live off his pension until he found a company he could run. (He had a short-lived and turbulent stint as the chief operating officer of Ross Perot's company, Electronic Data Systems, and eventually became CEO of a small Internet security company in Washington state called CyberSafe.)

When Cannavino's resignation was announced, Gerstner sent a memo to the workforce with the standard platitudes about Cannavino's career. But the CEO reportedly was "complimentary but cool" when assessing his contributions to Big Blue. Gerstner had no immediate candidate for the job of chief strategist, and it wasn't at all certain that anyone inside the company would want it. The position was looking like Gerstner's holding tank for expulsion.

For his part in approving Workplace, John M. Thompson, in one of IBM's more intriguing examples of FUMU, was rewarded

with a bigger playpen. As senior vice president and group executive in charge of software, he would eventually control $12.6 bil-
lion worth of IBM's revenues. In 1997 he received stock options
that made him the highest-paid executive in the company after
Gerstner.

Meanwhile, by 1994, for the first time in Gerstner's reign, sales
in IBM's mainframe business were on the upswing again. The
CEO took particular pleasure in tweaking his critics about this
last item. In one midsummer meeting at the New York Hilton,
he told a ballroom filled with CIOs, the corporate buyers of big
systems, "IBM and you all deserve a shot in the head for allowing this mythology that mainframes are dead." When he finished his speech, he was given a T-shirt that had a dinosaur and
the words "Mainframe Rex" on it. "Dinosaurs are back,"
Gerstner said.

There was another critical shift in Gerstner's business. Selling
components to competitors and licensing technology had been a
minuscule revenue source for IBM. Actively producing chips for
companies like Apple, Canon, Unisys, and Hitachi, it discovered
it could make money OEMing, becoming the original equipment manufacturer, for companies that wanted to buy only IBM
components and not necessarily its finished products. Licensing
revenues in 1994 doubled over the previous year.

By the end of 1994, Gerstner had to be feeling secure about
the company's progress. Big Blue was now squarely in the black
with $10 billion in cash on hand. IBM's total revenues had
increased by six percent, the first time annual revenue had grown
since 1990. The stock was trading in the low- to mid-$70s,
almost double the price of IBM when Gerstner took over. His
only disappointment was the PC Company.

11

Gerstner Grabs for Groupware

O n Thursday, September 15, 1994, Mike Szeto is feeling confident as he boards the shuttle at LaGuardia Airport, bound for Boston. A managing director at J.P. Morgan and Company, he is scheduled to meet with Ed Gillis, the CFO of Lotus, the software company with offices in a large, imposing red-brick building on the north bank of the Charles River in Cambridge. He is thinking about how he will pitch a merger. Szeto has a presentation entitled "M&A Discussion—Lotus Development Corporation."

The timing is probably right. Lotus's stock is depressed. It had reached $85 at one point, but it had taken a precipitous slide to $32 and is currently trading in the low $40s. The company is vulnerable. Lotus is under considerable price pressure from Novell and Microsoft. The industry's last hot product—suites, or groups of office applications—is losing steam, and groupware is the newest rage. Lotus's groupware entry, known as "Notes," has a lot of potential, but in its current version it is little more than a souped-up e-mail program. Two points of Szeto's pitch are titled "Lotus Remains a Market Leader, but Its Position Is Eroding" and "Lotus Appears Exposed in This Environment." The company is not in real financial trouble, but its future is certainly hazy.

Szeto's strategy is to persuade Gillis of the benefits of a merger with IBM. To him, the logic is irresistible. The two companies already are compatible business partners. Lotus had developed software for IBM's OS/2, including the OfficeVision suite. Lotus can benefit from Big Blue's marketing heft and deep pockets to promote Notes. Microsoft is planning to launch a competitive product, Exchange, but it won't be ready for at least a year. Such an alliance would give Lotus Notes a substantial head start.

This a deal that not only could bring in many millions in M&A fees for J.P. Morgan, but would create a substantial jolt in the technology industry and rattle the cages of Microsoft. Bill Gates would take notice.

Szeto has one significant advantage. He is an ex-IBMer, having put in more than eighteen years with the company, including a long stint as a strategy specialist. He recently left Big Blue to pursue a career on Wall Street. A slight, energetic man, he is not your typical IBM executive. He was recruited in 1976 for IBM Canada from a consulting firm, and though he was shifted through the usual course of assignments, he wasn't a spit-shined, wing-tipped sales caricature who sucked up to his general manager. He landed a coveted executive assistant assignment for a top executive. Szeto knew that EAs were glorified secretaries, keeping calendars, writing papers for their boss, functioning as a gofer. But you had to accept it; you needed your ticket punched to move up at IBM. He even resisted line jobs until a mentor convinced him it was the only way to get promoted. Finally, he found his way onto the corporate strategy team in Armonk.

Szeto was assigned to the M&A unit at IBM. It did not have an enviable history, as the record clearly showed. IBM's alliances with other firms stifled almost every joint venture. Prodigy, the joint online venture with Sears, ended with huge losses. And Taligent and Kaleida, IBM's efforts to develop an operating system and multimedia software with Apple, had been disasters. But given the former management at IBM, it wasn't Szeto's fault. Most of the time, nobody listened to his advice, anyway. Certainly not Ned Lautenbach, the IBM group vice president who was his boss for a decade, and the executive whom he blamed for his stalled career. To Szeto, Lautenbach was the ultimate empty suit-with-a-smile whose focus was always inward. He had become a classic FUMU. If you checked his record, Szeto said, Lautenbach managed to leave every business division he inherited in worse shape than he found it. And he was rewarded with promotions.

Szeto did not immediately hit it off with Jerry York. But York wisely deduced that Szeto wasn't promoting anyone's agenda. Szeto was merely the messenger for many of IBM's ridiculous blunders, not the architect. Szeto became an adept translator of corporate IBMspeak, which meant that he contributed invaluable insights to the CFO's thinking: Jerry, here's what they're saying. Here's what they think they mean. This is the marketplace reality. York tested him by assigning him the heavy lifting of the sale of IBM's defense business. He discovered Szeto was smart and efficient, and had the same low tolerance for incompetent colleagues. He knew who the pretenders were.

When Szeto arrives at Lotus's offices, he hopes that Jim Manzi, the CEO, also will be available. But Manzi is too busy to attend, or doesn't think the meeting is important enough to warrant his presence. He pokes his head into Gillis's office only once to check their progress. Szeto takes him through his pitch, reminding Gillis that in the past year Microsoft's software revenues are up twenty-eight percent while Lotus's are off by fifteen percent. He emphasizes that Lotus can respond in one of two ways, an "incremental approach" or the "bold stroke."

The latter means finding the right business partner. Szeto points out how IBM offers a number of opportunities to strengthen its competitive position, including an installed base to build software for its client-server franchise. Also, by eliminating redundancies, Lotus can save $350 million a year in SG&A and R&D. With nearly 50 million shares of Lotus outstanding, the company's market capitalization is just under $2.1 billion. Szeto is convinced he could get $3 billion to $3.5 billion for Lotus shareholders.

But after a couple of hours, Szeto senses that Gillis and Manzi aren't interested in a merger, at least with IBM. It is a pro forma meeting, a waste of time. They can't be this naïve, Szeto wondered. They are exposed to a hostile bid. Revenues are off due to the discounting of Lotus Notes. Manzi is trying to build market share, and Wall Street is looking askance at his business strategy.

Reflecting on that day, Szeto recalled, "They didn't think it was much of a proposal. It was the ego, a hubris thing. Manzi thought he was the equivalent of Gates and others. He didn't think he was vulnerable."

Szeto flew home disappointed, but he didn't let the idea go. He was still hoping to seed the rain clouds for J.P. Morgan, if not in Cambridge, then perhaps in Armonk. He scheduled a meeting for later in the year with Jerry York, partly to discuss a Lotus merger but also to present an overall M&A strategy on several fronts for IBM. He brought with him Roberto Mendoza, J.P. Morgan's vice chairman.

"Now, I've never known Jerry York to sit down for a three-hour meeting on any subject, but he stayed for our whole presentation," Szeto said. York was impressed enough to invite an entire team from J.P. Morgan back to Armonk to meet with several IBM senior executives, including Dennie Welsh and Steve Mills, to take a more detailed look at Szeto's plan. An all-day meeting was scheduled for January 9, 1995. Szeto's team had done extensive research. "When we made this presentation, it was like giving IBM free customer feedback," said Szeto. He also brought with him Peter Miller, the chief technology officer at Morgan, and another half dozen high-level vice presidents.

Szeto got to the crux. He gave IBM the bad news first. Out came the chart that said, "IBM's Participation Within the Client-Server and Networking Segments Is Mixed." The smart money was betting that two platforms, Unix and Windows NT, were going to capture the real growth opportunities in this market. In the next four years, J.P. Morgan predicted IBM would lose market share or stay even at best in its mainframe and midrange lines. Szeto's team had done thorough spadework in twenty mar-

ket segments, including LAN, server, database, and network services. Its conclusion was that IBM was strong in about half the
segments, weak or very weak in the other half.

IBM should make several acquisitions to position itself in areas
where it was weak, was the recommendation. In short, Morgan's
team suggested that Big Blue buy four companies: Sybase, Sun,
Lotus, and LDDS/Cable and Wireless. Sybase could give them an
advantage in the client-server database and application development space. Sun would advance IBM's market share in the workstation and server business. Lotus made all kinds of sense for the reasons Szeto had already made clear to the software firm. And LDDS
would help IBM provide a strong entry in the data networking
infrastructure field, a growth opportunity as the Internet expanded.
This last company was something of a throw-in because IBM had
been a disinterested player in the telephony side of technology. Its
Advantis unit was a distant fifth in global network outsourcing,
behind AT&T, British Telecom, MCI, and Sprint.

As Szeto worked his way through his presentation, one particular page in Szeto's bound booklet caught York's attention. It
was titled "A New Paradigm . . . the 'Glass House' of the Future."
In it the M&A people explained how the various technology
markets would expand, and where they saw business returning
to IBM's core strengths. York ripped it out and photocopied it.
Though the CFO was known as the cost cutter, he immediately
grasped the implications of growth through M&A. Perhaps IBM
could improve its abysmal track record, boost its market share
by buying other firms. If nothing else, giving his managers the
photocopied page would show them an outsider's point of
view—free advice, as his former colleague put it.

At the end of two hours, the Morgan team summed up. It had
evaluated the target companies and estimated that IBM could
acquire Sybase for $5 billion, Sun for $4.5 billion, and Lotus for
$4 billion. The more Szeto looked at Lotus, the more he thought
it was a good fit. Because he already knew there was resistance
from Manzi and Gillis, he had upped the purchase price by close
to $1 billion from his earlier estimate.

IBM could put together a $13.5 billion package that, with only a modest boost in the price/earnings ratio of IBM, could be worth $22.2 billion in a very short time. The downside was minimal, break-even at worst. Even without a bump in the multiple, the merger could save as much as forty percent in expenses in many areas. (Today, in hindsight, a Sun acquisition might have been something to contemplate. Thanks to the rapid growth of Java, IBM easily would have tripled its investment in just a few years, making at least $10 billion.)

IBM was still a cautious company in Mike Szeto's view, even though Gerstner and York were now running it. So many deals went sour that he had begun to agree with the critics. And now it was gun-shy. Szeto had great respect for York's and Gerstner's abilities, but he felt they would have only minimal effect as change agents for the long run. IBM's immutably conservative bent was one reason he had left. So he was not exactly crushed when the J.P. Morgan briefing went nowhere.

If nothing else, however, Szeto gave IBM the idea that if it wanted to give itself any chance at all in network-based software, even a glimmer of a competitive edge, it would have to buy another firm. And a large one at that.

John M. Thompson, now Gerstner's software guru, was asked to head a team to take a close look at Lotus. He was one of only a few IBM executives who had a reasonably cordial relationship with Jim Manzi. In March, he asked Manzi to dinner in Rye, New York, about twenty minutes from IBM headquarters. Manzi did not yet know it, but that meeting was the beginning of the end of his running Lotus. When Thompson broached the subject of IBM becoming a partner in Lotus, Manzi welcomed the idea of selling up to fifteen percent of the company's stock. He needed the cash to promote Notes. When the IBM senior vice president danced around the prospect of buying more, Manzi eyed him suspiciously. Thompson pressed further, wondering about buying all of Lotus. "What the fuck does that mean? Why don't you just buy dinner instead?" Manzi reportedly replied.

Then he forgot about it, or at least tried.

. . .

Lotus Development Corporation is probably the East Coast software firm closest in spirit to a Silicon Valley company, or at least it was during the 1980s. It was founded by Mitch Kapor, a guy who in earlier lives had been a disk jockey and taught transcendental meditation. He preferred Hawaiian shirts over suits. He had become fascinated by computers, dabbled in programming, and fashioned himself a software "designer." Kapor had seen the power of the first successful spreadsheet program, VisiCalc, which drove PC sales in the beginning of the computer revolution. In a bold move to improve it, he developed an application that added other elements, including a database manager. That way financial types could use it to crunch numbers and add graphs, as well as do traditional forecasting.

Lotus 1-2-3 was introduced at a lavish press conference in October 1982 at the World Trade Center's Windows on the World restaurant high above the New York harbor. The first "integrated" program, 1-2-3 was a killer app before that term was in vogue. By 1984, that single piece of software had propelled Lotus to $157 million in sales and a staff of seven hundred. Symphony, which included word processing, followed it, and so did Jazz, which ran on the Mac.

Two years later, Kapor decided that he wasn't much interested in being the CEO of a large company, so he turned to Jim Manzi, then only thirty-four, who was Lotus's president. Manzi was not at all like Kapor; he knew very little about the details of software technology. He was a businessman first, a guy with solid experience, someone who knew marketing. Manzi grew up in Yonkers, New York, and became a newspaperman, putting in three years at the *Portchester Daily Item* in New York's Westchester County. Then he abruptly changed course and decided to work for McKinsey and Company. Without a graduate degree in business, he had to suffer through more than the usual amount of scrutiny. Ultimately, he convinced the McKinsey partners he would make a decent consultant. He worked in the firm's small

Los Angeles office, then he was transferred back to New York. But he quickly became impatient doing studies for clients such as large oil companies, and he resigned after four years.

At Lotus, Manzi was known as an intelligent, hard-driving executive who was dedicated—perhaps quixotically—to positioning the company to compete with Microsoft. His strong suit was in analyzing the markets and mapping out big-picture strategies. His downside was an uneven record as a manager. On one hand, he went through several development heads in just a few years. But on the other, he did manage to keep a highly respected chief technology officer, John Landry. And he gave one of the industry's software superstars, Ray Ozzie, room to nurture an extraordinarily creative design team. Manzi could be charming and witty or crude and nasty, depending on the day. Paul Santinelli, a former marketing manager who worked for a Lotus subsidiary, said Manzi's "ego/ability ratio was way out of whack." After all, Lotus's revenues were only $970 million in 1994, far less than Bill Gates's net worth. Also, Lotus was on the decline, posting a first quarter 1995 loss of $17.5 million. Others agreed with Santinelli's view. Manzi had a tendency to hire high-priced advisors and ignore their input. Still, despite his foibles—perhaps because of them—he wasn't your typical CEO. Manzi's sense of humor was sly and subtle; those who liked him were extremely loyal. He was not afraid to look ridiculous either. He reached a high point of camp during Lotus's tenth anniversary party by getting on stage dressed in drag, miming the Aretha Franklin hit "Respect." His choice of song, according to some, was entirely appropriate.

If there is a single incontrovertible truism about technology start-up companies in American corporate life, it is how the early struggles shape the company's personality. In the beginning, there is a microkernel or code that defines a company's values. It's not exactly the same from firm to firm, of course. But you often see an informal work atmosphere and a loose hierarchy of control. Day care, dress down, flexible hours, free coffee and soda. At some usually imperceptible point, the start-up becomes subject to the laws and characteristics of a corporation. Somebody sketches an org chart. There's a need for ID badges, a human resources department, diversity training, and ice cream mall parties to welcome the employees of the small firm it just bought. The company shudders and shifts, and the founders, executives, managers, and employees either understand it and adapt to these seismic waves, or they abandon it, like Mitch Kapor.

Lotus was something like this. It courageously tried to operate with an eye on its founder's roots and progressive values. But as it grew and became more successful, it suffered from the vagaries of internal strife. It developed some of the worst behavior patterns of a company like IBM. In fact, Manzi actually hired an IBM executive, Frank King, as senior vice president for new product development. King was an old Boca Raton hand, home of the original maverick IBM PC team, and his claim to technology glory was the development of an innovative database language called SQL. King got the product out the door despite the classic resistance built into Big Blue's bureaucracy. He brought with him to Lotus two other IBM executives, Don Casey and Terry Rogers. King first began wearing suits to work, but in an effort to blend into the Lotus culture, soon changed his wardrobe to include leather jackets.

But even Lotus couldn't take the IBM out of a former IBMer. Lotus employees resented the influence of Big Blue managers, and they let Manzi know it. During a period when Lotus needed to make cutbacks, Manzi asked King to put a list of the seven or eight products under development on his whiteboard, top to bottom, in order of descending priority. The last item was Lotus Notes, which King knew was Manzi's baby. The list was meant to tweak Manzi. Sources who worked at Lotus said King resented the fact that Ray Ozzie was developing Notes under a separate company in another location. "He was a control freak," a former Lotus senior executive said of King. "He couldn't stand that Ray reported to Manzi and not him." Manzi decided to remove King a few weeks after that meeting, confiding to a source that hiring King had been one of his worst mistakes.

By the early 1990s, there were two distinct factions at Lotus, the desktop portion of the business—the bread-and-butter software that produced most of its revenues—and the Iris group, headed by Ray Ozzie, which worked exclusively on Notes software development.

Iris Associates was tucked away in Westford, Massachusetts, an hour's drive from Lotus headquarters. Notes promised to revolutionize corporate intranets, a package that would promote the concept of "collaborative computing." Ultimately, this software would allow users to create, modify, and send documents throughout cyberspace. Lotus Notes, when it reached its apex of power and flexibility, could change the way workers used their computers. Even change the way they worked. In short, Notes was heralded as the next killer app.

Ozzie, thirty-nine, was one of those quiet geniuses who had been distracted by computers as a college student. He dressed in jeans and sneakers, unless he went more formal, which meant downtown black. He kept something of a manageable profile until he was the subject of a long article in the *New York Times Magazine*. Even Bill Gates conceded that he was "one of the top five programmers in the universe." Manzi knew enough to stay away from Ozzie's playpen. It was Lotus's moon shot; only Ozzie could press the buttons that would result in a successful launch.

Iris, however, would cause a rift within Lotus. Notes was years in the making—Kapor had actually provided $1.2 million in seed money as early as 1984. Ozzie had asked the very best programmers and designers from Lotus to toil through nights and weekends on his brainchild. Iris turned into a hacker's paradise. There were no office hours, a big-screen television with a bunch of couches, assorted video games scattered around the room, even a pool table. The free vending machines featured pure junk food, the preferred diet of programmers. Anybody in need of inspiration could repair to the parking lot for a two-on-two game of hoops, weather permitting. Iris was what Lotus had been in its start-up days. So it was inevitable that Ozzie's elite, intensely focused group caused a high level of resentment led by the software geeks who weren't working in Westford. Iris folks were different from Lotus people. They had separate stationery, business cards, and benefits package—including a more generous bonus plan. And there was a growing feeling in Cambridge that the desktop products with a large installed base of loyal users were subsidizing a project that hadn't yet brought in any money.

Paul Santinelli said the chill was felt all the time. "Talk about animosity, you should have seen the animosity between Notes and the desktop at Lotus," he said. For example, there would be a marketing meeting, and someone would tell a product manager to cut X number of dollars from his marketing, promotion, and PR budget. The manager would calmly ask why. The reply was that Lotus didn't have the money for it. There were other areas that were hungrier for resources. The marketing manager, now miffed, would ask how much was getting taken out of the Notes budget. The answer was that even more money was being added to Ray Ozzie's project. And the product guys would steam and remind Manzi's senior execs that there wouldn't be any money for Notes without the success of their other products like 1-2-3, Approach, AmiPro, and so on. Worse, sometimes the best elements of their products were cannibalized so they could be integrated into Notes. The attitude of the people who did not see that Ray Ozzie's product was the future of Lotus was: The rest of the company is funding your R&D. Does that mean you screw Lotus 1-2-3, you bite the hand that fed you for fifteen years?

The short, cruel answer was, of course, yes. That's the way it is in this business. Silicon Valley rules apply. Manzi, as much as anyone, knew the only way to survive was to eat your own children before some other company did. Knowing that his desktop products were maturing, Manzi had to have a hit product that Lotus could ride into the networked world of the late 1990s and beyond. He had long since decided to bet the ranch on Ozzie and Notes. Lotus had poured $100 million into product development costs, and it had yet to see any real profits on that fall day when Mike Szeto knocked on Ed Gillis's door.

. . .

By April 1995, IBM's John M. Thompson and his software task force had thoroughly studied the idea of whether it should make a takeover bid for Lotus. Susan Fairty, an executive who had worked for Jim Cannavino, had been doing much of the preliminary work, along with a group of attorneys and a finance team. The conclusion was that Lotus's group of desktop products would be a good addition to IBM's portfolio. But if IBM ever was going to develop a networking presence, it needed Lotus Notes.

One question arose: What would the industry think? IBM had never made a hostile bid for a company, and neither had Gerstner. Jerry York saw no encumbrance. In fact, he welcomed it *because* IBM was a white shoe company. If anything, York knew it would be just one more statement that this was a new, meaner, more aggressive IBM.

Thompson's group had to educate Gerstner about Lotus Notes. One former IBM executive who was close to the Lotus takeover deal said that Gerstner had been primed by the failed Apple deal. "I think after that he felt bad, because he had gotten all of his juices up to wanting to do a big deal," an IBM manager who worked on the deal said. "He knew the only way we could grow was through acquisition. And then this Lotus idea came around, when John Thompson actually made a formal recommendation. He [Gerstner] actually was really intrigued with the idea. He couldn't even spell collaboration and Notes, and it was almost kind of hysterical to watch him go through the process. He had no idea this was a good idea, so the education process was just hard." Another former IBM executive said, "Lotus was just a flower to Lou."

A few weeks after Manzi's dinner with Thompson, there were rumors in the trade press that certain large companies might be taking a look at Lotus. In New York, Manzi had dinner with a group of investment advisors from Lazard Freres and Company. At the dinner was Felix Rohatyn, sixty-six, the man who was credited with spearheading the plan to save New York City from bankruptcy back in the 1970s. Rohatyn was head of one of the most prestigious deal-brokering firms, and few in the business commanded more respect. Manzi had been introduced to Rohatyn by Jerry Rosenfeld, an M&A specialist at Lazard. Rosenfeld was a former math teacher who had switched to a business career when several years earlier Lou Gerstner hired him as a consultant at McKinsey. His expertise was in doing financial workups of companies.

Manzi asked the key question: Would Gerstner make an unwanted play for Lotus? Rohatyn said that IBM would never do a hostile takeover. It was not the IBM way. Also, hostile deals in software were nearly unheard of. Software was less tangible than other kinds of assets; it was programmers and people. You could take over a software company, and if the key people quit, your investment could be worth considerably less very quickly. In Rohatyn's view, Gerstner definitely would call first with a friendly overture. At the very least, he'd send a formal letter.

Meanwhile, in May, IBM's board approved the hostile bid up to $65 a share, a large premium over the current stock price. IBM was prepared to pay more than $3.5 billion. Gerstner figured that a pre-emptive bid would seal a quick deal and discourage any other companies from jumping in and starting an auction. And after hearing rumors that Lotus was sounding out potential suitors, Oracle and AT&T among them, IBM stepped up the pace. Gerstner decided IBM had to act right after the Memorial Day weekend.

On Sunday, June 4, a casually dressed Gerstner assembled his takeover team to plan their strategy for the following morning. He spent a couple of hours with his public relations department, fielding questions in a mock press conference. David Kalis's people left nothing to chance. The questions were nasty and nastier. Gerstner excused himself, saying that he needed to go home and study some more.

IBM's hostile bid took advantage of a loophole in Lotus's bylaws. When the company was first incorporated by Mitch Kapor, a "consent solicitation" clause was included that allowed the board to be removed by a relatively simple process. A poison pill had been added, which is a complicated legal mechanism that makes it economically difficult for a hostile takeover to proceed without allowing the board to negotiate for a higher price. In Lotus's case, the poison pill could be removed with a simple legal maneuver. IBM attorneys could file a document that stated they had received the consent of fifty-one percent of the outstanding publicly held shares. This is done by tendering a cash offer for a much higher value than the stock is currently trading. The company making the hostile bid then can remove the board of the target company and insert its own directors. (In most hostile takeovers, it never goes this far.) In order to begin this process, the company initiating the bid files a lawsuit proposing to remove the poison pill.

IBM's lawyers had arrived over the weekend in Delaware, the state where many large companies, including Lotus, are incorporated. On Monday morning, as soon as the courthouse doors opened, they filed the suit. Then they informed Armonk. Lou Gerstner called Manzi precisely at 8:28 A.M. to tell him a fax was on its way to the office. Two minutes later it arrived; the essence of the letter was that IBM was making a bid for $60 a share for Lotus. The call and the fax shook Manzi. He had completely misjudged the timing, misjudged his relationship with Big Blue. IBM had acted faster than he thought was possible. In just a couple of weeks, he was scheduled to meet with Jim Barksdale to try to put together a Lotus-Netscape merger.

Five hours later, Gerstner held a thirty-five-minute press conference in New York City. After a brief opening statement in which he said the move "made an enormous amount of sense for everyone involved," he took questions from business reporters. He said that IBM could take advantage of Lotus's product line, while IBM could provide "financial and marketing muscle." He also maintained, "We wanted to negotiate a transaction. We were unable to do that." When Gerstner was asked about the background of the bid, he said that IBM began thinking about it "months and months ago." He later added, "We have been trying to get Lotus to consider such a transaction for over five months."

When Manzi heard this, he was furious. Gerstner was being disingenuous, at best, according to those executives close to Manzi.

A former Lotus senior official said a merger was never discussed, though several software agreements between the two companies were on the table. "There were OEM agreements being negotiated, pricing being negotiated, all sorts of things," the official said. "And four or five days before they announced the acquisition we had our final meeting, and we reached an impasse [on the OEM agreements]." This meeting took place in Cambridge with John M. Thompson. Except for Szeto's separate proposals to both IBM and Lotus, and apart from the single dinner that Manzi had with Thompson three months earlier (where Thompson suggested the possibility of an acquisition almost as an aside), there were never any serious, prolonged discussions between the two companies for a friendly merger. Certainly, nothing that approached the level of the IBM-Apple discussions of a year earlier.

Gerstner had been well briefed for the press conference. He did not once use the word "hostile." When a reporter asked whether he had talked with Manzi about the deal, Gerstner said the conversation was private, adding, "You should ask him what he said to me." The comment was unclear, yet sources at both Lotus and IBM say that Manzi's remarks to Gerstner were unprintable in a family newspaper.

So began one of the worst weeks of Manzi's professional life. After twelve years as the Northeast's major domo in software, he was about to lose his company to, in his mind, the least compatible suitor.

Over the following two days, Manzi's mood ranged from anger to despair. Felix Rohatyn's analysis had been wrong. He assembled a response team, a phalanx of advisors, and met with Rohatyn. At 11 P.M. on that Monday night, Rohatyn, who was also stunned by the IBM action, called Jerry Rosenfeld, who was in Canada winding up a Labatt deal. Rosenfeld was ordered back to New York to deal with the IBM takeover crisis on the following day. IBM's move—a "full-court press"—would result in a slam dunk for Big Blue. All of Manzi's available advisors told him that there was nothing Lotus could do except negotiate with Gerstner for a better deal.

For a day and a half, Manzi could not face the inevitable. He worked the phones, calling potential investors in Japan and in Silicon Valley. This is a standard reaction, known as the search for a "white knight," or a company that will make a friendly offer that tops the hostile offer. Just after Gerstner's fax arrived, Manzi had awakened one of his senior vice presidents in California and asked her to test Oracle's interest. But Larry Ellison was not about to face off against IBM, especially at this price. It was a desperation play by Manzi because according to a former Lotus official, "Larry has never bought anything but fighter jets and real estate." A call was also placed to Andy Grove, but Intel was not interested either. IBM was too big a customer to offend.

Lotus informally succumbed on Tuesday afternoon. Manzi asked to meet with Gerstner one-on-one at Gerstner's apartment at the Sherry Netherland Hotel in Manhattan. They had dinner in the room, and Manzi expressed the hope that Gerstner meant it when he publicly stated that he expected Lotus to operate independently with its headquarters remaining in Cambridge. When Gerstner wanted to know what jobs he was interested in at IBM, with a touch of bluster Manzi reportedly said he was only interested in two: Gerstner's and Thompson's. Gerstner apparently assured him that he would still run Lotus, as long as "he performed."

Manzi also wanted to find out just how much Gerstner knew about the assets he was about to purchase. "Lou, I believe, is clueless," a former Lotus senior executive said. "I remember during the merger, we used to say, 'Tell us again, why do you want Lotus? Tell us what the strategy is.' And he would look at us exasperated, bang his hand on the table, and say, 'Ugh! I have to do the vision thing again, one more time?' He didn't get it. I don't know if he gets it now. He sure didn't get it then."

What the Lotus team was trying to get across to IBM's CEO was that a software firm had no infrastructure; its lifeblood was intellectual property created by special people. Without them there is nothing.

Manzi wasn't surprised to discover that Gerstner had no idea who Ray Ozzie was. Later, executives at Lotus could not believe

Gerstner's ignorance. They did not expect Jim Manzi to accept a demotion and remain as a senior vice president reporting to Lou Gerstner. A CEO can be replaced. But if Ozzie quit, and the CTO, John Landry, walked, the next iteration of Lotus Notes—version 4.0—would be in jeopardy. It would be like buying a baseball team and having the two star players decide they don't want to play for the new owner. Meanwhile, you're worrying if the manager is going to walk. "I think it was a big shock [to IBM] to find out that the most powerful person in the Lotus organization was Ray Ozzie and not Jim Manzi," said a former Lotus executive. "And that was something that Jim always understood well."

A pro forma meeting with Ozzie and Gerstner was arranged. After all the briefing, Gerstner still had no idea what it would take to motivate him to stay. Perhaps thinking that Ozzie possessed the Holy Grail to future software development, he offered the only job he thought might entice him: a prestigious IBM fellowship. An IBM fellow gets a salary and a budget, and he or she sits around a lab and thinks for a living. There's no agenda other than pure research.

Ozzie already had made a lot of money, a lot more than an IBM fellow, and he had a bigger staff. "And he gets to do exactly what he wants to do every day," said a former Lotus executive who was involved in the takeover. "What was Lou offering him?" It was as if Gerstner was giving Ozzie the run of the castle when he already had the keys to the kingdom. Ozzie, however, had spent more than ten years on this project, and he was fully committed. He didn't need any motivation from Gerstner. He agreed to stay at least until the next upgrade of Notes was ready. Gerstner, in turn, promised not to drop in on him until it was shipped.

By midweek, the meetings among investment bankers, lawyers, and human resources executives had begun in earnest. Three groups of IBM-Lotus people had been formed to grapple with issues in three areas: personnel, finance, and legal. New contracts would need to be drafted for some key executives to stay. Buyout packages were necessary for those who would be asked to leave. Outstanding stock options held by Lotus employees would be vested. A $15 million package in "stay bonuses" was arranged for rank-and-file employees.

On Saturday night, six days after receiving Gerstner's fax, Jim Manzi rented a private room at the Four Seasons, an expensive and popular midtown restaurant for the city's power brokers. That was the last supper for the Lotus senior executives. Those who attended recall that the atmosphere was raucous but bittersweet. Manzi felt that whatever overtures Gerstner had made about Lotus's continuing autonomy and independence were pure fiction. If he had been less than forthright about the deal to the press in the first place, how could Manzi trust anything he said? Also, nobody pays $3.5 billion for a company and doesn't meddle.

As Manzi loosened up after several glasses of wine, he toasted his new boss, "Louie, Louie." Later, he referred to Gerstner as his "Uncle Louie," and it was quoted in the press. He was resigned about his defeat, but the sympathy at Lotus would be muted. He would end up with a lot of money, far more than anyone else. His 2.5 percent stake in Lotus was worth just under $75 million.

While Jerry York had insisted that IBM would pay only $60 a share, both sides knew the price would end up higher. It was traditional in any takeover that hoped to conclude with civil negotiations. The price was upped to $64, which left the IBM CFO somewhat relieved. He was able to leave a dollar on the table. If he had to go higher than another $50 million, he and Gerstner would be required to obtain the board's approval once again.

When he knew there was no way he could stop the deal, Manzi had made a series of personal demands, mostly to try to fluster Gerstner during the negotiations. Thinking Gerstner had no sense of humor, he expected the IBM CEO would take them seriously. He wanted to stick it to Gerstner. The demands were inspired by one of Manzi's colleagues, and some were so outrageous they were funny. They included unrestricted use of the corporate jet fleet, and an IBM senior vice presidency. (Manzi knew there was a Gulfstream IV in the corporate jet fleet restricted for use by the CEO. Gerstner had told Manzi he expected him to meet with a lot of customers, and customers don't want to meet with anyone lower than a senior vice president.) He also wanted John Thompson's job as the head of IBM's entire software business, and a seat on the board. A board seat was out of the question, and Manzi knew this. Oddly enough, Gerstner was almost tempted to yield on the job demand. On three separate occasions, Thompson had offered to let Manzi take complete charge of IBM's software. He told Gerstner that he was anxious to maintain corporate peace and see that the merger worked. He would take any equivalent assignment within IBM, including running the desktop business. Manzi was appointed an IBM senior vice president, still heading Lotus and reporting directly to Gerstner.

The boards of both companies approved the deal, and the papers were signed on Sunday, June 11. That afternoon, the public relations staffs of both IBM and Lotus debated how to handle the news. Someone suggested giving an exclusive overnight story to the *Wall Street Journal*. But this was quickly vetoed by David Kalis. Gerstner had been extremely displeased with recent tough coverage from the *Journal*'s IBM beat reporter, Laurie Hays. They decided to do a telephone press conference with several newspapers and broadcast media with both Manzi and Gerstner.

Manzi tried to maintain his sense of humor by perpetuating a myth that he was seriously religious. Earlier in the week on the way to visit a friend at his Manhattan office, he passed St. Patrick's Cathedral. Knowing that Gerstner was a serious, practicing Catholic, he mentioned he had been in church, even though he hadn't. During the press call, Gerstner, wanting the press to know that Manzi had sought spiritual guidance, pressed the mute button as Manzi was asked a question. "Tell them about St. Patrick's," Gerstner said. Manzi obliged, and his fictional story was repeated in the newspapers. One former executive who knows him well called this "classic Manzian behavior."

The following day, Manzi, Gerstner, and Thompson, all in shirt-sleeves, were seated onstage at the Wang Auditorium in downtown Boston. Some 2,500—most of the Lotus workforce in Cambridge—

were in the audience. When Manzi strode to the microphone, look-ing haggard with his tie loosened, he was greeted by a long, sus-tained ovation. He faltered slightly as he tried to put the week's events in perspective. "IBM has paid you an enormous compli-ment," he began, "paying $3.5 billion dollars for our company. It is by far the largest transaction in the history of our industry." As to the hostile-turned-somewhat-civil deal, he said there had been a "miscommunication" between the two companies. One of his biggest concerns was that Lotus maintain its unique culture.

Manzi continued, "In this agreement with IBM I can honestly tell you without reservation that we've taken care of our employ-ees, our shareholders, and our customers, and now I can tell you it is time that we take care of Microsoft." This comment prompted huge applause and cheers. His voice cracked when he said, "So when they wake up this morning in the Pacific Northwest, I hope they start asking themselves, where do they want to go today?" He ended by quoting his favorite poet, T. S. Eliot, "To make an end is to make a beginning. The end is where we start from."

When Gerstner was introduced, the first thing he said was that he "hoped that some of the applause was for us." A few uncomfortable laughs followed that remark. Gerstner was mag-nanimous in his praise for Manzi, telling the Lotus audience that their CEO had behaved impeccably all week long (even though he hadn't, and most of the Lotus employees knew it). He said he tried to put himself in Manzi's place to understand how he would feel if the same thing happened to him. He explained that IBM wanted to preserve Lotus's corporate culture, its name, and its product mix. Then the three took several questions from the audience. Quickly, the scene turned humorous when someone asked whether this meant the end of Manzi appearing in drag. Manzi ducked the question, but Gerstner said he wanted to see the tape.

"There's only one copy, and I have it," Manzi said.

"What we really want to know is whether we're going to see Lou in drag," someone finally asked.

Gerstner laughed along with the audience, which now was hooting wildly, as he walked to the front of the stage with his hands in his pockets.

"I'll make you a deal," the IBM CEO said. "The day that we have forty to fifty percent of the market, and the day that the guys on the West Coast throw in the towel, you'll see me any way you want to see me." The crowd erupted and cheered. Maybe this guy wasn't so ominous after all.

After the Wang event, the IBM helicopter ferried the three executives to Westford to reassure Ray Ozzie's Iris group. Gerstner had an investment to protect.

The mood was mixed within Lotus in the aftermath of the takeover. Some welcomed Big Blue, the "rich uncle," while others braced themselves for what was perceived as an unwelcome intrusion by Big Brother. Those with instantly vested stock options had become suddenly flush. Many middle-level managers lapsed into dysfunctional status, contemplating whether or not to take "the package," IBM's enhanced separation agreement. The software designers in both companies still eyed one another warily, even though there was no visible animus. Programmers like Bob Balaban, when asked if they had a few days to attend and present at IBM conferences in places like Austin, politely begged off. They always were behind schedule, they didn't even have time to return phone calls.

Gerstner had kept his word. IBM was still mostly hands-off. But the Big Blue culture began to creep into the corridors of Cambridge. "They wanted to have all these IBM information exchange meetings," Bob Balaban said. "They gathered people from all over the world on a particular topic, and they're all on the same project team. For a Lotus person it was bizarre because we were used to having everyone in the same building." It was also weird when Balaban and his fellow programmers discovered that IBMers just hopped on a plane at a moment's notice to go to a meeting. At Lotus they weren't accustomed to this extravagance.

Gradually, the relationship between the two companies began to warm. The Lotus-Iris people actually became interested in some projects within IBM, technology they wanted to incorporate into Notes. Soon, they began to trust each other, and at least the essential information began to flow between Cambridge and Somers, New York, where IBM's software group was located.

Manzi and his team spent the next three months in transition, working with John Thompson to develop a software strategy for IBM. High-level executives who worked with Manzi believe he had a sincere desire to see the merger work.

The Lotus CEO, however, had a difficult time educating Gerstner. Lotus executives put together a plan identifying a half dozen key initiatives that would dovetail with Gerstner's "network-centric computing," or NCC strategy, as it was then called. In one memo, Manzi cautioned the chairman to stay focused and beware of redundant and misdirected efforts, typical pitfalls he had seen in his years working with the company. He wrote, "Frankly, NCC is perceived as an amorphous concept that can be anything and everything at the same time. My sense, for what it is worth, is that the organization at large is dying for a rallying cry and we have one to give them—if we would just give it and then stop all the duplicative task force churning."

Manzi also had analyzed the worldwide software market and compared projected revenues (forecasted over three years) with IBM's R&D efforts. He was concerned that Big Blue was investing thirteen percent of its research budget in back-office software, a market that would account for thirty-four percent of sales. And in terms of total software spending, Manzi argued that sixty percent of its future R&D spending would end up chasing only twenty-one percent of revenues. In sum, IBM was investing too much in the wrong areas.

Gerstner did not take much of Manzi's advice. One Lotus executive, however, would have more influence on Gerstner's business strategy than perhaps anyone from Cambridge.

John Landry was a key figure in persuading Gerstner that he was wrong in his initial dismissal of the impact of the Internet.

Often portrayed as arrogant, obnoxious, and aggressive, Landry is something of the Elmer Gantry of the high-technology industry, one of the earliest proselytizers of the business potential of e-commerce. He preaches and bangs his fist on the desk when he makes his point, pontificating that he knows this stuff better than anyone else. But he's well prepared and a brilliant software strategist, a man with vision. "As much as people within IBM don't want to admit it, he's IBM's Internet division," a former Lotus product manager insisted. "I don't want to piss all over John Patrick [IBM's ranking Internet evangelist], but John Patrick couldn't shine John Landry's shoes, let alone wear them." Landry's great strength is his ability to explain technology so ordinary businesspeople can understand it. When Landry spoke, Gerstner finally understood.

Nobody at Lotus expected that Manzi would stay very long after the takeover, and this speculation was fueled by analysts and the trade press. Manzi had publicly insulted Gerstner during the takeover proceedings, and Gerstner had an elephantine memory for those kinds of put-downs. The two had massive egos, they did not particularly like each other, and they could never work together.

On Tuesday, October 10, 1995, Manzi traveled to Armonk to meet with Gerstner and tender his resignation. He had lasted with IBM for only ninety-nine days. Those close to Manzi said they were surprised it took that long. Gerstner said that he wanted him to stay, though this was a standard courtesy and a way of keeping their final meeting civil.

Other senior executives, most of whom were at Manzi's side during the takeover, left as well, though they insist their resignations were coincidental to their CEO's. K. C. Branscomb, Manzi's top lieutenant in corporate development, quit on the same day. Tom Lemberg, corporate counsel, Ed Gillis, the CFO, Russ Campanello, the head of human resources, all quit at about the same time. John Landry stayed on as a part-time advisor, and Ray Ozzie, as promised, did not leave for two more years, until Notes 4.0 was a product in great demand. (Notes made Ozzie fairly wealthy, though not nearly as rich as Manzi. In 1997, Ozzie and his brother, Jack Ozzie, began a small start-up called Rhythmix in the Boston area, apparently with Lotus's and IBM's blessing.)

Two Lotus executives, Jeff Papows, along with Mike Zisman, stepped in to run the company for IBM. Zisman eventually cut down his involvement and Papows assumed command. Papows reportedly felt refreshed that Gerstner and Thompson would continue their hands-off management policy. (Papows, however, was the subject of a damaging front-page story in the *Wall Street Journal* in April 1999. The newspaper claimed that Papows inflated his military credentials—including the fact that he was a fighter pilot—in order to enhance his status with Marine officials. His résumé padding apparently led to more lucrative Lotus Notes contracts. There was no immediate reaction from Gerstner about the story.)

Lotus flourished, due at least in part to IBM's major marketing push behind Notes. And as long as management continued to put fannies in the seats, corporate was pleased to let them operate autonomously. There were only 4.5 million Notes users in 1995. By the last half of 1996, Lotus had sold more Notes seats than in the previous six years. By 1998, there were 20 million users.

There was certainly a void after Manzi quit. John Landry was left to carry on what remained of the Lotus esprit de corps. At one of the company's Lotusphere events, where some five thousand or more employees, customers, business partners, and assorted fanatics gathered every year, Landry was asked to deliver the keynote speech. Since the theme was the World Wide Web, he was talked into making a dramatic entrance dressed as Spiderman. He was nervous about the stunt and didn't even want to rehearse it. When Landry was introduced, a hatch opened in the ceiling, and he began descending at the end of a wire. Halfway down, the cable got stuck and he was left dangling for what was a hairy half a minute. It seemed a lot longer to Landry. The audience cackled at their superhero flailing desperately like a frightened bug.

Though Lotus retains its independence, some feel it is now more IBM than IBM subsidiary. One ex-Lotus director said, "A lot of the good people have left. What remained were the IBM-like people. What a brain drain."

Today, Microsoft is quickly catching up with IBM in the groupware race. For the first time, its Exchange program outsold Lotus Notes by 300,000 copies during the first quarter of 1998. Half of the fifty largest companies in the United States are now using Exchange rather than Notes. And Lotus's once-dominant market share is shrinking. Some industry experts think Gerstner overpaid for Lotus; that, in fact, it was paying for a single product, Notes. It will take some time to assess whether this is true.

12

A Shifting Wind in Armonk

Lou Gerstner's sense of timing was always brilliant or lucky, or a combination of the two, so it wasn't surprising when the Lotus takeover coincided with a personal accolade. On June 12, 1995, only a day after the deal had been completed, the Harvard Business School Club of New York gave him its Business Statesman of the Year award. IBM aides liked to point out that he previously declined the honor—it wasn't yet appropriate. Now, however, he certainly was a deserving alumnus. In less than twenty-seven months, Gerstner's IBM had gained considerable momentum. Wall Street was pleased with Big Blue, if not yet delirious. Quarterly earnings were $1.72 billion, more than double the $689 million IBM made in the second quarter of 1994. The stock had reached $107, more than two and a half times higher than when Gerstner took over.

IBM speechwriters had planned on providing the Harvard B-School Club dinner speakers with some light material in order to roast the boss—jokes about his well-paid personal chef, for instance—but David Kalis vetoed this idea. Any remarks teasing the CEO were summarily jettisoned. The event was a formal, almost solemn occasion, an "international" dinner in the main ballroom of the Waldorf-Astoria. Other captains of industry were on the guest list, and Kalis did not want even the most innocent quip to be misconstrued by Gerstner's peers. Some things never changed. Humor at IBM was no laughing matter, at least for speechwriters.

Video testimonials were arranged by IBM's communications staff for two who could not attend, Gerstner's good friend Vernon Jordan, and Jim Burke, the board member primarily responsible for Gerstner's hire. When Jordan, who was traveling abroad, appeared on the giant projection screen above the dais, he reminded the audience that he, too, had had a hand in convincing Gerstner to take the IBM job. He called it a "rendezvous with destiny." At the beginning of the sappy speech, however, Jordan couldn't resist a subtle dig about Gerstner's need to control everything: "[And] knowing Lou as I do, he is worried about my remarks, which he has not seen, nor approved. Relax, Mr. Chairman. I've come to praise Gerstner, not to bury him. Trust me, I'm from Washington." Jordan's political crack fell flat.

Burke played it straight and lauded Gerstner's "passion" and his "complete intellectual integrity." He made a reference to the remarkable events of the past week, when IBM had dominated the headlines with the Lotus deal. But what really impressed Burke was Gerstner's "ability to look at virtually everything he does strategically. He literally thinks strategically all the time. I suspect he thinks strategically about his family, about his dog—I don't know if he has one. But he just plain looks at the world and says, how can we arrange things and do things better?"

As for Gerstner's propensity to strategize about everything, Burke was not exaggerating. Now that IBM had become respectable in both the investment and technology communities, Gerstner was busy rearranging the boxes on his own org charts once again.

For most of 1995, Gerstner did not have a chief strategist, a technology guru who could help him read the industry's often confusing tea leaves. To fill the gap, he called on specific executives depending on their expertise. For example, his advisor on the Lotus deal had been John M. Thompson, IBM's top software executive. The two IBMers who previously held the top strategy job, Jim Cannavino and Bernard Puckett, had quickly realized that the position was titular, a preretirement holding pen. Still, the outside perception of the job was different. Chief strategist at a company like IBM is potentially one of the most important senior advisors in corporate America. Microsoft's Nathan Myhrvold, for example, Bill Gates's muse, was considered critical to that company's success in recent years. Bill Joy performed this function for Scott McNealy at Sun Microsystems.

In September 1995, Gerstner finally filled the IBM position. He startled the high-tech industry by hiring Bruce Harreld, whose most recent job had been as president of Boston Chicken, a fast-food franchise. It was a baffling choice. Harreld, forty-four, had little experience in technology. He had spent most of his career in the food business, including a tour as the senior executive in charge of marketing and information systems at Kraft General Foods. Other items on his résumé, however, must have attracted Gerstner. Like Gerstner, he was a Harvard Business School graduate, and he had taught at Northwestern University's Kellogg Graduate School of Management. He'd done a tour at The Boston Consulting Group, dispensing the same kind of business advice Gerstner had for McKinsey. In short, Harreld was more of an academic and an intellectual than a businessman, somewhat like Rick Thoman.

On Harreld's arrival, IBMers already had envisioned the glib tabloid business headline, "Cookie Man Hires Chicken Man." (One senior IBM executive had seen Harreld's résumé and predicted the joke.) Industry experts also viewed the appointment skeptically. Dan Mandresh, the Merrill Lynch analyst, wondered what Gerstner saw that he didn't. Mandresh said, "His principal strength was that he was one of the world's most ardent supporters and users of Lotus Notes. He was a Lotus Notes maniac. He ran Boston Chicken with Lotus Notes. Too bad he didn't run it with some good recipes for food. My point is, Boston Chicken was a failure, right? If he stayed where he was, he'd be a failed executive at Boston Chicken. I don't know what Bruce Harreld does at IBM. I met Bruce, and I still haven't figured out what I've learned."

Steve Milunovich, the Morgan Stanley analyst, also was surprised by Gerstner's choice. Milunovich had an academic interest in corporate strategy, so he sought out Harreld at an analyst meeting. Harreld wasn't wearing a name tag—he was sort of working the room incognito—but Milunovich recognized him and introduced himself. The analyst was impressed with the fact that Harreld had implemented technology in the past; there was no doubt he was a fairly bright guy. Milunovich said he'd like to get to know his business better, perhaps accompany him on customer calls to see his strategy up close. Harreld balked at the request, preferring simply to meet and chat. Milunovich recalls, "The first thing he said was, 'I'm chief strategist of IBM, but I don't really do all that much strategy because Lou Gerstner's our chief strategist.' It's little bit vague what his role is." Harreld eventually described himself as something of a "utility infielder." Bob Djurdjevic, president of Annex Research, a consulting firm in Phoenix, said, "The last thing IBM needs now is another bureaucrat pushing paper." Harreld was given an extensive support staff, but it still isn't known exactly how much research and direction he provides for IBM.

During the same month that Harreld was struggling to understand his new role at the world's largest technology company, Gerstner's most influential colleague, Jerry York, was planning his exit. He had seen IBM through its darkest hour and had played an integral role in its recovery. But there was a tempting offer on the table. Kirk Kerkorian, the head of Tracinda Corporation, the largest shareholder in Chrysler, had made an audacious bid in April 1995 to take control of the nation's third-largest automaker. While the takeover attempt failed, Kerkorian wanted to extract certain concessions from Chrysler, including the promise of a major share repurchase plan and board representation. Kerkorian asked York to help him with these demands.

York originally had thought that the IBM turnaround would take three years, so he had planned to stay at least through the summer of 1996. That was almost a year away, and although most of the major surgery had been done, there was still plenty of inefficiency, a lot of bloat throughout pockets of IBM. Leaving the company wasn't easy, and he wrestled with his conscience for several weeks.

His CFO duties were almost pro forma at this point. Finding a replacement to handle the core part of the job wouldn't be that difficult. But Gerstner relied on him more as a chief operating officer. York was such an invaluable executive in terms of day-to-day operations at IBM, he enabled Gerstner to easily sidestep the delicate question of appointing a president (who would then expect to become the CEO's successor). Plus, there were still messes to be swept up. The server group was not performing particularly well, and the PC Company was a perpetual money trough. The CEO would have a difficult time replacing York.

Around Labor Day, when York had made his decision, he took a Friday off, planning to call Gerstner from home. When he reached Gerstner, the CEO asked the obligatory question, "Is there any way I can talk you out of this?" York said, "Lou, I have been thinking about this for a month, and it's the right thing for me to do."

The day that York's resignation was announced, IBM stock dropped two percent, even though most computer stocks advanced. One investment company president said he was "upset" by the departure. The reaction was understandable. Some thought York had been more critical than Gerstner to IBM's success during the first two and a half years of the new administration. The reductions in SG&A and R&D were largely York's initiatives. And when IBM's quarterly reports first showed that IBM was turning the corner, it was obvious why. Operating income was up and gross profit margins increased largely because expenses were greatly reduced. "I think a substantial part of my job is done," York told the *New York Times*. "The balance sheet is rock solid, and we have substantial liquidity." IBM had enough cash in the bank to buy two more Lotuses.

York left an indelible mark at corporate headquarters. Even those who disliked his management methods respected his tireless commitment to getting the company rolling again. Yes, he was remembered mostly for taking names and making painful and unpopular decisions, but he also managed to repair IBM's seriously damaged relations with Wall Street. He gave IBM credibility once again in the investment community. Previous IBM financial officers had always been trying to slough off bad news. A disappointing quarter was always an aberration, not a trend. York, however, was refreshingly candid about IBM's financial health, refusing to burnish less-than-acceptable results. He would go beyond the SEC's minimum requirements for public companies when it came to breaking down IBM's figures. Also, he returned phone calls. He was accessible. Gerstner met once a year with analysts, while York appeared every quarter. The financial analysts who closely charted the turnaround gave York very high marks. He was the ideal do-everything CFO. He took off the green eyeshades, walked into Big Blue's toughest trenches, and became an activist when the company needed it most.

So for IBM watchers, September wasn't a good month. Big Blue acquired a utility infielder and its star designated hitter became a free agent.

While York and Gerstner had a harmonious relationship, they differed over who should get the CFO job. York strongly recommended Wilson Lowery, whose most recent assignment was as IBM's vice president of quality and reengineering. Back in early 1994, York had examined IBM's Asia-Pacific unit, which included the very important Japanese market. Bob Stephenson was the executive in charge of Asia-Pacific, and Lowery was his number two man running the financial end. Stephenson and Lowery had made cost reductions and taken other extreme efficiency measures on their own. They hadn't waited for the draconian directives from Armonk. By the time York got to Tokyo, he found there was little for him to do. Unlike other IBM units, Asia-Pacific was a model of leanness, efficiency, and accountability. The business unit was sometimes hurt by dollar devaluations against the yen, but Lowery reported his numbers accurately, completely, and on time. After he pored over their books, York recalls, "I literally said to them, 'Well, if the IBM board had ever seen these numbers, they might've decided to put you guys in charge of the company.'" York was stingy with praise, so this endorsement counted for something.

Wilson Lowery was York's no-brainer pick for his successor, according to several sources.

Gerstner did not share York's opinion, however. He appointed Rick Thoman instead. Many managers at IBM thought Thoman's track record as a line manager was spotty at best. But it actually was an inspired choice. Gerstner took Thoman out of a job where his positive influence had been manufactured and exaggerated by the spin doctors in Armonk.

Thoman now would no longer be directly responsible for a business line. It was, some said, a classic FUMU, by any measure, but at least he was promoted to a job where he was actually well qualified. If you pointed to his various financial posts in his past, including his early stint in Gerstner's Finance Group at McKinsey, you found a CFO with solid credentials and experience. Even his detractors, those who thought he did a terrible job running the PC business, gave him high marks as the number two official at IBM. He was sincere, personable, and well liked by the Street. He welcomed input from analysts and put himself out to seek their advice. Thoman was masterful in schmoozing the financial community, and this is one of the prime elements of the job. It was also one of those obligations Gerstner didn't care to deal with.

Gerstner had changed much of the character of the company, and in order to compete with other firms, he had raised the ante the only way he knew how: He increased executive pay packages.

Executives with stock options were pleased. Gerstner understood the allure of monetary rewards, and they were a prime motivator for his senior managers. But he didn't necessarily understand their character. Top-performing executives at IBM, like anyone else, expect fair compensation, but for many, money is not the only item on the scorecard. In the high-tech industry, most overachievers who merely want to build net worth head for points west, to the Valley, where their market value is highest. IBM was not a place where you stayed if pure wealth was your goal. You stayed because of prestige. In the 1980s, Don Estridge, the father of IBM's PC, continually eschewed more lucrative offers because working for Big Blue meant more than any paycheck.

There still were vestiges of this mentality among the senior executives, especially the ones who were comfortable and didn't aspire to the wealth that Gerstner did. And Gerstner was mostly blind to it. This was evident when he held his annual dinner in the fall of 1995 for his high command and their spouses at the Blind Brook in Rye, a very tony and exclusive country club. Most members are CEOs or senior executives from the area's prestigious corporations. Sometime between the appetizer and the entrée, Gerstner tapped at his wineglass with a spoon to get everyone's attention. Then he gave a little speech, which began, "This is the IBM family. These are the people who make IBM work. Now listen, husbands and wives, because this affects you . . ." Gerstner then exhorted about IBM's stock price. He said, "If we could just get it to where it once was during its best days, get it back up to $150, our stock options, the options in this room, would be worth a quarter of a billion dollars."

Gerstner probably had no idea that his remarks could be construed as a faux pas. Though this was strictly a social occasion, he couldn't resist talking about business, because that was his consuming passion. The normal chitchat one would expect from the boss, the polite thank-you's, are just not part of the Gerstner modus operandi. One senior manager who was there called the CEO's remarks "inappropriate." Another former executive was much more offended, and so was his wife. He described it as an incredibly vulgar display, something Gordon Gekko might have recited in the Oliver Stone movie *Wall Street*. It was saying greed is good. He said, "I couldn't believe it. There's nothing behind him, he's this omnivore moving forward."

You could complain about Lou Gerstner's lack of social grace, but IBM stockholders were likely to overlook this flaw.

By the end of 1995, IBM had finished a record year with an outstanding balance sheet. Revenues had increased twelve percent, from $64 billion to nearly $72 billion, a growth spike the company hadn't experienced since 1984. Hardware, which accounted for half the company's sales, grew by ten points. System/390, the mainframe, was again selling well. Software, IBM's most profitable revenue stream, was also up by double digits. Net earnings per share in 1995 grew by forty percent, $7.23 versus $5.02 in 1994. "Most important, our quarterly and full-year results indicate that our fundamental strategies are working," Gerstner said in the accompanying statement. The doubters were beginning to believe him. It was okay to buy IBM again.

York's resignation and Thoman's promotion gave Gerstner the opportunity to further shuffle his lineup before beginning his third year in 1996. There now was a gaping vacancy at the Personal Systems Group, which included the PC Company. Still foundering, it desperately needed an infusion of tough management, especially since Jerry York no longer was around to help out on weekends. By now, the PC Company was referred to as IBM's "Vietnam" by executives and managers alike. Only those senior execs with the steeliest nerves and resolve even thought about going "in country." It was IBM's most difficult assignment because privately, most IBMers thought it was unfixable.

Gerstner turned to Bob Stephenson, a fifty-six-year-old veteran with one of the longest tenures at IBM. Despite a thirty-four-year career with the company, he was probably the least-known senior executive outside the industry. One reason was that Stephenson, a native of Kentucky, disliked speeches and interviews. When his appointment was announced, one news article began, "Bob who?" Despite his low profile, he was a very sharp businessman and more colorful than the typically bland IBM executive. A one-dimensional workhorse, he was nearly ecstatic when mandatory retirement at sixty years old was lifted. When asked to update his bio, Stephenson drew a blank on hobbies. Well, what do you do with your free time, he was asked? "Algorithms," Stephenson replied.

A former high school basketball player, Stephenson was physically imposing, close to six feet four inches tall, with a shock of white hair, always neatly trimmed. But now he contended with a substantial middle-age gut that was slung over his belt. He often prefaced his pronouncements at meetings by standing and hitching his trousers and pacing the conference room.

The wrath of Bob was widely feared. Anyone who didn't perform, anyone who obfuscated the truth about his business, could suddenly find himself "not one of my favorite IBMers." Stephenson was famously volatile, and if the answer to a question was a simple yes or no or I don't know, and the manager ran on with IBMspeak, Stephenson would furiously punch the pound key on the phone to cut him off. His language could make Jerry York look like a choirboy. Once, when he couldn't get a VCR to work in his conference room, he threw a tantrum. "This is the goddam fucking IBM company," he ranted at a pair of secretaries. "Get somebody in here right now who knows how to work this fucking thing." Despite these infrequent outbursts, however, he was well liked by nearly everyone who worked with him. Also, everyone in Armonk headquarters respected his business acumen.

He was the company's most notorious white-knuckle flyer, too. He turned red-faced whenever the smallest amount of turbulence jostled the eight-seat company jets he frequently flew on, and if the weather was really bad, his briefcase slammed shut and he gripped the armrests. "How can you stand this shit?" he once asked an aide during a flight home from Raleigh through a thunderstorm. It was comical when one of IBM's most feared and revered senior executives was reduced to a whimpering lump. When aides tried to relax him with a glass of wine, he insisted on coffee. If the Falcon 2000 was going down, by gosh, Stephenson wanted to be alert.

Few at IBM had a more eclectic background than Stephenson. He graduated from Yale in 1961, having majored in engineering and science. He boasted that he had been able to avoid almost every English course at the nation's preeminent undergraduate school in the humanities. He went right to work at IBM, and he programmed some of the company's earliest mainframes. Not only was he steeped in technology, he could sell it too, a rare double threat in any IBM era.

His ability to finesse Watson's rigid management system was demonstrated at IBM when he became a sales representative in his late twenties. He had long resisted Big Blue's required "sales school." It was a waste of time, he concluded, and for years all of his superiors looked the other way. Finally, a new manager heard about his insubordination and insisted that he attend. When he continued to defy the order, a threat of dismissal was issued. Stephenson's response was that IBM could go ahead and fire him. When the problem was bumped up a couple of layers of management, IBM executives discovered he was one of the company's leading salesmen. His absence at the upcoming Golden Circle awards would be embarrassing. The matter was quietly dropped. Nobody at IBM has ever heard of any sales rep getting away with what Stephenson did.

Once, a small-town government manager wanted to buy an IBM computer, and he needed to convince the elected officials to commit to the expense. He called Stephenson to arrange a demo of one of the company's most advanced computers. Stephenson was honest. The machine wasn't yet ready; there wasn't even any software written for it. The manager didn't care; he wanted his people to see it immediately. So Stephenson reluctantly arranged a meeting, flipped on the switch, and a bunch of numbers even *he* didn't understand popped up on the screen. Pure mumbo jumbo. He bluffed his way through the presentation and, of course, made the deal.

As an executive on a steady arc, Stephenson was a company man who stood firmly behind the IBM logo. In addition to tours in Europe and Tokyo, he became controller of the company. When he returned to the United States, he was appointed general manager of IBM North America, a high-visibility post for anyone other than a Bob Stephenson.

Gerstner, however, impressed with his considerable business ability, raised Stephenson's profile when he appointed him head of the Personal Systems Group. Eventually, Gerstner added the Storage Solutions division, Networking Hardware, and the new Network Computer unit to Stephenson's mix. In sum, he would take charge of between $17 billion and $20 billion in annual revenues (it depended on the accounting, which until new regulations were issued in 1999 could be broad and vague in the company's annual report), the greatest single chunk of IBM's business. According to the company's proxy statement in 1998, after exercising a large block of stock options, Stephenson took home the third-highest paycheck after Gerstner and John M. Thompson.

When Stephenson moved into Rick Thoman's fourth-floor corner office in Building 3 in Somers, many of the problems he discovered could be traced to Thoman's lack of experience in the computer business. Thoman also was not particularly adept at judging managerial talent. He had hired a group with considerable marketing experience, but who in fact had the same weaknesses he did. They were bright young guys from outside the company with a lot of energy, and little understanding of technology. They were deep thinkers like himself, but not terribly good at making and selling computers.

David Winn was tapped to run IBM's European PC Company. Winn was a warm, refined guy who was a serious amateur classical musician. He was not particularly dynamic, and he failed to energize the overseas sales force. Jim Firestone, forty, a brainy go-getter who was fluent in Japanese, was hired to run the new consumer division in August 1995. Firestone had worked with both Gerstner and Thoman at American Express, but he had next to no experience in the computer business. David Hoyte, who had been an executive with Frigidaire, was hired to run manufacturing.

Stephenson inherited James Corcoran, a British executive who had never earned a degree, as vice president of marketing and communications. Corcoran, whose wife worked at Ogilvy and Mather, had been one of two finalists for the job when Thoman turned to Shelly Lazarus for advice on whom to hire. Lazarus said that if he wanted someone who could "move a building across the street," then Corcoran was his man.

He immediately made a terrible impression on Stephenson. At a Worldwide Operations Meeting, an internal summit for top managers in the group, Corcoran unveiled his new marketing strategy. His opening gambit included stepping off the stage, reaching into his pocket, and tossing pixie dust in front of Stephenson and his colleagues. It was as if he were the Merlin of marketing, and he promised nothing less than magical results.

Corcoran wasn't much interested in new technology; nobody ever saw him with his ThinkPad open. His secretary printed out his e-mail. He was frequently inaccessible. Subordinates thought it was laughable when he claimed he could be an "eight-hundred-pound gorilla" if necessary. He couldn't move his chair, let alone a building across the street. He alienated several of the Ogilvy staffers who created his ads. Privately, they thought he didn't have a clue how to market computers. He made a big point of his bootstrapped career and how far he had gone without a degree. If he didn't like an ad, he wondered how the "guy from Manchester" would react—meaning the unrefined, underprivi-leged buyer. Corcoran took six months and spent $4.2 million to produce two thirty-second TV spots for the Aptiva. They fea-tured a Peruvian Indian chanting and a cowboy singing. "It was a joke," recalls former Ogilvy hand Steve Sonnenfeld. "We referred to it as the *Waterworld* of advertising," a reference to the Kevin Costner box-office bomb that cost a fortune to produce.

Stephenson, however, had a number of other far more press-ing problems.

IBM's channel partners complained that the company's direct sales force was competing with them and eating into their prof-its. The company had not been a reliable supplier. Products were still too expensive. IBM was still between thirty and seventy-five percent slower than its competitors in getting products out of the factories. Low-cost PC servers, for example, a burgeoning market, lagged behind Compaq's in performance. Every iteration seemed to be a generation behind. The marketing department was constantly searching for the most esoteric benchmarks that the sales staff could use when they pitched IBM's servers against the competition.

The reengineering effort that Thoman had begun (with York looking over his shoulder) was far from complete. When Stephenson heard the results of an outside consultant's preliminary assessment of the PC business, he shared them with three or four of his senior managers. IBM had made substantial improvements in improving its product cycle times, the consultant reported, but it had started from such a low point, it was now merely bad instead of absolutely horrible. When one executive said he'd never heard of the consultant, Stephenson stood up, hitched his pants, and drawled in his Southern lilt, "Well . . . if we're paying these guys millions of dollars to tell us what's wrong with our business . . . and we don't believe them . . . then maybe we ought to be examining our own fucking navels."

At the 1996 senior managers event, Stephenson's assigned topic was "speed to market." In front of a worldwide audience of six hundred of the highest ranking IBMers, he reported, "I did a CD-ROM search of the news clips . . . over the past two years. Guess what? There were dozens of success stories, many of them about our competitors. IBM was conspicuous by its absence. We were a no-show." Stephenson went on to tell a story about how Chrysler, in a $1 billion reengineering project, used IBM's Catia workstation package to get its Neon off the assembly line a year faster than usual. "You'd think that if we could do it for Chrysler, we could do it for ourselves," Stephenson lamented.

No wonder the PC Company was still in a quagmire.

Stephenson was rigorous in cutting costs. To get better pricing and deliveries on components, especially chips, he had no qualms about calling Andy Grove at Intel and threatening to take his business to a Korean supplier.

But he had to grow market share and revenues, and this was difficult because IBM was committed to third-party resellers. Compaq was trying to eliminate the middleman; IBM embraced him. Stephenson was open to any new suggestions, and in internal meetings he implored his troops to think out of the box, go for the big idea. The way to gain market share, he claimed, was not to dig the ditch a little deeper every day but to come up with some brash new approach to excavation. His campaign slogan was "Plus 10 by 2000." He wanted to increase his desktop business by ten percentage points in less than four years. A huge banner was hung in the lobby under the atrium in Somers Building 3 proclaiming his goal. He was not against cutting prices and shrinking his profit margins to next to nothing, if it meant turning his inventory and gaining share.

In April 1996, in one of Stephenson's most forward-looking decisions, he appointed Sam Palmisano, a forty-four-year-old IBM executive, to run the PC Company. He'd begun his career as a data entry clerk in 1973, went through management training school at IBM, and quickly gained the attention of senior officials. Palmisano was widely known throughout IBM as one of the company's big producers, and like Stephenson, he was one of the few who had been able to successfully bridge the cultural gulf between Akers and Gerstner. *Business Week* held his latest promotion in such high regard, its headline read, "Golden Boy at Big Blue." Palmisano would assume control of about half of Stephenson's piece of IBM, around $10 billion in sales. It would include ThinkPads, Aptivas, commercial desktop units, and PC servers. He'd attempt to create a profitable business model where Thoman had not.

Palmisano had been a history major at Johns Hopkins University, and had played center on the football team. As a young man, he'd invested in government-subsidized real estate in the Maryland area and learned how to make money. Not only did Palmisano have a nose for property investments, he was adept at playing the stock market, as well. Plus he had the kind of social pedigree that endeared him to old-line IBMers.

Palmisano's wife, Missy, was the daughter of a prominent bank CEO. They lived in Southport, a small, exclusive community on the Connecticut coast. The Palmisano family knew George Bush's family well before he was elected President. They'd bought a summer house owned by the Bushes in Kennebunkport. There was no doubt that Palmisano came from a privileged background, joined all the right clubs, and played golf with the industry's elite businessmen. Groomed from the start to be a top-level executive, he was the highest of the "hi-po" (high-potential) talent at Big Blue. He had been John Akers's executive assistant, and he and his wife were still close to the Akerses, even after John was deposed.

In addition to his social advantages, Palmisano had the requisite sales personality and an affable smile. He stood six feet two inches tall, and a pair of large eyeglasses with thick lenses framed his boyish face. He had a more collegial style than other IBM execs, dressed casually, and traveled without an entourage. He refused an executive assistant because he had been one himself. He didn't need someone to pack his underwear for a business trip. He was a quintessential regular guy, well liked by aides. Palmisano also was not a meetings guy. He was known for snapping pencils when an IBMer was in full drone, and when he could no longer stand it, he excused himself and called customers. In a refreshing departure from most senior execs, he spoke without notes or slides unless he was addressing the IBM board. He would not travel halfway around the world to a Leadership Forum just to shake some dignitary's hand. If it had nothing to do with his business, he avoided it. He'd cut short a business trip so he could be with his kids on Halloween.

Palmisano's social contacts undoubtedly helped bring in lots of business, but he was a natural salesman, a closer. He understood just how far high-pressure tactics could take him. Once, he was in the middle of a dinner with a potential client, the CIO of a large company, and he wanted to sign the deal before dessert. He sketched out the terms and conditions of an outsourcing contract on a cocktail napkin.

"I'm ready to sign off on this right now," he said. The customer balked, wanting more time to think it over. "Then you're telling me you're not in charge," Palmisano said. "I can sign off on this piece of paper right now. I can do this deal." Eventually he earned the business.

For twenty-two years, he put up with the worst aspects of IBM's polite, insular management. Long before IBM got in trouble, he was one of the few who warned that the company was consumed by revenue growth while disregarding profits and competitors. Despite his close ties to Akers, he welcomed the Gerstner regime and remained loyal to IBM. Headhunters had tried unsuccessfully for years to lure him to a bigger playpen. As CEO of another company, he easily could have earned more money than Gerstner was paying him (though he had a substantial golden handcuff at IBM, including bonuses that netted him at least $1.5 million to $2 million yearly). When Gil Amelio was ousted as CEO of Apple, Palmisano's name appeared on top of the short list even though he never considered the job. (And today, he is often mentioned as one of the only possible in-house heirs to Gerstner's office in 2002.)

When he took over the PC Company, Palmisano could not believe what he saw. Eight or more layers of management for seventeen thousand employees. In his previous job in the services division, there had been forty-nine thousand employees, and only four layers of management. Human resources? In services, it had been one for every two thousand; in the PC Company, it was one for every five hundred. In his old shop, market research was outsourced. Here, the equivalent work was done by a staff of two hundred. At one briefing, Palmisano allowed that he was disgusted that his managers did not understand what it took to run a profitable business. "We were on the plane last night coming back from Raleigh," he began. "Everybody who works for me is in first class; I'm in seat 10D. Think they get it? I don't think they get it. I go to the city on the Harlem [railroad] line, $4.50 on the Harlem line. I go to the same meetings they go to. They take the helicopter."

Palmisano also could not fathom the rationale behind "Rally" and "Kickoff" events, traditional IBM extravaganzas that cut directly into the company's bottom line. He understood the value of esprit de corps. But three or four days in a warm resort, a couple of lectures or seminars, team-building workshops, maybe a celebrity guest like astronaut Jim Lovell, and what is the take-away? A blue windbreaker. Not to mention the three or four days those top performers wouldn't be designing, building, and selling computers. Do we need all these retreat-cum-vacations masquerading as motivational safaris? Wouldn't the troops rather save a few million and see it added to their bonuses?

"We've got to become a high-performance, in-your-face, speak-your-mind culture because that's what this industry requires," Palmisano said. But he was also practical. "I'm not going to change the IBM company," he added. "That's Lou Gerstner's job."

Palmisano, like Stephenson, was incredibly direct, but he preferred to deliver his pronouncements without histrionics. At one meeting, one of his managers balked at a suggestion, and Palmisano immediately cut him off. "I said, 'You lost $20 million in the first quarter. You don't have any opinions until you make money,'" Palmisano said. "I'll respect you if make money."

Privately, Palmisano viewed Stephenson's goal of gaining ten points in market share as a lost cause. Still, he made changes that enabled the PC Company to win back three points the year after he took command. He shuffled his top managers, implored them to speed up their cycle times, and kept reminding anyone who would listen that increasing inventory turns was critical to a successful business.

In one season under Palmisano, IBM's PCs were the first to market for the first time in seven years. New approaches such as the "authorized assembly program" allowed channel partners to sell made-to-order desktop machines. This was not a new concept for other PC makers, but at least it finally made IBM's desktop business customer-focused again. Under Palmisano, the PC Company was not as nimble or efficient as Compaq, Dell, and Gateway. It could never hope to compete with any company selling directly to customers. But it was run far better than under Rick Thoman's aegis.

After Palmisano's team began posting better results, they were given bigger bonuses than they thought they'd ever see in that division. Making money, in the world according to Sam, was more fun than not making money.

13

New Images in the House That Lou Built

It is a balmy summer morning in downtown Atlanta, and the spring temperatures are already in shirtsleeve territory. But the dozens of IBM managers, programmers, and technicians who are intensely tapping at their keyboards and snaking cables across the floor of the Control Room are oblivious to the weather. They haven't been outdoors much. With the 1996 Summer Olympics less than three months away, they're too busy putting in overtime in this top-secret expanse—about the size of a typical high school gym—that houses the central neural network for the entire Games. The privileged few who are allowed a peek at this installation cannot bring cameras. IBM is taking no chances. In the unlikely scenario of sabotage or a security breach, a disaster recovery site has been constructed several miles out of town.

IBM is providing all the technical support for the Games, the complete package. It's the first time in Olympic history that the Games' organizers have entrusted the entire task to a single vendor. And IBM hasn't taken the responsibility lightly. It has been preparing for this moment for at least five years, well before Gerstner's command, and there are dozens of special teams working on nothing but the Games. All told, some two thousand employees are involved in the effort.

One could argue that no other company has the breadth and experience to even contemplate the huge data requirements for the seventeen-day competition. There are 271 medal events, and as many as twenty-two occur simultaneously. "These games actually wouldn't happen without IBM and IBM support," says Eli Primrose-Smith, the company's director of Olympics and sports operations. "This will show the world what we can do," says IBM's Ron Palmich. "This is for bragging rights."

IBM's task is mammoth: wiring a city within a city, one where 130,000 athletes, coaches, officials, journalists, and support staff will test modern technology's limits. IBM not only is responsible for providing scores, it is printing badges, accrediting athletes and other personnel, performing security chores, and handling ticket sales. Through IBM's Net.Commerce clearinghouse, 130,000 seats worth $5 million are sold over the Internet.

The stakes are upped by the World Wide Web. This is the first Olympics that connects the world via computer and modem. While some of us are asleep, users from Sri Lanka to Sarajevo will log on to IBM's Web site to seek the results of sporting events, order souvenirs, or to send e-mail to their favorite athletes.

We have indeed traveled some distance in Olympic technology. All this was unthinkable in 1960 at the Winter Games in Squaw Valley, when data management was a far simpler task. Computers were less powerful and did a lot less, of course. Also, there were fewer events, and a state-of-the-art IBM mainframe handled most of the basic computational chores. Back then, Walter Cronkite marveled at IBM's ingenuity, programming, and planning. IBM also had implemented the technology for the 1994 Winter Games in Lillehammer, but that was merely a warm-up for Atlanta.

Almost all the information related to the Games is routed through this central control floor. The technology is complex, intimidating. It's as if IBM rebuilt the glass house. All those monitors—banks of screens, actually—sheer computing muscle. This is Big Blue in its 1990s glory, all squared at the corners, behind the scenes with seamless solutions. There are herds of techno-wonks with their minds on the mission, and some of them actually know how it all links together. Though this site does not house all the gear, it includes two WANs (Wide Area Networks), two hundred and fifty LANs, four System/390 mainframes, eighty AS/400 midrange machines, another thirty RS/6000s, and about seven thousand assorted PCs and ThinkPads. It's a a virtual flotilla of technology. There are another eighteen hundred touch-screen terminals and electronic kiosks throughout the Olympic Village that will transmit news and results worldwide in French and English.

In addition to the command center in Atlanta, IBM also is plugging in large systems at six locations around the world to handle the anticipated record traffic on its Web pages. The added sites are designed to accommodate as many as ten thousand hits *per minute* from Internet users. A young IBM research team manager from the Yorktown Heights labs, Scott Penberthy, has spearheaded the development of a unique software management tool, the "Web Object Manager," or WOM, which administers and integrates thousands of templates, graphics, data objects, and Java applets (mini-applications written in the Java programming language). This allows for updates to Web pages without downtime as the Games go on. Penberthy has a terrific dog-and-pony show where he enthusiastically explains how it works, and everyone marvels when he's through with the last slide. But nobody really understands it. Even Bob Stephenson, a guy who thrives on the mysteries of math and programming, looks perplexed when he is given a one-on-one spiel.

IBM has spared nothing. Its Olympic technology represents "bulletproof reliability" with "failover" capability, the same commitment it makes for its largest corporate customers. This means if a server goes down or is overloaded, you won't even know it. At trade shows, IBM intentionally crashed a server during a demo, and the backups kept everything online. The data kept flowing so smoothly that nobody even knew. So, if a server collapses while you're touring the virtual Olympic villages, you'll be routed through another part of the planet. Web denizens will take for granted IBM's network, as it does the telephone system. They just assume it will work.

Still, with a system like this, glitches are likely to slip in, and when a number of small things go awry and multiply unchecked, major problems can occur. The trick is to root out the smallest bugs and eliminate them before they slip into another system and infect some other application. No other company understands this better than IBM. And nobody understands this basic daisy chain of failure more than Gerstner. Before the annual shareholders meeting in Atlanta in April, David Kalis excised all the references to the company's role in the upcoming summer Olympics. In his view, the downside was far greater than the upside. If everything went right, the news story would be a yawner. IBM was expected to deliver.

Although Gerstner avoided the topic in his opening adress, however, it came up later during the Q&A part of the program. When the CEO was asked about IBM's involvement in the Games, Gerstner cautiously replied, "Half the world's population will be watching. We both have a lot on the line. It's a chance for your city and our company to show their very best. . . . I don't need to tell you there's an element of risk in stepping onto a very visible world stage." *Datamation,* a trade publication, was more to the point: "Depending on whether Big Blue scores a perfect 10 or flops with a 1, it will be either a public relations coup or an international embarrassment." And a spokesman for the Games, Scott Mall, added, "There's no room for error. If their system fails, it'll be like being undressed in front of the whole world."

The executive in charge of IBM's Olympic effort is Dennie Welsh, the senior vice president of the Global Services division, now Gerstner's most successful business unit. Welsh, fifty-three, commands ninety thousand IBMers, some forty percent of the workforce. Welsh, along with Sam Palmisano, first built the company's services business from nothing into a thriving revenue stream. A Tennessee-born engineer, Welsh came from a small town and played high school football. He joined the Army after earning a degree, and then IBM hired him to help NASA design space capsules during the Apollo program. As one of Gerstner's key executives, Welsh understood the technical nuances and challenges of large IT installations at Fortune 500 companies. Nobody at IBM was better at big systems integration than Welsh. With that Southern drawl of his, he exuded astronaut-like confidence.

IBM's Olympic investment in technology was at least $40 million, but much higher when you add in the accompanying expenses (housing, entertaining customers, and so on). Insiders within the company put the final figure at close to $300 million. It was a significant enough expense for Gerstner to highlight at a subsequent quarterly meeting. It had an adverse affect on the company's earnings. Despite the hefty price tag, this was a good investment. IBM's contract effectively shut out other vendors, including Hewlett-Packard and Microsoft. And as a primary sponsor, Big Blue saved some money. The Olympic organizers waived IBM's sponsorship fee in return for providing complete technology support for the Games. IBM paid only for advertising and air time.

The summer Olympics is a marquee event anywhere in the world, but because the centennial Games are held in the United States, the attention is even greater. IBM's publicity is impossible to calculate in pure cash terms. Customer goodwill is another immeasurable by-product. Of all the world's companies showcased at the Games, IBM will occupy the spotlight.

As expected, IBM takes advantage of every publicity opportunity. Senior executives are encouraged to carry the Olympic torch. A Winnebago that showcases the technology is parked outside the New York Stock Exchange. Well before the Games begin, an Executive Briefing Center is set up in Atlanta. Customers and dignitaries are invited for VIP tours, and IBMers painstakingly explain how every crouton of information will be created, entered into a computer, transmitted, and consumed by voracious fans the world over.

In retrospect, with such an immense buildup, with so many cautious comments and advance warnings, it will be a small miracle for

IBM to achieve an error-free operation. And not long after the opening ceremonies, there are portents of Lou Gerstner's worst fears. Reports begin to trickle onto the TV networks and in the sports pages of daily newspapers.

It is as if the ghost of bad luck has paid a sales call on Big Blue. Perhaps unfairly, IBM is immediately called to task for a series of nonfatal screwups that result from data entry mistakes and minor programming faults. A twenty-one-year-old athlete suddenly ages seventy-six years, a German medalist switches nationalities to Ghana. A polo score is either 12 to 7 or 11 to 8, according to one confused printout. Beach volleyball is different from conventional volleyball, but nobody bothers to inform IBM's computers. Some of these mistakes are almost comical and do not threaten anyone's enjoyment of the events. Many aren't even Big Blue's fault. They're caused by volunteers doing data entry.

Individually, these gaffes might have gone unnoticed. Yet the one critical area where IBM cannot afford miscues is in the information stream that constantly feeds the fifteen thousand journalists covering the games. The World News Press Agency system, called "WONPA," is the clearinghouse for results. And there are significant software problems with WONPA right from the first day of competition. The necessary information just isn't flowing. Server traffic is not managed properly; system clogs are commonplace. The sportswriters are in a panic. Event results begin moving by hand, on paper. Worse, the more problems they uncover, the more they complain about them to their readers and viewers. IBM's systems are completely useless, some of them write. The situation is rapidly escalating into a public relations crisis.

After being confronted by frustrated, angry journalists, Fred McNeese, the senior IBM public relations manager at the scene, finally calls Armonk for reinforcements. A high-level manager who takes the call is first unconcerned. McNeese is telling him he has a four-alarm fire. The scene is a mess, results reporting is out of control. McNeese is frequently given to hyperbole, so it cannot be as bad as he claims. But the manager and a colleague immediately fly down to Atlanta anyway. When they reach the IBM command center, they discover that McNeese has not been exaggerating. They find a floor of computers, and the screens are either blank or full of gibberish. "It was an amazing scene," says the IBM manager. "We screwed things up royally. We coped with some of it and threw more programmers at the problem, but even working around the clock, sleeping on cots, they couldn't get it fixed in time. I mean, sixteen days." They were still working on the problems during the closing ceremonies. Somebody had to tell them, It's enough, it's all right now. You can stop.

By now, a good part of the free world has seen IBM undressed. It is particularly embarrassing because this has turned into one of the largest customer events Big Blue ever conceived. The fleet of Falcon 2000s has been operating a shuttle service, flying VIP customers between Armonk and Atlanta, throwing lavish buffets and providing them great seats for the Games. IBM has commandeered the Swissôtel, a luxury hotel in the fashionable Buckhead section of town. Here, IBM executives entertain their most important guests, and in the dining room they punch their dinner orders into computers using touch screens at the tables. IBMers even set up video cameras to project images of visitors on giant screens. Then they digitize them, and place them into a movie scene of their choice. It is an amusing idea, and even Gerstner reportedly succumbs to the gimmick. The whole town is gaga over IBM's Olympic technology.

But when the CEO flies back to Armonk and hears about IBM's problems on the six o'clock news, his mood sours. The embarrassment is considerable, and he is angry. In fact, IBM sources say he goes ballistic and tells Dennie Welsh it is *his* responsibility to fix the problems. Welsh is the senior executive now in the forefront; anything else that goes wrong is his fault. Gerstner wants nothing to do with the mess, and David Kalis bunkers him in his office. The CEO's name is barely mentioned in any of the negative news stories.

Meanwhile, damage control to IBM's image continues apace. Gerstner confers with Abby Kohnstamm. Kohnstamm calls for overnight research from focus groups convened in key countries, seriously contemplating a response campaign where IBM can apologize and explain the problems. The feedback is more positive than she anticipates, however. Most viewers receive their Olympic news from TV; a majority of the respondents have a "positive" impression of IBM's technology. Some people haven't heard anything at all about IBM's problems (they are probably not even casual sports fans). Also, there is a general feeling that ads calling attention to the debacle can only make things worse. Already in the defensive mode, IBM does not want to be accused of bad taste, especially after the bombing that occurred in Centennial Park.

After Bob Stephenson, the Personal Systems Group head, returns from the Games, he is in the elevator in Somers, scanning the news clips. He stares at one headline: "IBM: Web site wins gold." Nearly 100 million visits were tallied. He asks nobody in particular whether this headline is true, whether the company was, in fact, that successful. Nobody riding with him says anything. Later, an aide reminds Stephenson that in some cases there are problems that were far worse than anyone but a few IBMers knew. For example, IBM had not anticipated the magnitude of Web traffic during peak periods. Many sites suffered from overload, including the FanMail program, which was impossible to access for most of the two weeks. Here, at least, IBM is a victim of Olympic popularity. This was a system that could not entirely be tested in vivo, and there were situations that were difficult or impossible to simulate in advance of the Games. (On the other hand, faulty IBM security systems were blamed by one newspaper for contributing to the bombing. This was untrue.)

In Gerstner's view, the mistakes that mushroomed into a PR meltdown should have been anticipated and expected. His disappointment and fury emanated from two fronts. First, he had been humiliated among his peers, other CEOs, and this was obviously painful. IBM had promised in its ads that its systems provided "bulletproof" reliability, and it had been anything but that. So Gerstner had to have winced when *Fortune* magazine reported, "If self-parody were an Olympic sport, IBM would have medaled." Second, perhaps more important, he analyzed the event from the purely intellectual and pragmatic aspects of business. In this, his view of the events from forty thousand feet was clearer than everyone else's. Gerstner had correctly surmised that IBM had made its most grievous errors many months, even *years,* before the midsummer of 1996. There was a gross breakdown in both basic strategy and the reporting chain. IBM had simply been the victim of its own "very bad technical planning," said one corporate manager. From a management point of view, Gerstner trusted Welsh, and Welsh empowered two or three levels of executives below him to ensure that work proceeded properly and on time. There was a breakdown somewhere in the matrix. The technology worked well only as an intranet, an internal network. IBM had tested it and retested all the parts in it, and of course it functioned perfectly. Taken outside the walls of IBM, however, it behaved far differently. Despite all of IBM's state-of-the-art machinery, the system "fundamentally didn't work," a vice president said.

Imagine a custom-built, very expensive automobile. It starts up and works perfectly in the garage, maybe around the neighborhood streets. But it doesn't function once it gets out on the highway, where the engine and the transmission are taxed and tested. "We never ever asked those guys down in Atlanta, the NBCs, the APs, what they wanted format-wise," the corporate manager said. "We never asked NBC, are you having a live feed on this event? Or with AP, how do you want the stuff, in agate type, in columns, or what? We never in the planning stages approached them and asked them what they were using, or what they wanted. And they were our customers. It was the old IBM saying, 'Here, we'll give you this.'"

Gerstner's two most important business maxims are to find out precisely what the customer wants and then deliver the same. He had been pounding the divisions for three years about this. IBM did neither. Gerstner had always cautioned his workforce to underpromise and overdeliver. Here, it did the opposite.

Those who know Gerstner say these are not mistakes IBM was likely to repeat, at least on his watch. Two years later, IBM's technology worked nearly flawlessly at the 1998 Nagano Winter Olympics. For those Games, IBM was so confident that it mailed out a glossy catalogue hawking pins, caps, coffee mugs, watches, and wallets. And it made certain that the company logo appeared below the five Olympic rings on nearly every product. Later that year though, IBM announced that it was giving up its technology sponsorship of the Games after 2002. Gerstner felt that the investment ultimately wasn't providing enough returns.

Anxious to recover from the publicity disaster of the Atlanta Olympics, IBM turns to its research labs and rolls out the heaviest chess player that had ever pushed a pawn. It is called Deep Blue, and it is a publicist's dream. It is only a machine, and people either love or hate what it represents, but they cannot stop talking about it. Unless Deep Blue crashes, IBM can achieve a public relations coup that will erase the sorry memories of Atlanta. Even if the computer loses, the sheaf of news clippings and network news tapes will be a terrific consolation prize.

In May 1997, a pair of souped-up RISC System/6000 SP computers, weighing in at 2,800 pounds, is dispatched to the thirty-fifth floor of the Equitable Center in New York City to oppose the reigning world champion, Garry Kasparov. The colorful thirty-four-year-old Russian is the highest-rated grand master, and perhaps the greatest who ever played the game. He has held the world title for twelve consecutive years. Kasparov is an ideal opponent, a media chess darling. He has an acceptably crabby personality. He's more socially reliable than the reclusive Bobby Fischer. He craves public attention and fat appearance fees, and he is no stranger to the PR gimmickry behind computer chess. He had beaten a predecessor of Deep Blue, called Deep Thought, back in 1989. The machines got a lot better in the next decade. In 1996, an earlier version of Deep Blue (slightly less powerful than this one) had squared off with him in Philadelphia, at a historic meeting of the Association of Computing Machinery's fiftieth anniversary celebration of the invention of ENIAC. Kasparov easily won that event, but the earlier version of Deep Blue drew human blood. It managed to eke out a win.

Computer chess has a long, fascinating history. Technology and chess are a natural combination, attracting similar quirky, somewhat geeky personalities, those who love gamesmanship, numbers, and computer programming. Alan Turing, the renowned British mathematician, developed a chess algorithm in 1948. It wasn't very good, however, and when he tested it against an amateur, it was beaten rather handily. But the technology progressed steadily, and for many years computer experts had been predicting that at some point a sophisticated program coupled with a powerful group of processors would eventually dethrone a world champion. Few, however, thought this would happen before the turn of the century.

For several years, the hothouse of computer chess research was at Carnegie-Mellon University in Pittsburgh. But IBM hired away several members of its team, and it worked diligently to build the state-of-the-art chess-playing machine. The Deep Blue project leader, a professorial-looking man named Dr. Chun-Jeng Tan, confidently predicted that the computer would prevail. This was standard prematch braggadocio, however, as harmless as Muhammad Ali building the gate for a heavyweight title bout. A year earlier, Tan had made the same boast and lost.

The rematch has captured the public's attention, and even Jay Leno and David Letterman crack jokes about it. IBM has put up $1.1 million in prize money, with the winner's share $700,000 and $400,000 going to the loser. Since IBM wasn't clear how it was distributing its share of the purse to itself, this is the company's way of saying that it is still a fun contest. In essence, it is simply paying Kasparov appearance money on an incentive basis for an exhibition match. Kasparov's contract also shrewdly has ensured that he is a partner with the ancillary media rights and related products sold by IBM.

The debate among chess and computer mavens is high-minded and spirited, of course, because it conjures up the age-old question about man versus machine. In a prematch cover story, *Newsweek* dubbed it "The Brain's Last Stand." Artificial intelligence, or AI, the concept of "thinking machines," and computer programs that can "learn" from their mistakes are normally the focal point of this debate. But IBM programmers insist that a chess-playing computer—at least this one—is less reliant on AI, which has taken on more of a philosophical rather than mathematical bent in recent years. The concept of a "thinking machine" that can learn from its mistakes has become a scientific subdiscipline with an ample number of supporters and detractors.

Deep Blue has more to do with standard "brute-force" programming. There is nothing intellectual about this style of computer chess. Brute-force programming is mainly related to processing speed and power. It concentrates on four basic areas—piece value, board position, king safety, and game tempo—and assigns numerical valuations to each. Deep Blue's 512 processors can analyze 200 million moves per second, twice the number in the computer Kasparov has previously beaten. The human brain can only "tree search" so fast. Kasparov, it is said, typically considers only two moves per second.

"This match is a demonstration that intelligence is not the only way to win at chess," remarked David Gelernter, the Yale art historian and computer scientist, after the first showdown between the two. "Brute force is dirt cheap, compared to human intelligence." As a custom device built specifically to do one thing, Deep Blue is a marvel in design, truly a supercomputer. IBM hopes its power and potential will compare favorably with other supercomputers from Cray and Fujitsu.

Tan's team has hired Joel Benjamin, a grand master and former U.S. chess champion, to help program Deep Blue. Yet it isn't until the match ends that IBM discloses it had used at least two other chess consultants in prepping the computer. Kasparov has an entourage of talented chess advisors as well, so this isn't exactly a stunning admission. But it opens the door to making a strong case that this is nearly a team match among some of the world's top chess players. Purists can argue that the computer's presence is almost incidental. But Kasparov immediately dispels the idea that the match is about anything else but man against a couple of sophisticated metal boxes, two black, six-and-a-half-foot-tall monoliths.

Deep Blue is cold and unfeeling, but it is charming to speculate that a computer has assumed the personality of those who had lovingly taught it to play chess. When Tan and his cohorts assimilate the "we" in discussing the contest, they include Deep Blue. The world champion, on the other hand, is given over to incredible mood swings and emotional outbursts. In other words, he behaves like a talented chess champion. Chess is nothing if not intensely psychological, and in warfare of this nature, at this level, man can quickly find himself at a disadvantage. As long as the air-conditioning is working properly, Deep Blue does not break out in a cold sweat.

Kasparov wins the opening game, but fate intervenes. Kasparov appears to be flustered in the second game, and then he astonishes analysts and grandmasters by resigning in a board position where any highly accomplished player easily could have forced a draw. This blunder, according to some, is the beginning of the end.

Meanwhile, Big Blue now has managed to firmly grab the world's attention. Some twenty-two million chess fans log on to IBM's Deep Blue Web site during game three. When the match is tied at 2 to 2, Gerstner makes an appearance. Perhaps sensing victory, the CEO cannot restrain himself. He says, only partly in jest, "I think we should look at this as a chess match between the world's greatest chess player and Garry Kasparov."

One has to admire the buildup of intrigue. The event has both sides flinging accusations at each other. Kasparov's camp all but accuses IBM of cheating. It is reported that the IBM team has said it has the ability to tweak the program between games to adjust to Kasparov's strategy. So Kasparov naturally asks if he can examine the printouts that determine the computer's moves. Tan refuses. Are Deep Blue's consultants—all very accomplished grand masters themselves—enhancing the program in between games? If so, what's wrong with that? Doesn't Kasparov consult with his seconds during the course of the match, and aren't those conversations confidential?

Kasparov suddenly decides that the playing conditions favor Deep Blue. It is like a scene out of Frank Baum's fictional Oz; IBM has Kasparov wondering what kind of wizard is lurking behind the curtain. The world champion becomes distracted to the point where he completely loses his concentration. Amazingly, Deep Blue has taken him out of his game. Kasparov, now completely unglued, admits he is "afraid," hardly the kind of reaction one expects from a world champion playing against an inanimate object. He is flirting with disgrace under pressure.

Before game four, Kasparov is so frustrated that he actually quits the match. "He told them, 'I'm not coming back,'" recalls Jeff Kisseloff, a writer hired by IBM to cover the match for its Web site. "And they [IBM] threatened him and screamed at him, and his people threatened him and screamed at him." Kisseloff unearths this fact and many others involving backstage pyrotechnics between the two teams, but they go unreported because Big Blue censors his dispatches (and eventually withdraws his services). Kisseloff concludes that IBM is treating the champion "poorly" and "horribly" and "monkeying with his head." IBM was desperate for a victory, he recalls.

When Deep Blue finally vanquishes an exhausted and bitter Kasparov, the victory delights millions of chess fans, not to mention IBM's image shapers. A photo of Kasparov, his face buried in his hands, runs on page one of the *New York Times*. But IBM's media people, ever so politically correct, are careful to downplay the result. Big Blue is publicly humble, so it sloughs off the postgame analyses about the machine-versus-man confrontation. Rather than simply basking in the headlines, IBM chooses to spin it as an experiment with important future uses.

Gerstner's e-mail to IBMers congratulated the Deep Blue team and thanked Kasparov, who "never considered this match a sideshow," and "took it seriously." The CEO wrote, "As much as I love to win (and I'm glad we did), I don't think the triumph of the match was that Deep Blue won and Garry Kasparov lost." Gerstner's mind already was spinning with ways to adapt Deep Blue to other tasks.

A few weeks after the match, Kasparov wrote a piece in *Time* magazine where he argued that "IBM owes mankind a rematch." He was bowled over by how well the machine played, its ability to exhibit the nuances of a seasoned competitor. He offered no excuses for losing. But he accused IBM of creating, either intentionally or incidentally, a "hostile atmosphere that was very difficult for me to bear."

IBM seriously considered a rematch, and it polled a number of executives, managers, and outside observers for their opinions. David Kalis was in favor of a third showdown. As a dedicated—and now elated—PR man, he believed that the Deep Blue–Kasparov series was akin to a sensational sporting matchup, a classic confrontation. This event had legs. Can you imagine the press IBM will get in the rubber match? It just doesn't get any better.

In the end, Kalis was overruled, however. Big Blue staked out the intellectual high ground by claiming its marvelous computer could do more good in solving mankind's more pressing problems in scientific and medical research. IBM even suggested that Deep Blue could simulate underground nuclear tests, thereby placating the world's most ardent environmentalists.

But those who craved another mano-to-mouse confrontation could not help but think that IBM had simply chickened out.

With David Kalis as the architect, IBM's public relations machinery was as professional as any other in corporate America. In contrast to the arrogance often displayed by previous IBM administrations, many technology reporters felt, the company finally had made an effort to reach out to the press. In the past, IBM never rushed to return journalists' calls. When a press issue appeared before managers, doing nothing was always the preferred mode. Now IBM was proactive.

The chairman's office, however, was another matter completely. Kalis's principal assignment remained protecting Gerstner and fashioning coverage of the executive suite to suit the CEO's and the company's ends. Almost everyone who has worked with Kalis, inside and outside of IBM, has given him high marks during his four years at Big Blue. This is no small accomplishment, given what many business journalists perceived as Gerstner's absolute distrust and general distaste for the press.

So it had to be one of the worst days of his long career with Gerstner when Kalis faced his boss after reading the cover story in *Fortune* magazine dated April 14, 1997. The eleven-page article had a coverline that read, "The Holy Terror Who's Saving IBM." As a business piece, it detailed how Gerstner breathed new life into a dying company. The writer, Betsy Morris, had interviewed dozens of customers, friends, and senior executives at IBM. It was a thorough piece of reporting, and the result was an eminently fair, and for the most part extremely complimentary, assessment of the CEO's many abilities. Even many PR professionals agreed, including some at IBM, who are naturally biased toward the client. IBM shareholders were certainly reassured that the company was in strong, capable hands. (IBM's corporate media relations department, which compiles the clips on a daily basis, put the *Fortune* story on its front page on March 24, 1997. While the department regularly includes noncomplimentary stories about IBM or Gerstner, they're usually relegated to the back pages.)

As a profile, it was slightly tougher. It brought out the gruffer side of Gerstner. He can be rude on the golf course, he is pompous, he is arrogant, and he has an air of royalty about him, the kind that makes certain he has a reserved seat on the corporate jet. Only a few sources contacted during the course of researching this book, all of whom are fairly close to Gerstner, said they felt the story was off the mark. One who knew him well at American Express—but has had little contact with him recently—commented, "That's not Lou."

Gerstner was appalled by what he read about himself. In fact, he was deeply upset. The tip-off to his reaction might have been during an early meeting with Morris when Gerstner warned, "You're not getting inside my head." Though IBM would not comment publicly on the article, sources in Armonk said Gerstner felt betrayed by the magazine's editors, and not for the first time.

At first, *Fortune* had assigned David Kirkpatrick, its technology writer, to research a piece about IBM's PC business. But eventually, the magazine dropped the idea, thinking it was unfair to single out one of the company's struggling business units. There was a bigger and better story in the CEO and the company's eye-opening comeback. Before the research began, there were extensive negotiations and at least two meetings between David Kalis and the magazine's editors. In order to elicit IBM's cooperation and to schedule interviews with Gerstner and other key senior executives, *Fortune* and IBM first had to agree on the writer. Kalis suggested Carol Loomis, a highly respected and well-known business journalist who was friendly with Warren Buffett. This choice surprised the editors because in the past Loomis had been extremely tough on John Akers. In fact, her reporting had helped lead to Akers's removal. Loomis, however, was not interested in the assignment. The editors then suggested Betsy Morris, and after reviewing her work, Kalis consented.

IBM sources claim that *Fortune* had been asked to accede to ground rules that specified not delving into the CEO's intensely guarded private life. Editors there, however, disagree. They contend there was no such deal. They said they would not be preparing a *People* magazine type of piece, but because the focus was on Gerstner, there were standard background and biographical details they would be obliged to report. Gerstner's older brother Dick was quoted in the story, but there was no indication that Morris had interviewed the subject's parents, his children, or any other relatives. Also, the editors say that Morris would have revealed any such restrictions either to her staff or to her readers.

One editor said, "She's Outward Bound, a field hockey player, Stanford, just a Girl Scout, a grown-up Girl Scout, but a tough Girl Scout. She wouldn't break any rule about anything; she's just totally straight." And Morris was scrupulously honest and fair. She had profiled several other CEOs, without repercussions.

In retrospect, it is difficult to ascertain exactly what Morris had written that so angered the CEO. One source said that when Gerstner's wife, Robin, read the piece, she burst into tears. There was a single paragraph about her. Morris wrote, "Robin is the spoonful of sugar that makes his medicine easier to take."

One plausible explanation is this: Sources at both IBM and the magazine speculate that Gerstner's wrath could have been the culmination of what Gerstner considers continuously negative coverage. This idea, however, is hard to accept. Previous articles about Gerstner and IBM were analytical and mildly critical, but again, generally quite laudatory about his performance as an executive and the company's comeback. *Fortune* is usually thorough and tough, but also fair. And there are easier targets than Lou Gerstner. At least one senior executive and confidant of Gerstner felt that he had overreacted.

Even given Gerstner's distaste for the *Fortune* story, had he just let the matter drop, even the half dozen or so negative paragraphs would have had limited impact.

Instead, Gerstner ordered a retaliation on two fronts, both advertising and editorial. First, Abby Kohnstamm was told not to renew any advertising contracts with the magazine. This stung some Lotus executives, who thought it was one of their most important advertising venues. Bill Gates even confided to a *Fortune* editor that the magazine's Lotus coverage had cost him more money than any other single piece of journalism. (Though now, given the negative publicity from the Justice Department antitrust suit, Gates might qualify that statement.) The advertising embargo alone was not much punishment, and it was not unique. Plenty of customers pull their ads after stinging stories. *Fortune* stood to lose about $6 million a year without IBM's and Lotus's ads.

Gerstner also sent word through Kalis that until further notice, IBMers were no longer allowed to return phone calls from anyone at *Fortune*. The penalty for violating the embargo was loss of badge. The same order was given to the entire staff of IBM's ad agency, Ogilvy and Mather. This amused some Ogilvy staffers, who wondered what their connection to this brouhaha was about. Only Shelly Lazarus was quoted in the *Fortune* piece, and she did not say anything remotely uncomplimentary or controversial.

The impact of Gerstner's retaliation was not widespread, at least at first. Gerstner's anger and vindictiveness were still largely a private affair. Despite several attempts at a rapprochement, the magazine's editors and writers were now persona non grata at IBM. The Time Warner empire, which publishes *Fortune*, and IBM did upward of $100 million worth of business with each other. They were each other's customers on dozens of deals. This was one reason why both IBM and *Fortune* did not want to see the imbroglio go any further.

But the contretemps took on a far greater import when the *New York Times* published a story on the front page of its business section about advertisers' increasing propensity to retaliate over aggressive reporting. The lead example was Gerstner and *Fortune*. Now far many more were aware of IBM's thin-skinned CEO, including those who had never read the supposedly offending article. *Fortune*'s advertising agency did not help matters when it ran a full-page ad in the *Times* heralding John Huey's award as *AdWeek*'s "Editor of the Year" for 1997. Smack in the middle of the page, in a huge medieval typeface, it boasted that Huey called Gerstner a "Holy Terror." By the end of December 1997, the CEO's low regard for the press was solidified in the *Times*. In its annual "Financial Follies" roundup, the editors cited the *Fortune* affair and gave Gerstner the "Henry VIII Award for Dealing with Critics."

Gerstner's hatred for *Fortune* continued into the following year, manifesting itself in ways that exasperated and perplexed IBM managers. The CEO was scheduled to give the keynote at the 1998 PC Expo, held annually at the Javits Center in New York. It was one of the most important industry trade shows of the year. A month before his appearance, he abruptly canceled, citing a scheduling conflict. The truth required a longer explanation. When he learned that *Fortune* was sponsoring his address, he refused to appear unless the magazine's banner was removed from the meeting hall. The show's organizers first tried to placate IBM and void their contract with *Fortune,* but the magazine refused any offer to return the check. As a compromise, the editors replaced Gerstner with Compaq's CEO, Eckhard Pfeiffer. A staunch IBM competitor, Pfeiffer was happy to oblige.

The affair has mushroomed to a point where IBMers are not only embarrassed, they are frustrated because this kind of petty, intractable stance already has cost the company a considerable amount of goodwill, and perhaps business as well. In a sarcastic piece about Gerstner's behavior, Ziff-Davis's online publication ZDNet summed up the situation with a headline that read, "Lou Gerstner, Grow Up!"

It isn't exactly a grudge match, but in September 1997, New York Governor George Pataki challenges "Junior," a scaled-down version of Deep Blue. After nine moves, he wisely decides to retire while "holding my own." It's an overly optimistic assessment of the board, however. Murray Campbell, one of the Deep Blue researchers who programmed the supercomputer that beat Kasparov, does not want to embarrass him, but the governor's game clearly is not in Junior's league.

Pataki has joined Gerstner in the lobby of IBM's new headquarters in the ribbon-cutting dedication ceremony. When Pataki defeated Mario Cuomo in the 1994 election, he made a call to Gerstner to assure him that his administration would be user-friendly to business. The new governor was concerned that IBM might abandon New York and take tens of thousands of jobs with it (an oblique reference to defections that occurred under Cuomo's administration). Local officials, too, had been worried that IBM, one of Westchester's largest taxpayers, might relocate to New York City where it once had its worldwide headquarters.

Negotiating against these fears, Gerstner was able to extract large incentives before IBM broke ground for a new headquarters building in Westchester. The company was allowed $30 million in tax abatements and other infrastructure subsidies. To further sweeten the deal, the state spent $13 million to buy 1.3 million square feet of vacant IBM buildings in Kingston and Endicott. In return, IBM gave the town of North Castle a twenty-three-acre recreational facility. The deal with the state subsidized the $75 million outlay for the new building. (IBM might have done even better had they found a buyer for the old site, but no company was interested, and it was finally taken off the market.)

The new high-tech design, hidden in the woods only a mile from its old site in Armonk, had been in the works for two years when it was finally opened in the late summer of 1997. The gun-metal-gray Z-shaped building is elegant and functional with a special foundation built into the natural stone of the landscape.

If anything, the new building reflects the direction in which IBM is now headed, as well as the CEO's style. Gerstner, who reportedly helped with the design, wanted it to make a bold statement, and it certainly does. Gone is the stodgy, institutional feel of One Old Orchard Road. Old Orchard stood on a flattened hilltop, isolated, nondescript, a three-story box resembling a government building. One New Orchard almost blends into the wilderness. It has dark green granite floors, a copper leaf ceiling, loads of glass and stainless steel, and wooden doors that seem to disappear in the walls. There's a mile-long jogging path as well, but you rarely see anyone on it. The new headquarters was reviewed by architecture critics. One from *New York* magazine raved about the design: "It's Silicon Valley come to Armonk. . . . It says viscerally . . . that corporations have to be lean, fast, and mutable." Employees who are lucky enough to have a view can stare into the woods and imagine they are working in Santa Clara or Cupertino.

In sum, the new headquarters reflects all of the contradictions and small hypocrisies of the chairman's often enigmatic personality. It was intentionally downsized to 283,500 square feet, more than thirty percent smaller than the old building. The new IBM is functioning in a leaner, nimbler fashion, and the physical plant must echo this as well. Built to house six hundred employees, it left two hundred from Old Orchard to find office space elsewhere. The head librarian was forced to deaccession hundreds of books when she moved to far smaller quarters. The new split-level cafeteria is cramped, but at least the dining area is wired for laptops to accommodate the absolutely compulsive. And there are far more cubicles than enclosed offices, ostensibly to promote open exchange among workers. Gerstner doesn't want the corporate staff to become too comfortable; it might encourage complacence. But several employees groused about work space demotions, even though the cubicles are constructed of expensive blond mahogany and the chairs are designed to state-of-the-art ergonomic standards. The bathrooms would not be called spacious. There is also a gym, which Gerstner frequents regularly, and he is known to become agitated if someone dawdles on an exercise machine he's waiting to use.

The building is undersized, but Gerstner's office complex, which includes a private bathroom and shower, is not. Instead of being bunkered near the end of a long corridor as it was in the old building, it is on the top floor in the center slab of the Z. Putting the CEO in the middle allows him easy access for impromptu meetings with senior executives.

Except for the ancient electronic integrators and calculators—ghosts of IBM past, and favorite Gerstner artifacts—which are displayed like museum pieces in the hallways, the building is a paean to high technology. There is barely a need for a receptionist; visitors sign in on a ThinkPad. Conference rooms are equipped with electronic whiteboards where IBMers can store, erase, and recall their doodles, and even share them with colleagues at other company sites. Offices are wired for high-speed Internet feeds and videoconferencing. "I wanted this building to be a living example of the strategy of the company, which is built around network computing," Gerstner said.

It is, as a *New York Times* headline proclaimed, the "House That Lou Built."

14

Leadership—At Home and Abroad

he trees are beginning to bloom at IBM's Executive Conference Center, the sprawling facility just off the west bank of the Hudson River a few miles north of New York City. If *Better Homes and Gardens* ever had a special issue for corporate design and interiors, the Palisades Center easily would be a cover candidate. Beautifully landscaped with specimen trees and sculpted cedar columns, it has a serene, understated elegance, like a Japanese garden. Had there been a religious shrine on the property, a visitor might think he or she was in the Far East. When spring comes, it feels like an ideal spot to meditate. Inside, there are reminders of once-unlimited decorating budgets: extra-long conference tables with inlaid tiger maple, birch paneling, marble stairwells, and the obligatory oil portraits of the company's founders. Upstairs, there are small bedrooms for overnight stays, and several meeting rooms. In many ways the Palisades is a throwback to Big Blue's glory years.

Secret Service agents are strolling the property, and occasionally they acknowledge some of the dozen or so landscapers and groundskeepers who keep the vast lawns meticulously manicured. Before the President's arrival, every last visible patch of dirt is filled with fresh sod.

Lou Gerstner, along with Wisconsin Governor Tommy Thompson, is the host of this event, the National Education Summit. The mission is to assemble the nation's governors, each of whom will bring one private sector representative from his or her home state. Normally, it might have been just another gathering to discuss the demerits of academia. But it is a high-profile event because President Clinton is the keynote speaker. In all, forty governors and forty-nine corporate executives are at this two-day conference. Another thirty-five school superintendents, teachers, and parents are on the guest list as "limited" participants.

Though technology is not the raison d'être for this assembly, IBM sees the occasion as an opportunity to showcase its wares. Event organizers take advantage of the expansive hallways to demo IBM's latest computers. There are a slew of IBMers who are eager to log visitors on to the site's home page.

This is understandable. Big Blue's reputation in the classroom ranges from wanting to worse. Educators have spurned its PCs for years mainly because they could not afford them. And Gerstner watched IBM continue to stumble in the education market during his first days as CEO. Before his arrival, IBM had formed a business unit to sell Eduquest, a PC brand targeted specifically to schools. The IBM PC Company, however, demanded a royalty from the Eduquest division for using the IBM logo. (It was a typical sell-to-itself scheme.) But in order to save licensing fees, Eduquest spurned the deal, and the company trademark never appeared on the product. (It was also a typical internecine snub.) Gerstner immediately scrapped both the computer and the business unit.

When Gil Amelio, CEO of Apple, heard about the Education Summit, he decided he had to be there. Despite flagging profits and revenues, Apple is still the leading brand in the classroom. It achieved its dominance through ease of use, discounting, and sensible marketing. Amelio wasn't invited by California Governor Pete Wilson, but he finally wangled a badge from the South Dakota governor (who for some reason does not bring Gateway's founder, Ted Waite). At the conference, when Amelio hears about IBM's technology display, he politely complains. Shouldn't Apple get the same opportunity to show off its Macintoshes? He argues that if only IBM is represented, it will appear as though Gerstner is simply commercializing the event for his own interest. This isn't in the spirit of the conference. The appeal works, but the planners allow Apple only about a tenth of the exhibition space that IBM takes up. Apple wisely recruits kids from Tennessee and New Jersey inner-city schools to run its machines, a stark contrast to IBM's buttoned-down marketing and sales reps.

Gerstner opens the conference and asks, "What do we want to accomplish at this meeting? Well, let me tell you it's not thinking up more ideas for changing schools. Over the last twenty-five years, there has been no shortage of ideas. And some of them are probably pretty darned good ones: longer school days, school choice, charter schools, competency exams for teachers."

President Clinton says in his remarks, "Here in 1996 you are saying that you can have all the goals in the world, but unless somebody has meaningful standards and a system where you meet the standards, you won't achieve the goals." Well briefed, the President is in sync with Gerstner's thesis.

The conference is top-heavy with dignitaries—there are captains of industry from all over the United States—but Amelio works the other end of the crowd. He isn't surprised to learn the educators are "very turned off by the pomp and circumstance of the whole event." The conference is a bit stuffy, formal, limned with rhetoric and speeches. The governors' positions are lofty and predictable: The schools are failing; we need to raise the academic bar considerably if the United States is to compete with Germany, Japan, and other nations with high-achieving children. An education summit is important, the educators concede, and it's even an important political statement. But as bystanders, they are not included in key deliberations and discussions. As second-class attendees, it is not very productive for them. We already know what's wrong with public education, they say. You've got to get the pontificators to act.

279

By the end, the National Governors' Association executive committee has adopted a resolution to create a nongovernment organization to serve as a clearinghouse for standards information, performance benchmarks, and public reporting.

It will take several years to find out whether Clinton's belief that the event was indeed "historical," and whether Gerstner's passion for accountability in grades K–12, become a reality. Chances are, however, few people will remember it.

Gerstner's education commitment began in the early 1970s. While at American Express, he had been encouraged to latch on to a pro bono cause, and he chose the schools. It was a good choice, and it consumes much of his limited free time. While he was at AmEx, his son graduated from high school, and Gerstner was asked to give the commencement speech. His staff spent weeks preparing, according to former AmEx spokesman Harry Freeman. "Gerstner said, 'I want to give the greatest speech ever heard at a high school commencement, and I want to talk about education,'" Freeman recalls. Gerstner also is one of four coauthors (along with Roger D. Semerad, Denis Philip Doyle, and William B. Johnston) of a 1994 book, *Reinventing Education: Entrepreneurship in America's Public Schools.*

In it he explains that his "interest in education reform is not just philanthropic: it is fueled by intense anger, and frustration as well."

He does not hold exactly the same view of private institutions of higher learning, however. Another dimension of the IBM CEO's intense anger and frustration was manifested when he agreed to make a speech to a large group of college presidents in Chantilly, Virginia, near the end of his first year at IBM. On the way to the hotel ballroom, he complained bitterly that it was a speech he felt forced into. The universities were in the habit of holding up IBM to donate computers, or sell them at significant discounts, and of course, this coerced philanthropy cost Gerstner's company millions of dollars. (This may help to explain why his alma mater, Dartmouth, is an "Apple campus.")

At the time, IBM was finishing its worst year ever, so it was perhaps understandable that he was in a foul mood.

When he stepped up to the podium, he never delivered anything close to the prepared text. Gerstner admitted that he did not know much about the business of higher education. His area of special concern was K-12. He was certain of one thing, however. "When it comes to grades, we [meaning corporate America] get a D, but you get an F," he said. Gerstner thought he was self-effacing in a generic way, but he apparently forgot that college presidents were IBM customers, or potential ones. He insulted most of the audience. His insensitivity shocked some. Later, when he realized that he had bombed, he ordered tapes of the speech destroyed.

He was far more confident and in control when he spoke about the public schools.

Fourteen months after the President's visit, Gerstner is again at the Palisades. Again, the subject is leadership, but this is not a public event in any way. In fact, it is a highly elite meeting. It is May 1997, time for the annual senior managers meeting, also known as "Lou's Show," and it is the single most important—and exclusive—internal company gathering of the year. It is a traditional no-frills retreat and quasi–pep rally, and top managers from all over the world flock to IBM's Palisades Executive Conference Center to take stock of themselves, their company, their challenges, and their goals.

A wisp of a breeze comes off the cliffs of the Hudson River, and as the late-afternoon sun winks through the oaks on a warm spring day, Gerstner moves easily among the crowd of 295 IBM executives. It is a very homogeneous group. Most of the attendees look as if they could be in today's IBM print commercials. They're wearing pastel Ralph Lauren Polo dress shirts, button-down with open collars, slacks, and sport jackets. The typical executive is male, approximately forty-eight years old, and has an average of twenty-one years with IBM. Only twenty-nine women are included; Gerstner admits this isn't nearly enough. It is an intriguing revelation. While IBM has one of the best records of any major corporation in recruiting the disabled, it is also woefully backward in promoting women in the executive ranks.

On this occasion, the chairman of what is now the sixth-largest U.S. corporation has to be feeling especially pleased. Earlier in the day, he sent an e-mail to his entire workforce of 242,000. The subject: "Stock Milestone." The company's share price reached an all-time intraday high of $177 1/8 on May 13, surpassing the previous record made nearly a decade ago. The message was terse and typically Gerstner: "The next milestone I am looking forward to very much is just ahead when the total number of IBM employees will be larger than when we began building the new IBM in 1993." Then he wrote, "Thank you. Take a bow. You've earned it. And, of course, I can't resist: Let's all get right back to work because we've just begun!"

Gerstner has been with customers all day, so he seems over-dressed in a gray business suit for an informal opening-night barbecue and buffet. He is one of the few in the "business casual" crowd wearing a tie. He makes his way over to the food tent, fills his plate with chicken and a couple of spoonfuls of salad, grabs a bottle of beer, and crosses the lawn toward the dining room. On the way, he approaches several IBMers, and after a warm greeting, he asks, "How's your business?"

This is his fourth senior managers meeting, and aside from the excellent news he is savoring about the company's stock price, this gathering is different from the previous three. In the past, the meeting was twice as large, some six hundred managers worldwide. This year, the human resources staff lopped off half of the lower-level vice presidents, making it a much tougher club to join. Gerstner explains this by saying that leadership was being concentrated into yet a smaller, more rarefied group; but, in fact, the downsizing suggested that he was still mindful of the corporate excess he inherited.

After three years of IBM's recovery and growth, this meeting originally was scheduled for the well-appointed Ritz-Carlton in West Palm Beach. Gerstner decided that it sent the wrong message. Previous senior managers meetings had been held at the serviceable Hilton in Rye, close to corporate headquarters. It has the largest ballroom in the area. This meeting focuses on high-level problem-solving; it is about IBM's constant—and often frustrating—struggle to become nimble and competitive, and not about congratulating one another during lightweight morning meetings. There is no golf on the agenda. No, this is not a traditional "recognition" event. It is a serious search into the upper echelons of the company's soul.

At last year's senior management meeting, Bob Stephenson had issued a grim warning to the group when he said, "When IBM was bleeding red ink just three years ago, our consultant . . . went around asking our competitors what they thought would happen to us. He said, in effect, our competitors were quaking in their boots. They knew with our backs against the wall, we'd reemerge as competitive as ever. And they were right. Recently, he's been asking them the same question. The consensus is this: Now that business is good again, IBM may get fat, dumb, and happy . . . and we're licking our chops, hoping they do." Stephenson's message was to step up the pace: When you're going well, you don't let up. When Stephenson held the lectern, Gerstner had been in the front row, scribbling notes at a furious pace, barely looking up.

Now a year has gone by, and from the tone of his recent all-hands e-mail, Gerstner surely agrees.

On the following morning, at 8:30 Gerstner strides across the Watson Auditorium stage, hands in his pockets, and opens his speech with the following remarks:

"Good morning. Welcome to Palm Beach . . . I mean, Palisades."

There is polite, subdued laughter.

"May fifteenth, 1994. Fifty-eight and a half dollars.

"May fifteenth, 1995. Ninety-five dollars.

"May fifteenth, 1996. One hundred and nine dollars.

"May twelfth, 1997. One hundred seventy-three and a half dollars."

The room erupts with cheers and resounding applause.

No wonder there is so much noise in the room. Gerstner, of course, does not need to tell them what the numbers mean. The stock options among the attending executives are worth $783 million dollars. In just fifteen months, the group has increased its net worth by $500 million. While their compensation varies widely, the average IBM senior manager is $1.69 million richer. Counting all the bonuses from long-term incentive plans, Gerstner says, "We've already got a billion dollars racked up." Personal gain is still a main motivational speaking tool, at least among senior staff. The boss isn't minting millionaires at the pace Bill Gates does, but these results get everyone's attention. Four years ago, their shares were at forty and going nowhere.

When the room quiets down, Gerstner emphasizes the theme of leadership, how leaders are different from managers, and how he needs everyone's best efforts to move forward. He has pressed this leadership string about as far as he can, and now it's up to the others in the room. This is very similar to last year's message, he admits. He finds humor in Japanese management. He mentions a wonderful little brochure published by Toyota that is entitled, "Ten Principles of Leadership." He refers to principle number two, which says that one of the most important functions of a division manager is to improve coordination between his division and other divisions. He quotes, "If you cannot handle this task, please go to work for an American company."

Now he's implying that IBM—and American business—is back, but not yet all the way back. "We needed a group who would stand up and be counted as leaders, who would energize and change the company. In my opinion," he says soberly, "this will be the fundamental determinate of where our 'Reinventing IBM' story goes. Will it end in a ho-hummer? Or will it be spectacular?"

Privately, Gerstner has been concerned. He does not want to see a repeat of the Kodak story. George Fisher stepped into the Rochester firm and had three great years, only to see Fuji brazenly eat its lunch in the international consumer film markets.

A few minutes later, he tempers the room's enthusiasm: "Every day the bar is being raised for IBM. At fifty-eight we could be sloppy. At a hundred and nine, they were still skeptical. At a hundred and seventy-three, there's nowhere to go but leadership. There's nowhere to hide anymore. We've fixed all the big problems." He is pleased with the company's comeback in "customer satisfaction." In 1993, IBM was in ninth place among major vendors. Gerstner was displeased and "very taken by the fact that we were four levels behind Unisys." IBM now has moved up to fifth, though it is still behind Hitachi, Dell, Hewlett-Packard, and Compaq. There is still a lot more to do here. IBM merely has gone from miserable to acceptably competitive.

Gerstner then refers to a special issue of the employee publication, *Think* magazine, now in its second printing, a sixty-six-page tract entitled "One Voice." Nothing like it was ever published and distributed at IBM. Much of the reason for doing such a project was Gerstner's grave concern about IBM's continual tendency for the divisions to remain disconnected. "One Voice" has the tone of IBM's advertising, only it's inner-directed. It was composed in a small format, more like a booklet than a magazine, and it could have been subtitled "Sayings from Chairman Lou." There is a lot of big, boldfaced type:

"In business, as in life, success depends on asking the right questions."

"In this new era, customers want help dealing with complexity."

"Think in big shifts. Then go invent."

The booklet goes on to summarize IBM's strengths, the business opportunities in network computing, the urgency in getting to customers before the competition does, and the need to "think like one team."

Continuing his speech, pacing the stage, Gerstner explains that the challenges are just coming, that IBM is in a big catfight, and that everybody is "in this pool." The pressure is on since IBM began talking about network computing two years before most of its competitors. Gerstner actually confesses that perhaps IBM talked about it because it had nothing else to say. Just a day earlier, Hewlett-Packard and Microsoft nailed down the Barnes and Noble e-commerce business. Also, Microsoft came to New York and announced it was aiming for big customers. The Microserfs called the event "Scalability Day," and it was an attempt to prove to potential clients that it could compete with the big computer makers by installing its NT operating systems. The pitch made an impact within the business and technology community. "Microsoft Aims for Bigger Share of Corporate Computer Sales," read the *New York Times* headline. "Microsoft Begins Push to Show Skeptics PCs Can Handle Biggest Corporate Jobs," said the *Wall Street Journal*. IBM was mentioned prominently as Gates's target in the stories.

Gates hasn't fired a salvo across IBM's bow since Gerstner took command in 1993. Gerstner makes sure that his managers know that Microsoft is trolling for the bigger-ticket "banking and distribution" business, traditional IBM strongholds. He quotes a memo from an IBMer who wrote, "Make no mistake: the folks at Microsoft are aggressive and relentless—not just in recruiting, but in business practices and in their desire to take what we have, our database leadership as a company. The battle lines are drawn and the field is NT. We can and must win this war." Gerstner reminds everyone that just the other night somebody told him: "I'm really pissed that Microsoft's trying to make a mirror IBM." Gerstner obviously is pleased when his senior team gets angry and pumped up.

Then the CEO makes an attempt at warmth, taking a tacky page from the human resources manual. Gerstner winds down by asking his colleagues to turn and shake hands with the person closest to them.

"That's your partner! That's your team!" he exclaims. There is a mawkish moment as IBM's most senior personnel oblige their boss, grin and greet one another. Gerstner is probably the last CEO to embrace all this human resources mush, and they all know it.

Gerstner closes, uncharacteristically, with a literary metaphor. He quotes from Shakespeare's *Julius Caesar*:

THERE IS A TIDE IN THE AFFAIRS OF MEN,
WHICH, TAKEN AT THE FLOOD, LEAD ON TO FORTUNE;
OMITTED, ALL THE VOYAGE OF THEIR LIFE
IS BOUND IN SHALLOWS AND MISERIES.

Gerstner's character imbued the IBM of the 1990s; his impact has been felt in every one of the 160-plus countries where the company sells its technology. And because this is a CEO who revels in staying in close contact with all of his business units, an unfortunate paradox has emerged. From his first days on the job, Gerstner made the courageous decision to centralize what was about to become a splintered corporation. He decided to instill tighter controls—more rigid, in fact, than any of his predecessors, especially the Watsons who, with their laissez-faire management styles, believed in a loose confederation of self-standing international subsidiaries. This confederation worked well for many decades, and contributed large returns to shareholders.

For the first time in its distinguished history, IBM, long venerated for its business propriety, appears to have lost control beyond its American borders. It must be especially dismaying for Gerstner that he stands alone in a line of seven CEOs to endure the embarrassment of three bizarre, politically charged scandals, in Argentina, Mexico, and Russia.

The one that has remained in the news longest first began in 1994 in Buenos Aires, when IBM was awarded a $250 million contract to revamp the computer system of Banco de la Nación, Argentina's largest bank. A $21 million IBM check was paid to a subcontractor for work that apparently was not performed. The money was paid out in bribes, and cash reportedly was laundered through bank deposits in the United States, Switzerland, Luxembourg, and Uruguay. Some twenty former government, banking, and IBM officials in Buenos Aires have been indicted so far. Gerstner fired the twenty-six-year veteran who was IBM's vice president of operations in Argentina, and other company officials were removed or forced into retirement in the United States. The judge, who also serves as prosecutor, even tried to extradite four IBM executives to testify in Buenos Aires, but the company has so far resisted. "I have many suspicions that this was too big a project for IBM in the United States not to have known a great deal about it," Argentinian Judge Adolfo Bagnasco told the Gannett newspaper chain in Westchester County. Company officials in the United States steadfastly denied involvement.

As the case went on, a number of ugly occurrences were reported. An explosive device was left at the door of Judge Bagnasco's home. He was ordered to halt his investigation, or the next time, the caller said, the grenade would be put in his secretary's mouth. A journalist who published a book on the scandal, called *La Nación Robada* (A Nation Robbed) was attacked by a gang who carved the letters "IBM" in his chest. And a bribe suspect in the case hanged himself. The deposed Argentinian IBM vice president wrote his own book about the case, entitled *The Corporation,* claiming he was made the scapegoat by IBM in the United States. Two more books reportedly are in the works.

Robeli Libero, an IBM senior vice president and general manager of Latin America, officially retired in the wake of the scandal. Libero, a Brazilian national, worked in the United States under a foreign visa. A former IBM manager who had worked in IBM's Latin American operations said that he did not believe Libero knew about the bribes. His resignation followed the scandal. "But because it happened on his watch, he had to take the hit," he said.

A similar incident occurred in Latin America within the IBM de Mexico subsidiary. In 1997, IBM received a $27 million contract to install a computer network that was supposed to modernize and streamline the city's vast criminal justice bureaucracy. But when the system didn't work, Mexican officials became suspicious. IBM claimed that there were minor technical flaws. The Mexican district attorney disagreed, and in June 1998 issued arrest warrants for three IBM executives and nineteen former city officials. Kickbacks and bribes were suspected. At the time, IBM was not required to bid on the contract—there was no bidding at all—and it has since reformed its business procedures in its entire Latin American operations. It denied any charges of wrongdoing and settled the case a month later by paying the city $37.5 million in cash and computer products. A Mexican economist told the *New York Times,* "This agreement makes clear that IBM's dealings here were a flop if not completely fraudulent."

The coup de grace in a stream of astounding misdeeds conjured up images of Cold War politics between the United States and Russia. Early in 1997, Russia's nuclear agency, Minatom, reported that it had purchased several powerful computers from American companies. Eventually, it admitted acquiring machines from Silicon Graphics and IBM, including a $7 million RS/6000 SP2. (Russian nuclear weapons experts had actually been invited to IBM's Kingston, New York, facility for demonstrations.) Though U.S. law barred sales of supercomputers to Russia, it was disclosed that IBM sold sixteen more RS/6000s. The computers were manufactured in IBM plants in Europe, were shipped to Amsterdam, and finally made their way to the city of Arzamas-16, some 240 miles east of Russia. Arzamas is highly secret site where nuclear weapons are designed. A Russian computer dealer told the *New York Times,* "IBM was very pushy. They thought Arzamas could be like Los Alamos, a very prestigious customer. That's what this job was all about." After an eighteen-month investigation, IBM was found guilty of illegal sales. It paid the maximum fine, $8.5 million.

The fine hardly mattered. It was the first time IBM had suffered the indignity of a criminal conviction. The last time an RS/6000 had received front-page news was when it defeated Kasparov in a chess match. This was not something Gerstner had in mind when he hoped that the machine could be put to other, more fruitful uses.

Gerstner, knowing that his foreign subsidiaries produce fifty-five percent of IBM's revenues, has traveled hundreds of thousands of miles traversing the globe. Given his propensity to take the pulse of every business throughout his organization, these incidents certainly make one ponder how different the new IBM is from the old. Big Blue has been doing business abroad longer than most American concerns. It has a history of trudging through the backwaters of even the most modest of emerging cultures.

IBM has been contrite about these misdeeds; the company usually takes an unusual degree of pride in holding to high standards of business practices, higher than the law normally requires. And there are these unexplainable lapses, which have to have embarrassed the CEO. Still, Lou Gerstner himself has not publicly acknowledged or apologized for them.

15

Network Computers and
Big Blue's Servers

By the end of 1996, Lou Gerstner was beginning to resemble
a CEO who was blessed. Despite international scandals, the
Olympic PR debacle, hardware units that had relinquished
their leads to competitors, he was doing all right. Better than all
right. Gerstner's three-year record at IBM was enviable by most
financial measures, and it easily exceeded his earlier career tri-
umphs at American Express and RJR Nabisco. And while he had
first cautioned shareholders and observers that the company's
recovery would take a long time, the speed at which he accomplished the feat was clearly remarkable. "Once-ailing computer
giant" was now a recurring phrase in news articles about the
company. His turnaround of Big Blue sanctified his status as a
captain of industry. He and his wife were on the White House
guest list for state dinners, and when he visited the Far East he
met with Chinese President Jiang Zemin. There was nothing
glamorous about his methods, however. Along the way, he made
the cover of *Newsweek* as one of a new breed of "Corporate
Killers." The theme of the article was the downsizing of the
American workforce.

A few cynics were compelled to point out that a large workforce reduction had caused immediate and substantial gains, an
action that makes any CEO look efficient. Still, Gerstner made

money while Akers had lost billions. And one glimpse at the ratio of revenue produced per employee revealed that Gerstner was far more effective than his predecessor. Selective downsizing was, in fact, continuing on an ongoing basis, especially throughout IBM's foreign units. Overall, Gerstner was hiring again, and there were display ads in the classified sections of large-circulation newspapers recruiting for specialized programming and service jobs. In the five-year period from 1994 through 1998, Gerstner actually increased his worldwide payroll by a third, an additional 71,000 employees.

The workforce was rewarded with an eight percent pay raise. The IBM board was far more generous with Gerstner. In 1995, the chairman was paid $4.8 million in salary and bonuses, plus stock options and other incentives that would be worth more than $13 million. Some executive compensation experts raised their eyebrows—one even called his package "enormous" for "an incumbent CEO"—because IBM stock, though now quite healthy, still lagged the S&P 500 index by ten percent. But as long as Gerstner continued to grow the company and return shareholder value, a few minor complaints hardly caused any guilt or anxiety among the directors.

In his 1996 annual meeting with analysts, Gerstner was upbeat about IBM's future. He had just announced the $743 million acquisition of Tivoli Systems in Austin. It did not draw the attention that the Lotus deal had a year earlier, but it was just as significant, if not more so. Tivoli, which had been founded by ex-IBMers, filled a niche software gap. It developed management applications that controlled complex computing environments that could include mainframes, client-servers, and individual desktops. Since CIOs were custom-assembling more of their company's systems in parts over a period of time, Tivoli saw an opportunity to manage the diverse components. It had only $50 million in sales, but the multiple in the purchase price was far less than what Gerstner had paid for Lotus. Given the immediate return on investment, many analysts think Tivoli was a better deal for IBM than Lotus.

Also in 1996, Ray Ozzie, after two years of refinement, finally finished his upgrade of Lotus Notes. Version 4 was a vastly more versatile and powerful application than its predecessors. It was as close to a killer app as IBM could claim. During one Q&A session at an internal meeting, an employee asked Gerstner when Ozzie's new product would arrive at his desk. Gerstner, of course, had no idea, but he winged it, putting the pressure on the internal crew responsible for the companywide rollout: How about getting every IBMer connected within a year? Deployment in IBM's own house was accelerated, though it would take considerably longer than Gerstner hoped. Two years later, while much of the U.S. workforce was equipped with Notes, many foreign locales were not. IBMers worldwide were still coping with the clunky VM mainframe system that was in many ways strangely incompatible with Ozzie's marvelous handiwork.

On the other side of the ledger, in a March 4, 1996, meeting with Wall Street analysts, Gerstner conceded that the company had missed valuable markets in storage, networking hardware, and desktop software, and he pointed out that the PC business, especially in North America, had been disappointing. But he was not one to dwell on past defeats. He only wanted to look ahead. He was reasonably sure about two things: First, the technology was still too complicated. Second, there was a lot of business potential in a networked world. The Internet was exploding and IBM would not miss out under Gerstner's watch.

He had logged hundreds of thousands of miles on the company Gulfstream, and he had spoken with enough CEOs who echoed the same refrain: The technology was aggravating and difficult. We'd rather just get the experts in here to make everything work, they told him. In the three years since Gerstner had started at IBM, systems integration hadn't gotten easier. In fact, given the thousands of companies that built and sold technology, it was more difficult. "Until we make computers that work like toasters, it is going to be a great business," he clucked about his Global Services unit.

IBM is at its best when it is a systems integrator, even when this means selling a competitor's products. For example,

Microsoft's NT operating system is designed for bigger work-loads on PC servers and midrange systems. Though IBM has criticized NT as not being "robust" or reliable for industrial-strength computing, the Microserfs are putting in long days to improve it. And Microsoft's sales force is knocking on the board-room doors of larger customers. Bob Stephenson had aggres-sively adopted IBM's new agnostic attitude, telling customers he'd be glad to employ NT wherever they wanted. Privately, he'd boast that IBM was selling more NT for Microsoft than Microsoft itself. In the new spirit of "co-opetition," this was not lost on the powers in Redmond. "We're not complaining about that," laughed Jonathan Murray, a Microsoft vice president in charge of the company's enterprise business. IBM had even sent a small team of programmers to Kirkland, Washington, near Gates's home court, exclusively to learn how to implement NT solutions. In terms of Big Blue's financial commitment, it wasn't much. This was largely a symbolic gesture.

As for the Internet, Gerstner was at first not convinced of its business potential. Part of this attitude stemmed from early business trips, where corporate customers did not see the market possibilities. Gerstner remarked at one meeting in 1995 that he hadn't met a single CIO or CEO who cared about the Net. Executives like John Landry at Lotus and IBM's John Patrick had been evangelizing about the Net's business potential for years. Those guys apparently convinced him IBM was about to miss another huge market.

A year later, Gerstner's attitude changed. He began to believe.

The hardware piece of the Internet puzzle intrigued large companies like IBM. The question most asked in 1996 was, "How can we connect the world as cheaply as possible?" The immediate response was, with the network computer, or NC. NCs look like PCs but they have limited innards, no hard drives, not even disk drives. The storage chores are handled far away from the desktop. NCs are a throwback to the ancient dumb ter-minals—like Wang word processors—that were powered by back-office computers. Known formally as "nonprogrammable terminals," these individual desktops can be supported by a single server. Each has its own local memory and a high-speed processor. The systems administrator installs whatever operating system a company desires, and he deploys software from his own desk to an entire farm of these "Internet appliances."

The raison d'être for the NC was the reduction of office overhead. IT operating expenditures were out of control. IBM, Sun, and Oracle seized on a new business phrase called "total cost of ownership." This was largely an invention of technology consulting firms like IDC and the Gartner Group. They had been asked by their clients to research the actual expenses of owning and maintaining corporate PCs. After a number of surveys were made, it was estimated that each PC cost anywhere from $6,500 to $13,000 a year to run. (There was a large gap in the figures because they depended on how many PCs were serviced in a given environment. But it was generally agreed that the initial cost of the PC was only twenty to twenty-four percent of the overall expense.) If a company had eight thousand or eighty thousand PCs, it was expensive and time-consuming to roll out an application for all of them. Stripped-down NCs cost as little as $400 to $500 apiece, or even less, and are extremely cheap to deploy and maintain. Upgrades are a cinch, and sneakerware is no longer necessary. ("Sneakerware" is slang for the tedious process of technicians installing applications to every user's desktop by going from office to office. IBM and other companies still maintain their PCs this way.) The theory is simple: If you want access to your company intranet or the Internet, this uncomplicated device can do it in the cheapest possible way.

The initial purveyor of the NC concept was Larry Ellison, the splashy and very public CEO of Oracle. Ellison did not have a specific corporate agenda for the NC, which was refreshing in an industry where few heads of state ever made a pronouncement without an ulterior motive. He became the first visible advocate somewhat by accident. Ellison was a brilliant businessman and a Silicon Valley original. He had an affinity for Japanese culture, big houses, and a tumultuous personal life. He raced big sailboats and flew fighter jets. And he had Big Blue to thank, at least in part, for his success. He'd made his fortune selling software that IBM had developed and dismissed. Ellison was refreshing in that his public appearances weren't scripted or ruled by a cadre of speechwriters and publicists. He spoke from a few notes outlined on index cards. He was accustomed to popping off about whatever issue consumed him at a given moment. His candor was refreshing. Occasionally, his pontifications were sensible. One day, he just seized the NC issue. Ellison said, "When you suddenly have a network-centric point of view, you don't need a device anywhere near as complicated or as expensive as a personal computer. You can build a multimedia Internet terminal for about four to five hundred dollars."

After he had repeated roughly the same spiel a dozen times, the trade press, the business press, even *Newsweek* and *Oprah,* wondered whether Ellison had gone over the top, or was in fact ratting out the entire IT industry. Hadn't the high priests of technology been telling us that if we didn't buy a new, more powerful, feature-laden box every two years (or less) at $2,500 to $3,000, we'd be hopelessly left behind?

At this point, Sun Microsystem CEO Scott McNealy, who could be as outspoken as Ellison (but was far less flamboyant), began pushing his own NC. Sun actually released a machine for only $742 without a monitor or keyboard. He was blatantly upfront about the advantages of NCs. Deploy these sealed boxes and you won't have to worry about computer viruses, hackers, and high-tech chicanery. "What's a floppy disk?" McNealy said. "It's a way to steal company secrets." Behind the glib comment, however, was this incontrovertible logic: The business world can function fine without PCs. NCs are cheaper and do all but the most complex tasks just as well.

Meanwhile, IBM had been testing several versions of NCs with customers, one code-named "Redcliffe." IBM wasn't as brazen as McNealy about the advantages of this platform, at least publicly. It did not play the security or privacy cards in its sales pitches by telling its customers they could more closely monitor employee behavior in front of their screens (not to mention getting rid of all that time-wasting game software).

The most promising of IBM's NC entries was known as a "thin client," high-concept terminology that described an upright flat package, something about the size of a laptop standing on its edge. This was the design that IBM eventually chose to promote. But these limited deployments were kept fairly quiet; neither IBM nor its guinea pigs wanted too much attention. The early concern was not reliability; the technology was hardly a challenge. The question was, will the NC drain away sales from the IBM PC Company? This was vintage IBM fear. Bob Stephenson crafted two short memos to Gerstner, explaining why NCs could make sense. His view was that NCs would not compete with PCs; they're replacement items for workstations that do not need fully capable PCs. Both could coexist in today's technology world.

Gerstner did not want the NC train leaving the station without IBM on it. He approved the formation of a separate division, and placed it in Stephenson's Personal Systems Group. This was less a financial commitment than a psychological one. While IBM reorganized with regularity, an additional pillar of this size in the company infrastructure was unusual. IBM did not cavalierly start new divisions. Bob Dies, an executive who once headed IBM's AS/400 division and had been with the company for twenty-eight years, took charge.

Staffers spent months working up strategies to explain to customers all the different user situations that could help them decide whether a specific technology solution required a PC or an NC. It was obvious that NCs were sufficient for simple data input and updating, back-office tasks done by low-skilled employees. This might include processing health insurance claims, for example. It was also a given that an engineer drawing the horizontal stabilizer on Boeing's new jet would need a high-end PC workstation with computer-assisted-design software costing ten times as much, or more. But there were so many users who fell into the shaded areas in between. IBMers developed a single chart that outlined tasks and potential customer categories. The slide was debated, agonized over, and rejected by executives for weeks. No IBM executive wanted to be accused of stealing his colleague's business.

When Dies went on road shows to introduce the NC to potential customers, he defused the issue by saying that the NCs were not going to replace PCs any more than television replaced the movies. There was room in the technology universe for both. Sam Palmisano, the PC Company maven, and Dies would be competing for some of IBM's same customers, though neither could admit it. After one meeting with Stephenson, the two emerged laughing, with the towering six-foot-seven-inch Dies playfully putting Palmisano in a headlock.

Palmisano already had an established business, despite the continuing challenge of trying to squeeze profits out of thin margins while competing with Dell, Compaq, and Gateway. Dies, of course, had to create product demand and build a client base. One of the first moves was to try it out on IBM's own workforce. Dies installed NCs in secretarial bays and asked a group at the Watson Research Center to test-drive them. The secretaries' PCs were replaced over the weekend with NCs. He assumed that they wouldn't notice the difference when they turned on their machines Monday morning and saw the same familiar icons on the screen. He was right. He expected hostility or at least resistance from the wonks and researchers in Yorktown Heights, however. They took the "personal" in personal computers more seriously than anyone else. Surprisingly, they didn't mind, mainly because while they gave up the privacy of their own data storage, they gained flexibility they hadn't had before. They actually liked the NCs because the machines enhanced the collaborative part of their work habits. They would frequently find themselves in a colleague's office saying, "Let me show you something." With the NCs, they didn't have to trudge back to their office to pick up a floppy. With passwords or smart cards, they could log on to someone else's NC and replicate their own desktop and files anywhere in the building. Gerstner himself has warmed to the NC. He keeps one in his office (though it's not certain how much he really uses it), and he trumpets its advantages to CIOs whenever he meets with them.

Inventing an NC market outside IBM's research walls has proven to be a lot more difficult. Two and a half years after the first machines were shipped, IDC estimated that only a little more than a half million were in use. IBM made about 250,000. Despite the attractive pricing and small footprint (a boon in foreign locales with limited office space), customers are still lukewarm to the NC concept.

Big Blue is leading a parade with few others in it. What do Ellison, McNealy, and Gerstner know that other high-tech CEOs don't know? As a "category," as the analysts call it, the NC is a nonentity. At least so far. Forrester Research wrote in one report, "The NC/PC debate will be anticlimactic. NCs will replace dumb terminals and a few low-end PCs—grabbing no more than 15 percent of large companies' desktops by 1999."

Peter Lowber of the Gartner Group put it this way. "The PC culture is like the mainframe culture back in the 1980s, and it's holding everybody back because of the cultural resistance," he said. "They [CIOs] think they're losing something by going to a thin client. Even though the technology is applicable for eighty percent of the PC users across the board right now, a lot of IT organizations have invested so much money in supporting a PC infrastructure that they're embarrassed to junk it."

Forrester's prediction of a $1.2 billion NC market by 1999 was overly optimistic. Full-function PCs, which were destined to become almost as cheap as NCs, still rule the nation's cubicles. (By 1999, no-brand PC prices had dropped to below the level of NCs.) They leave management to muse over the total cost of ownership, while the price of PCs continues to decline.

Though modest as a start-up, even by IBM standards, the NC was supposed to dovetail with IBM's servers. The theory was that Bob Dies could sell a few thousand of these cheap terminals to a customer, and then the customer would buy either IBM's

PC servers to run them, or other bigger engines in the Server Group, from midrange computers to mainframes.

The Server Group is in Building 4 at Somers, just one building over from where Dies ran the NC group in Building 3. The Somers operations site is a mammoth five-building complex, each with a trademark I. M. Pei atrium shaped in a towering pyramid, in the northernmost reaches of Westchester. The buildings have jagged sides that allow for multiple corner offices, far more than the normal four per floor. The Somers site was advocated mainly by Jack Kuehler, Akers's technology maven, who envisioned a collegial atmosphere that would be useful for product development. For example, the guys working in mainframes in one building could stroll over and brainstorm with the team working on servers or software in another. To enhance this exchange of information, ultrawide, carpeted, glassed-in hallways connect all of the buildings. On a rainy day, teams could meet in the Central Services Building cafeteria and exchange ideas, or "noodle," in IBM parlance. It was a nice enough plan, but it never worked. IBMers were nothing if not territorial, and throughout the turbulent 1980s, there were huge turf battles and internecine conflicts.

Cynics from IBM's corporate headquarters, only twenty miles to the south, wonder if the Somers location is merely one big make-work meeting place, where thousands of pages of paper are spewed out of printers, copied, circulated, and finally discarded or shredded. There are several large pockets of empty offices and deserted secretarial bays, a not-too-subtle reminder of the old IBM, when the word "budget" was simply not in the company's vocabulary.

Under Gerstner's stewardship, business in certain pockets of Building 4 has gone wanting. The senior vice president and group executive for the Server Group was Nick Donofrio. He was one of the few digitheads who had risen through the ranks to the highest levels of management. He was a thirty-year veteran at IBM, and nobody questioned his ability to manage the design of semiconductor logic and memory circuit chips. He was a fellow of the Institute of Electrical and Electronics Engineers and a member of the National Academy of Engineering. But he wasn't what the high command called a "good businessman." Donofrio had an outstanding background in computing per se, but he just wasn't a topflight line manager.

About the only good news coming out of Donofrio's group was from the System/390 division. The mainframe had come back from the dead, partly because it was subject to the vagaries of the market cycle. (At the time, IBM began using the phrase "enterprise computing" to describe it, as if mainframes had a bad name.) Also Linda Sanford, the highest-ranking woman line executive at the company, had aggressively campaigned IBM's new strategy. She had seen the competition, lower-cost Unix machines and Windows NT, eat into her market share. So she responded by speeding up the development of the G4 line. She lowered the price by using the kinds of chips found in PCs; they were cheaper, but more important, they were compatible with Unix-based platforms. They could run some of the more popular software being created by SAP, Lotus, PeopleSoft, and Oracle. And she understood the importance of Java for her customers.

Donofrio also had responsibility for the midrange servers, the AS/400 and RS/6000 divisions. Compaq, Hewlett-Packard, and others were growing at a nineteen to twenty percent annual rate, while IBM had but single-digit increases. Big Blue was losing ground; nobody was doing anything but watch some of its most reliable cash generators begin to bend under increasing competition. The worldwide server market was about $50 billion, and IBM held a twenty-three percent position with $12 billion in revenues. There was a lot of overlap between the midrange systems, and IBM could not always differentiate the advantages for confused customers, who were shifting loyalties to Big Blue's competitors at an increasing rate. Many thought AS/400 and RS/6000 could be combined; and if the lines couldn't be integrated, certainly many aspects of the two manufacturing operations could. The group was full of redundancies. And, per the model of the old IBM, there were far too many marketing people to support an efficient SG&A model.

One of Donofrio's weakest links was the RS/6000 workstation. It had been losing market share, not so much because of what it did wrong but because of what it never did right. While IBM debated and dawdled over marketing strategies and the color of casings, Sun, Hewlett-Packard, and Silicon Graphics had gotten into the Unix and advanced workstation market before IBM, and IBM continually had to play catch-up.

The RS/6000 business was run by Dr. Mark Bregman, a guy who had come up from research, a typical IBMer in love with technology. He had the same kind of background as Donofrio, and that was one reason why Donofrio hired him in late 1995. In an earlier era, he'd have been the guy with the pocket protector and the slide rule on his belt. For a short time, he was advising Gerstner on technical matters. Bregman had a streak of digital elitism that did not serve him well. He liked to hang out primarily with engineers and other vice presidents. He insisted on using his doctoral title, for example, an affectation not even normally associated with other IBM Ph.D.s. Bregman's view of his business was limited; he liked to travel only to see a few select high-end customers in Europe and Asia. He rarely went to the Austin manufacturing facility for even pro forma visits. This was not wise if he expected to inspire the rank and file to be more productive. His detractors snickered when IBM saw a huge part of his market share dissolve. A joke went around the RS/6000 group in Somers: "How do you turn a $4 billion business into a $3 billion one? You get Mark Bregman to run it." An ex-IBMer who worked for him lamented, "He just didn't know how to be a vice president. He should have stayed in research."

By late 1997, after two years of watching the Server Group's management adrift, Gerstner had finally seen enough. He called on Bob Stephenson, now the company's best-known troubleshooter, to take over the group. Both Bregman and Donofrio were moved to other positions. Today, Bregman is in charge of "pervasive computing," a broad IBM term that encompasses the chip technology that goes into such things as cell phones, web TVs, screen phones, and wearable computers.

Donofrio is now the senior vice president for technology and manufacturing, no longer running a line business but probably in a role better suited to his skills. Donofrio's move to research was more titular than anything else (the labs are still run by Paul Horn). When a shareholder from Indiana at the 1998 annual meeting asked about the status of IBM's superconductivity research, Gerstner hadn't the faintest idea. He scanned the audience and searched for Nick. Donofrio gave a long, detailed answer that not one single person understood.

16

A Loss Leader Even Lou Can Live With

By mid-1996, Lou Gerstner was totally baffled by his inability to solve the problems of the PC Company. It was the one business unit that seemed to elude all of the brainpower in Armonk. His brightest executives couldn't make any money selling these boxes. IBM could design high-quality commercial desktop PCs, whether they were advanced workstations for complex engineering tasks or simple machines for rote data management. But Big Blue didn't lead—in fact, it lagged—in almost every market niche.

The one space where Gerstner really hated to lose, however, was in the home—the PCs that were targeted for living rooms and dens. The consumer was a wildly unpredictable beast, and Gerstner, one of the brightest, most successful CEOs in America, could not tame it. All of his years of experience with packaged goods did not make a difference. Despite all the hard work Gerstner and his team had accomplished to restore the company's reputation, its consumer flagship—the Aptiva—was overdesigned, overbuilt, overpriced, and somewhat overpraised. This did not mean that the Aptiva wasn't a good computer. On the contrary, it was an excellent machine.

But it was a brand that was always in search of a larger market. You could tell it was in trouble when even IBMers, especially secretaries in search of a computer for the whole family, didn't buy the employee-discounted models. After scanning the ads, they found a Gateway, Dell, or Packard-Bell that delivered nearly the same features for substantially less. Not only was technology changing at a rapid pace, the demographics of the consumer were broadening as well. The home user who was buying his or her first machine was very different from the one who was upgrading. Cheaper products allowed lower-income people to get in the game. What Gerstner's marketers did not understand was that fewer PC customers could afford to pay extra for a status nameplate.

As a former consumer manager summed up, "Even though Aptiva cost $30 million to build and lost money, it got great reviews. It was a loss leader even Lou could live with."

The home of the Aptiva is in the Research Triangle Park, or RTP, in Raleigh, which is also the locus of high technology in the mid-Atlantic states. A number of firms like Compaq and Cisco are located in the RTP, and IBM has eleven thousand employees there designing, manufacturing, and marketing PCs, components, and peripherals. They are housed in several windowless complexes with tiny offices and cardboard-thin walls that IBMers, when they're in a charitable mood, describe as "severe" or "institutional." On an overcast day, the insides of these buildings can resemble a dungeon. When it rains and IBM's RTP buildings leak, it can be a depressing scene. Managers run for cover when they're asked to transfer from the northern reaches of bucolic Westchester County to North Carolina.

One out-of-the-way nook in IBM's Raleigh is worth a detour, however. Perched on a second-floor balcony is an area nicknamed the "mezzanine." The mezzanine is a showcase for new consumer products, or other gadgets that are in the testing stage. By inviting influential technology analysts and journalists into the lair, Big Blue trades on the feeling of exclusivity. The message is clear: This is hallowed ground. Not everyone gets an advanced look at what's coming next. At first, anyone with an IBM badge could climb the stairs and open an old fire door and tour the goodie room. Then someone had the clever idea to install a metal plate and a lock on the mezzanine. At least now it has a special aura.

Early in 1996, the PC consumer marketing team installed a full-scale living room in the mezzanine to display its newest computer, the Aptiva S series, code-named "Stealth." This update of IBM's home PC had been a year in the planning. Much of the design was the result of extensive focus-group testing by Ogilvy and Mather. Consumers, the agency learned, wanted a quiet machine. Potential buyers said they weren't interested in a conventional computer. They wanted it to be as snazzy as their stereo systems. In fact, high-level stereo sound would be a nice touch. They did not want clutter or the usual unsightly array of cables anywhere near their desk. It should be part of the décor, something they wouldn't be uncomfortable leaving out in the corner of the living room.

An IBM consumer strategist had spent months investigating home building trends. He concluded that the home office wasn't the critical "extra room." Builders were accommodating dwellers' desires to have a library. The home computer should be targeted toward family leisure pursuits and education, not necessarily spreadsheet work taken home from the office.

Most of all, focus groupies demanded all this for far less than IBM had priced its original Aptiva. Instead of $3,300, they wanted to pay closer to $2,000, depending on the features.

For once, an IBM code name for a new product was apt. The Stealth was created to be the harbinger of cool, at least as far as a home PC went. It was as close to a hip, suburban family appliance as IBM could envision. The monitor was black, not the ubiquitous beige favored by most makers. Unlike other clunky machines with detached speakers, it had built-in Bose speakers with woofers that blended in with the Stealth's monitor. The mini-tower was separated from the other components, and it could be hidden under a desk or up to six feet away from the monitor and keyboard. That way, the noise from the cooling fan would be less bothersome.

The main attraction was the media console, which housed the disk drive and a pop-up CD-ROM drive. The console drove what IBM called "Total Image 3D." The machine also was designed with teenagers in mind, those with insatiable appetites for the most compelling and realistic graphics, with games like Mech Warrior 2 and Virtual Reality Soccer. Well before the launch date, Walter Mossberg, the critic who wrote the influential "Personal Technology" column for the *Wall Street Journal*, was invited to the mezzanine to preview it. IBM managers and executives were encouraged when he told them that the company was on to something good.

Publicly, Stealth had the blessing of the chairman. Gerstner had passed down a mandate, first by separating the $4 billion to $5 billion consumer division from the PC division to give it more visibility. At an analysts meeting, Gerstner declared that the consumer market was "a growth opportunity we cannot and will not ignore." The original Aptiva, sold in 1995 and early 1996, had been highly regarded by critics and consumers, but IBM had underestimated its popularity, and profits were penalized because of supply shortages. "The first year of Aptiva, the demand was so strong, they could have sold five times as many as they did," said a former Ogilvy manager who worked on the advertising. "But they stopped ramping up production. They lost so much money because they never thought about just getting a big installed base."

America's living rooms and dens were a highly competitive arena for computer makers, however, and Gerstner was determined to succeed the second time around. The consumer division's general manager, Jim Firestone, declared, "We can dazzle the world, and we will." Gerstner and Abby Kohnstamm committed $70 million to advertise and promote Aptiva, consumer software, and related options.

Stealth was unveiled at a press conference on September 26, 1996, in a loft in lower Manhattan. It was different from other splashy product introductions that took place in midtown hotel ballrooms with elaborately staged special effects. This time the nifty multimedia was on the computer monitors, not on the overhead projection TV screens. It was a casual setting, where the Aptivas were displayed on pedestals around the room. The idea was to convey a living room–like setting. The executive in charge of IBM's consumer products from Raleigh, Jose Garcia, was beaming. He knew he had a hit. Critics loved the clean design of the Aptiva S series. The reviews were almost universal raves; the machine eventually won a number of computer press awards. At the end of several enthusiastic notices, reviewers commented that all the new features were great, but the Aptiva was still somewhat expensive.

There were a few minor quibbles, mostly small inconveniences. The CD drawer was at the bottom of the monitor; and with most computers a simple push of a button opens or closes it, but with the Aptiva you had to open the tray door manually before you pressed the button. And while you could place the mini-tower anywhere, the six-foot power cord did not allow for much flexibility. (There was talk about substituting a twenty-foot cord, but this went nowhere.) Users could avoid the fan noise, but they couldn't escape the loudly whirring disk drives, which were right in front of them.

In a rare press outing, Gerstner appeared on Tom Brokaw's network newscast to promote the Aptiva and the viability of what IBM called the "information furnace." This notion emphasized America's living room as the locus of the networked family. Media consoles could be located throughout the house, in every room, powered by a PC server, perhaps located in the basement. The home server—where a single unit accommodated the entire family's computing needs—was not far off, Gerstner said. In addition, IBM's Home Director software would be available in just a few months, which would allow Aptiva and other PC users to control all kinds of appliances in their homes, from toasters to TVs to thermostats.

IBM had announced that the world of the Jetsons was coming, and Gerstner heralded its arrival. Big Blue had innovative, powerful technology that the entire family could use and enjoy.

IBM's CEO was a consumer technology advocate, though he was far from from a devotee. Gerstner had an Aptiva in his Greenwich home, but a technician who had installed and maintained it was hard-pressed to say whether it was ever turned on.

The buzz was encouraging. Aptivas were sent to TV newscasters such as Chuck Scarborough and Bryant Gumbel. Gerstner even made sure that one was delivered to his friend Vernon Jordan. So many promotional machines were given out that at the November 1996 COMDEX trade show, IBM's public relations managers found themselves short of demo models. Hurriedly, they went to a local Las Vegas retailer to buy them. Executives were feeling especially confident. The consumer division, after losing money for most of 1996, reported a third quarter profit.

Initial sales in the fourth quarter Christmas season were brisk, but soon after the opening rush, demand began to slow. A couple of flaws were apparent. Some Aptivas had faulty speakers. They were shipped with plenty of software, but most of the applications were non–mission-critical or just plain useless. Savvy users deleted much of it soon after they opened the boxes. Many of the best features were options that cost extra, like the wireless mouse. IBM justified the higher price tag by emphasizing its heralded service and support, but this was a difficult concept to sell in a world of commoditized, discounted hardware. Customers who comparison-shopped saw the Aptiva and got sticker shock.

The consumer division reacted quickly, however, and there was a scramble to fix some of the shortcomings. The microprocessor was upgraded from a 166-mHz Pentium to a faster 233 mHz chip, so the graphics would tile on the screen more quickly. IBM switched from Intel as its chip supplier, instead using National Semiconductor's Cyrix. Aptiva no longer boasted the "Intel Inside" sticker—which earned a modest royalty of between $6 million and $12 million from Intel—but it saved far more in production costs (around $200 per machine) by using the lower-cost vendor.

Eventually, to further lower hardware costs, IBM allowed Acer to become its OEM. The low-cost Taiwan supplier was not known for its reliability. When Acer became an OEM for IBM it was the end of a long period of denial. Big Blue finally conceded that it could not produce a low-cost home PC on its own. The first Acer machines were rolled out in Europe. (The Acer-built machines were discounted for sale to IBM shareholders in 1998.)

There were other problems.

An internecine struggle developed over whether to ship Aptivas with Netscape's browser or Microsoft's Explorer. Netscape dominated the market, and Microsoft was looking to cut into its share. Some of IBM's sales teams preferred Microsoft, partly because they were trying to build a partnership with Gates's crew in Redmond, and partly because Explorer produced revenues while Netscape cost them money. (Gates paid vendors to bundle its Explorer with new computers, just to gain market points on Netscape's stronghold.) A year later the pressure to use Explorer apparently was stepped up. IBM testimony at the Microsoft antitrust trial in the spring of 1999 accused Microsoft of threatening "repercussions" if IBM did not use Microsoft's browser in 1997.)

The consumer division discovered early on that it preferred using Netscape for one very important reason: It worked, while Explorer caused the Aptivas to freeze or crash. The consumer division lost the argument, however, and Aptivas were shipped with the problem browser. IBM received at least $2 million in incentive pay from Microsoft for using its Explorer. But these insignificant revenues easily were offset by the flood of phone calls to IBM's hotlines from helpless customers who found themselves constantly having to reinstall all of Microsoft's software.

The Aptiva team knew it had to offer better applications. IBM acquired Edmark, a small educational software maker whose programs appealed to yuppie parents who wanted to use computers as reading, writing, and math tutors. The consumer division also cut a deal with Crayola to create a drawing and painting program, which even allowed children to design dresses. In a more ambitious move,

IBM formed a partnership with World Book, where it sold its encyclopedia on CD-ROM. The problem was, recalls a former consumer
marketing manager, "It was an awful encyclopedia. The second edition was much better." Even after the improved version was published, IBM was forced to compete with Microsoft, which had
achieved considerable success with the Encarta encyclopedia.
Encarta already was bundled on the Aptiva, the result of a previous
deal with Microsoft. Why would anyone buy *another* encyclopedia if
the computer already came with one?

Even the World Book ads were controversial. Ogilvy and
Mather had prepared a TV spot in which a little girl discovers an
injured owl in the woods. She brings the creature back to her
house, and turns on her Aptiva to browse through the World
Book CD-ROM to search for a remedy. When IBM previewed the
commercial, one manager immediately red-flagged it. First, owls
didn't fly during the day, they flew at night. Second, the owl was
an endangered species, and you couldn't just bring wayward
ones home as pets. The National Wildlife Federation would complain. While Ogilvy was asked to correct the problem, for some
reason it was not immediately fixed or pulled. It managed to run
just long enough for the Wildlife Federation to threaten legal
action.

This was not a strategy that would make headway against
Microsoft's dominance in this product category. "We felt the
World Book was problematic to begin with," said Steve
Sonnenfeld, a former Ogilvy advertising hand who worked on
the account. "Even though you had two good brands merged
together, the product was late to market. Microsoft already had a
seventy-five percent share with Encarta."

In November 1996, IBM also made a management change
that perplexed dozens of IBM managers in Raleigh, and it might
have been one that cost the company any real chance of success
with Aptiva. Jose Garcia, probably the most respected and well-
liked consumer executive at IBM, was shunted aside, ostensibly
because of flawed chemistry with his boss, Jim Firestone. Also,
Garcia worked with the troops in the Raleigh trenches, while

Firestone's office was in Somers with the bureaucrats. Garcia felt that he should have Firestone's job, and many IBMers who had worked with both of them agreed. Garcia, and not Firestone, really had run the consumer division during the few quarters when it returned scant profits. His abilities were well respected throughout IBM. Also, he was one of the few executives who truly understood the consumer PC market.

Since Firestone had been a marketing prodigy when he worked at American Express, it may have been more difficult for either Bob Stephenson or Sam Palmisano to remove him than Garcia. Gerstner might have questioned the shifting aside of Firestone. To the dismay of many at IBM, Garcia was replaced by Brian Connors and James Corcoran, neither of whom had extensive knowledge or expertise in consumer technology. Connors's experience was in selling to business customers. Corcoran hadn't even managed a business. He had dealt only in advertising and public relations. Corcoran's promotion did not quite qualify as a FUMU. He went from a non–bottom line business to one with cash responsibility, which one IBMer called a "lateral arabesque." This arabesque would put Corcoran to the test. If he had his pulse on the market, if he knew the business, let him run it, was management's logic.

Garcia's loss was felt more abroad than at home. One of his real strengths was in his leadership among IBM's foreign subsidiaries, where a large number of sales were expected. When Big Blue's country managers met with Garcia to discuss how many units they felt they could sell, they had a tendency to promise only low numbers. It was much easier, of course, to fulfill a modest quota than a high one. Garcia badgered and cajoled them into setting higher, yet still realistic sales goals. He constantly helped them by asking what he had to do with the product line to increase volumes. He demanded excellence, much the way Gerstner did. He made them feel that he was their partner, and he wanted them to succeed.

The incoming executives, Connors and Corcoran, did not understand this traditional intracompany dance with IBM sub-

sidiaries. "It was very clear early on that they had trouble managing the business," Rob Carpenter, the former technical manager
on the Aptiva, said about the two. "The geos [foreign sub-
sidiaries] immediately started reducing their volumes, and they
basically let themselves go into a tailspin. The geos essentially
reduced volumes from two and a half to three and a half million
for the year on Stealth, down to about forty thousand units.
Now, that was like half the line, so it became a self-fulfilling
prophecy."

They were about to go down in flames in Europe, and they
didn't even know it.

There was a sea change in the consumer marketplace, and it
occurred abruptly. By 1997, only four months after IBM introduced the Aptiva S, the price war in home computing had begun.
Packard Bell/NEC cobbled together a PC for $799, and AST
Research was crowding Wal-Mart's aisles with $999 computers.
But when Compaq announced that it was about to deliver a
$999 PC, everyone in the business took notice. Finally, a large-
scale computer maker had cracked the magic thousand-dollar
threshold. True, the fine print in almost every ad disclosed to
consumers that the monitor—starting at about $225—was not
included. But this did not deter the anxious first-time buyers
who were searching for something they could simply afford. Sexy
features they could worry about later.

Other makers would follow with bargain-basement prices as
well, catching IBM totally unprepared. It had no such competitive product, nothing in the pipeline. For the past two years it
had been banking on the faith of customers willing to pay more
for IBM because of its perceived brand quality.

By March, Bob Stephenson had read enough of the trade press
clips to realize that IBM's home PC strategy was seriously deficient. He called a meeting with the half dozen top managers of
the consumer division in his Somers conference room. Others in
Raleigh were on the phone. He wanted to know why IBM had no
under-$1,000 PC and what it was doing about getting one.

Stephenson polled Firestone, Corcoran, Connors, among others. When the technobabble began to disguise excuses, he angrily punched the pound key on the phone. He wanted a simple explanation, but unfortunately, there wasn't one. There was a long silence from the Raleigh team. Finally, everyone agreed that even though Compaq had taken the early lead, IBM had no choice but to follow. But decisions kept getting deferred until July, when a deal with Acer was made to supply low-cost machines.

IBM announced its sub-$1,000 machine, the Aptiva E16, in November 1997, and the following month, the *New York Times* gave it an excellent review. Grouping it with the similarly priced Hewlett-Packard Pavilion 3100 and the Compaq Presario 4500, technology critic Stephen Manes wrote that "IBM's competitors clearly have some catching up to do."

Despite this glowing endorsement and IBM's rapid recovery, the home PC business continued to flummox the company. After every small step forward, there was another larger step backward. "Firestone and his team missed that one," says an IBM vice president who worked in the Personal Systems Group, "suggesting that our customers wanted features and functionality over price. We were ten months late with our sub-$1,000 offering, but by that time, well, you know the rest." A year late, and there go your profits.

It wasn't all IBM's fault. Retailers, who by now were accustomed to guiding nervous first-time buyers away from more expensive IBM machines toward cheaper models, now saw easier sales in the sub-$1,000 market. It might take a salesman several customer visits to make a computer sale that ranged in the $2,500-plus category. An entry-level machine was by comparison almost an impulse buy.

IBM, however, did not have a good feel for its retail outlets, however. In a single deal, the company gave up mindshare, eyeshare, and a massive amount of shelf space.

With seven thousand stores throughout the United States, Radio Shack was by far IBM's largest retailer, by a factor of three or four over other large chains like Circuit City, Best Buy, and CompUSA. If IBM had any chance to sell computers with "value-add" (meaning enticing customers who were willing to pay more for quality and extra features), it was in a Radio Shack. Radio Shack's sales personnel were well trained, and they could patiently explain the differences in features among the various brands to computer buyers. They tended to attract wily buyers rather than less sophisticated shoppers who prowled the aisles of discount chains in search of the cheapest box. Aptivas were still costlier than other machines, so the Radio Shack relationship was critical, and the contract was about to expire.

By early 1998, Radio Shack was being heavily wooed by Compaq. The retailer held intensive negotiations with both IBM and Compaq for an exclusive arrangement. Compaq promised to provide a cheap, solid, reliable machine (and one not built by Acer). It even matched IBM's warranty. According to a former IBM manager close to the negotiations, Compaq won the new contract not merely because it equaled or topped everything IBM offered. IBM simply did not negotiate in a way that left Radio Shack feeling there was a strong desire to continue the relationship with its consumer division. There was a crucial time during the discussions when the Radio Shack deal could have gone either way. "IBM sent two lawyers and two accountants, and no computer people to an important meeting," the marketing manager said. Compaq only had to sweeten IBM's existing deal slightly. In the end, it topped the co-op advertising part of the deal by raising IBM's $20 million offer by only $2 million—hardly significant when several hundred million dollars in revenues were at stake. At the time, IBM probably did not realize that losing so many storefronts would cost Aptiva so much in mindshare, not to mention lost sales.

"The returns that we'd get out of Radio Shack were miniscule compared to a Circuit City, Best Buy because Radio Shack had a personal relationship with most of their customers," said Rob Carpenter. "I think they [IBM] lost focus on that relationship with Radio Shack."

Gerstner's patience was wilting. It became harder for Firestone's marketing team to pry more money loose from corporate headquarters. Every time the wind shifted, Firestone suddenly needed to expand his ad budget. It cost millions to buy TV time, but that was the fastest way into the nation's living rooms. Since he had exhausted their budget, on two occasions Firestone and James Corcoran had to appeal directly to Gerstner. Ogilvy and Mather's consumer account team had prepared an elaborate marketing plan for Corcoran, "designed to save his ass," according to one source who worked on Aptiva. It included branding, sub-branding, and a means to push IBM's Authorized Assembly Program to compete with Dell's phenomenally successful "build-to-order" computers. But Corcoran ignored it, preferring a grand scheme he called "integrated marketing" through third-party vendors. (Corcoran eventually was shunted aside to a job marketing accessories, and he left IBM shortly thereafter for Citigroup.)

All throughout 1997, the brands and sub-brands complained as Abby Kohnstamm continually trimmed their budget, mostly at Gerstner's behest. The consumer division originally expected to receive an additional $20 million, but the bad numbers were already in, and Kohnstamm and Gerstner appropriated less than $4 million (mostly to promote Home Director). Frantic for cash, the ad team began raiding the PR department's budget, which was minuscule by comparison. It was like panhandling for spare change.

This kind of desperation ultimately found its way into the narrow corridors and rabbit-warren offices in Raleigh. The rank and file in the division began to get disillusioned. Middle managers felt the distant chill from Armonk's decision makers, and they were angry because they felt orphaned. Here was a corporation that spent $900 million on advertising in 1996, and more than half went to support IBM's image. When an individual product was in trouble, and its future was in doubt, the spigot suddenly was turned off.

Perhaps Gerstner finally decided that enough was enough?

It hadn't been long ago that Gerstner was gung ho about the consumer business, crowing about it on national television. Now here was this vote of no confidence. "Gerstner sent mixed signals to the consumer division," recalls Steve Sonnenfeld. "At times he made a zero commitment to the space, but he refused to kill it. But it was clear to many in the consumer division he had no respect for it." A former consumer manager added, "They know he won't go into the trenches for them. He's paying lip service to the division."

It was worse than that. Soon even the lip service budget was reduced.

By the fall of 1997, Gerstner had decided to fold the consumer division back into the PC Company. Word filtered through the hallways of Building 3 in Somers that this probably was for the best; it might help cover the fact that Firestone's group would be more than $300 million in the red for the year. Firestone's star had finally dimmed. His responsibilities were greatly reduced. He no longer ran a division. He was given the marketing job for Aptiva and ThinkPad, but he was stripped of all other management duties. Firestone was replaced by a former IBM executive named Mike Braun, whose experience in the consumer products was not extensive. A twenty-year veteran of IBM, he had headed the ill-fated multimedia software company, Kaleida, a joint IBM-Apple venture.

Employees in the Personal Systems Group worried about how much the steep losses on Aptiva would lower their annual bonus. Suddenly, they had a new respect for the prosaic options division, which consistently turned out useful peripherals and sparkling profits.

Sam Palmisano, now in charge of the Personal Systems Group, however, had been busy doing what he does best: pushing computers. If enough commercial desktop units could be sold in the fourth quarter, it could make up for the weak sales in the consumer division. In December 1997, word soon filtered down that the "channel was stuffed." The inventory was in the dealers' hands, and not in IBM warehouses. Determined to make his numbers, IBM sources say, Palmisano had no real concern about any slowdown in sales this strategy was likely to cause over the next two, possibly three, quarters.

One reason was that Palmisano knew he was leaving the division three months before it was publicly announced in January 1998. Palmisano was promoted to senior vice president in order to run the Global Services unit (replacing Dennie Welsh, who had become ill with a serious disease). The PC problems of 1998 would be his successor's problems. In retrospect, Palmisano couldn't be blamed. He was merely following typical executive protocol at IBM. Look at the mess he'd stepped into when Rick Thoman left the PC Company to become the CFO.

The defunct consumer division and the company's subsequent restructuring were eventually made public, and while the losses were significant, they were more of a blow to the company's image than its bottom line. *Business Week* surveyed the carnage with a headline that appeared to sum up IBM's main mistake: "I'm not going to pay a lot for this Aptiva." The *Wall Street Journal* reported that first-time Aptiva buyers in 1995 did not necessarily stay loyal to the IBM brand. Other PC makers were out there offering the same quality, the same features for less. Even their service and support were comparable to Big Blue's. A consumer was quoted as saying that IBM's reputation made it worth paying more for a PC, but only by about $100. Rob Carpenter said, "IBM hasn't stepped up to the fact that their name just does not carry the premium pricing that they want to charge. You know, it really came right down to that."

In 1998, IBM announced that it no longer was installing a fancy exhibit at COMDEX to show off its latest wares. The 1,200 or 1,300 IBMers who filled up so many rooms at the Hilton, the Flamingo, and Bally's just to entertain customers and collect a bunch of brochures from other companies were told to stay home. IBM saved $30 million a year by withdrawing from the world's biggest PC trade show. But it was not the figure that would concern the CEO of a company of IBM's size. It was more than that. There would be no Aptivas on display in Las Vegas in November. Gerstner was making a statement to the IBMers in Raleigh who worked in the consumer division and to the technology community as well. He'd lost the battle for Middle America's living rooms.

There's No Place to Hide

In the spring of 1997, IBM's Rick Thoman called Merrill Lynch's Dan Mandresh, seeking some advice. Mandresh remembers it was more of a personal matter than a business one. The IBM CFO wanted to review some of the stocks in his investment portfolio. After a few minutes, Thoman honed in on Xerox. Mandresh was Merrill's in-house expert on Big Blue, but he was one of a few Wall Street analysts who also tracked Xerox. Thoman asked some pointed questions about the copier company and its office products division, and its stock price potential.

It wasn't until two months later, when Mandresh was on a business trip in Boston, that he finally figured out what that call was about. His secretary caught up with him to tell him that Rick Thoman was frantically trying to reach him. When they finally connected, Thoman told Mandresh that he would be making an important announcement the following day, but he couldn't tell him what it was. He was hand-delivering a package with updated biographical material that evening. (Thoman used the same faux cloak-and-dagger technique with Sam Albert, a favorite media source on IBM matters.)

By 7:30 the next morning, Mandresh's phone began ringing. Reporters were seeking comments because Thoman was leaving

IBM to become president of Xerox, a newly created number two spot under chairman and CEO Paul Allaire. Thoman would be in the waiting room to run the company when Allaire retired. (Thoman took command in April 1999.)

After laboring in Lou Gerstner's shadow for nearly his entire career, Thoman wanted to run his own shop. He had gone a long way since giving up on his early ambition of becoming a diplomat. This was a chance to prove to his doubters that his business career was something more than a long apprenticeship to Gerstner. He was fifty-three, and opportunities like this one did not emerge every day. Gerstner, of course, was nothing less than gracious. (Not long after moving to Xerox, Thoman hired Jim Firestone, with Gerstner's blessing, rescuing him from exile in IBM's hapless consumer unit. It cannot be said that Gerstner's people do not take care of their own.)

Larry Ricciardi also called Mandresh after the Thoman appointment was made. This was an important courtesy call. Ricciardi was Gerstner's choice to replace Thoman, as acting CFO, though he did not want the job indefinitely. Like Thoman, Ricciardi had long been one of Gerstner's most trusted and loyal executives. But he didn't particularly like coddling analysts. He was purely an inside guy, a "technical lawyer," according to Harry Freeman, an attorney and former colleague at American Express. "The last thing he wants to do is go to an analysts meeting and talk," Freeman said. "His attitude would be, we have to live with them, but we don't have to talk to them. He's a buttoned-up, no comment guy." Ricciardi wasn't comfortable carrying the company flag in public.

For starters, he hardly looked like a CFO. He had been a literature major in college, and before becoming an attorney, he attended the East Asian Institute of Columbia University's Chinese Culture and Language Program. At Columbia, he had developed an affinity for Asian art, which he avidly collected. He wore a scruffy beard and often walked around in cardigan sweaters. He had an image of a frumpy, college professor. In fact, his outfits clashed. Sport jacket, loafers, and William Faulkner–wide khakis. One former IBM manager called Ricciardi an "Italian mensch," while another said that he was more like "Lou's consigliere." Ricciardi could be tough when necessary, and he had earned Gerstner's confidence over many years at both RJR and American Express.

As a behind-the-scenes operator, Ricciardi was more of a deal maker, well versed in Gerstner's fiscal strategy. As general counsel, he had been involved in all of IBM's major deals. He had batteries of lawyers to handle all the drudge legal work. His interest was in the financial part of IBM's acquisitions and alliances. Ricciardi was affable, but the rumpled, tweedy look was also a pose. "He can be a hard-ass," according to Dan Mandresh, and several others who knew him agreed.

Several present and former colleagues describe Ricciardi as a very shrewd negotiator. When IBM put its outdated Global Network operation (a telecommunications and data network) on the block in 1998, IBM's asking price was $5 billion. Business analysts expected it might bring bids between $3 billion and $4 billion. It was Ricciardi who insisted on holding out for the $5 billion price tag. AT&T CEO Mike Armstrong paid Ricciardi's price, though the deal was predicated on a quid pro quo. IBM signed a contract—$5 billion over five years—to remain as one of the division's biggest customers.

Until Gerstner found a permanent replacement for Thoman, Ricciardi kept a low profile on Wall Street. Not long after he assumed his new position, Ricciardi abandoned the traditional face-to-face quarterly meetings with the 160 analysts who tracked IBM. He used the Internet and telephone conferences instead. And he met with them less frequently than Thoman had. During his first conference call, he admitted that a lawyer discussing financial performance was Wall Street's "greatest nightmare." As a lawyer, his instincts were completely the opposite of Jerry York's. If there was any doubt about what to say or how to say it, he'd kept his mouth shut.

Thoman's departure did not raise nearly as much concern on Wall Street as did Jerry York's two years earlier, when IBM was still involved in major cost reductions. With IBM once again respectable as a component of the Dow Jones Industrial Average, the CFO position was not the pressing issue it once had been. Gerstner took ten months to find a permanent CFO. Douglas Maine, the former CFO of MCI Communications, became IBM's main face to Wall Street. (Ricciardi's parting words to the analysts were, appropriately enough, "See you in court.")

The CFO now had a conventional job description, which mainly consisted of wooing the investment community and serving as Big Blue's top bookkeeper. The company was now cash rich, and there was no real plan to put the cash to work, other than to buy back its own stock. In 1997, IBM's board sanctioned two stock buybacks, one in March for $3.5 billion, and the other in October for the same amount. It already had made several such large buybacks since 1995. The additional repurchase of its own shares sent the message to Wall Street that company officials still felt the stock was a bargain at its mid-March price of $144. (In 1997, Gerstner also gained board approval for a two-for-one stock split, the company's first since 1979.)

All told, IBM's buyback program reached around $25 billion under Gerstner's administration. Some analysts criticized this strategy, claiming that Gerstner was more interested in short-term returns than IBM's future. This is something of a legitimate complaint. Buybacks artificially inflate the company's earnings by reducing the number of shares outstanding. During analysts' phone calls, IBM was forced to defend the practice, which had been called "financial engineering."

Howard Anderson, founder and president of The Yankee Group, a Boston-based consulting firm, has tracked IBM since 1968. He criticized the buybacks, saying that at first they made sense. Anderson said, "Without IBM's stock recovering, there would have been the biggest brain drain in twenty years. IBM's never paid all that well, and he needed a way to lock in his key managers. And he actually did lose a lot of key managers. When the [stock] options became worth a lot of money, it was a way to hold on to a lot of people. So that's one reason to do this. We've bought back our stock, too, and essentially we're sending a signal to the market that we think our stock is undervalued. But to buy back $25 billion seems excessive." In June 1998, Anderson wrote a critical piece in *Network World* that accused Gerstner of "playing it safe" with this strategy. He even suggested, "Maybe IBM needs a gutsier, younger guy whose idea of vision is more than a healthier bottom line."

In addition, cash used to repurchase shares might be put to better use making other investments, including buying other firms. Skeptics maintained that Gerstner should have been trolling for deals along the lines of Lotus. (In 1998, IBM spent $700 million on acquisitions, but it still has not made any investment that could be deemed a major strategic deal.)

Despite these few barbs from afar, IBM's board gave Gerstner a high approval rating, and the board was the only critic that counted. Gerstner had been maniacal about providing shareholder returns, and from that standpoint, the CEO had performed admirably. During the boom years on Wall Street between 1993 and 1998, which corresponded almost exactly with Gerstner's tenure at IBM, the Standard and Poor's index of five hundred companies averaged an 18.57 percent increase annually. During the same period, IBM's stock returned 35.98 percent. IBM's directors could boast that Gerstner almost doubled the rate of return of the S&P index. In five years, Gerstner increased IBM's market capitalization more than fourfold. At the end of 1993, it was $33 billion. The market cap at the end of 1998 was $169 billion.

For this he was generously rewarded.

Gerstner had been granted 200,000 stock options early in 1997, part of increasingly large annual compensation packages that dovetailed with IBM's continued improvement. Fearing that after five years Gerstner might become disinterested or look toward early retirement, in late 1997 the board issued two million more options, which could be vested over a five-year period in equal parts. When Gerstner reaches sixty, in 2002, he'll also be awarded a ten-year consulting contract for per diem work.

Stock option grants are based on a corporation's future returns, and they are not worth anything until a specific date. So their value varies with the volatility of the market, and it is difficult to accurately gauge their exact worth. Gerstner's options fluctuate at a rate of at least a few million dollars a day. Based on his last award, however, Gerstner clearly was now one of the nation's richest hired hands, according to Graef Crystal, the executive pay expert and consultant, who conducts periodic surveys. Of the 279 public corporations he analyzed in 1998, Gerstner's pay that year ranked third, at $91.5 million. Four other CEOs in the top ten were paid less, however, and reaped greater earnings for their shareholders. In Crystal's 1999 survey, it appears that Gerstner's pay/performance ratio improved. Gerstner ranked seventh among CEOs on his "High Performance/ Low Pay" chart.

Even if IBM continues to make only modest gains, Gerstner will easily exceed $500 million in personal earnings during the decade he plans to rule Big Blue.

So using Graef Crystal's options pricing methodology, one could ask whether Gerstner is worth what he's being paid. Most investors might say yes. At this time, however, it is too early to argue the point. It is a question that will be better answered as IBM forges into the next century with Gerstner in command. If IBM continues to grow and reward shareholders over the next few years, it's likely he will receive at least one more large stock option grant before he retires. As far as the generic debate goes— are large-company CEOs overpaid?—the answer depends on one's politics and views. (As the nation mints more Internet wealth because of ludicrously high stock valuations, Gerstner's high compensation may look like a bargain.)

The more pertinent questions, and some are multibillion-dollar ones, are these: Where in the technology universe is IBM headed as a corporation? In which businesses will it succeed in the coming years? As technology continues to rapidly evolve, can Big Blue adapt quickly enough to take advantage of new market opportunities? Can Gerstner completely reshape IBM into something new? Or will all his efforts result in returning the company to a more efficient example of what it was in the past? Is he one of America's most creative business leaders or just an extremely good manager? Will he merely be a caretaker for his successor, stuck with the label of "turnaround artist"?

At the time of this writing, Gerstner has been in charge of IBM for six years. During his first four years, the company's financial report card slipped ever so slightly from spectacular to excellent.

It was spectacular in the first two years because he (along with Jerry York) resuscitated, at remarkable speed, a dying patient. As the company stabilized, however, there was less fat to trim. Still, the results were near-stellar, given the challenge of integrating IBM's many businesses.

I had the occasion to ask Sun Microsystem CEO Scott McNealy about Lou Gerstner's performance during a press conference in December 1998. I reminded him about the "International Biscuit Maker" comment he had made when Gerstner was appointed. He has since revised his opinion. He said, "After my first meeting with Lou Gerstner, I came away thinking this guy is very, very smart, and one of the most impressive CEOs I've met. And I've met a lot of them, and some of them don't impress me.

"IBM has basically changed a lot from the days where they invented all their own technology and were strictly a product company, to becoming a reseller, integrator and user of other people's technology."

Overall, the company's recent performance over 1997 and 1998, however, is only "good." (As this book was being completed, IBM's first-quarter 1999 results were reported. Earnings were up forty-two percent over the comparable 1998 quarter, and the stock price reached its all time high of $246 in the spring of 1999. Revenues were up substantially, including hardware sales. Obviously the outlook for the year is excellent once again, but a single three-month performance does not reflect an entire year.)

Even with IBM's great core strengths, the technology business still is in continual flux. Gerstner's top line was acceptable, with record revenues of $81.7 billion in 1998. But the rate of increase has slipped. After a 12.3 percent boost in sales in 1995, IBM grew by only 5.6 percent in 1996, 3.3 percent in 1997, and 4 percent in 1998. (IBM says it lost five percentage points in 1997 because of currency devaluation in its foreign divisions. But every global concern suffered from the same handicap.) Revenues are vitally important, but not the only absolute by which you judge a company. Net earnings and returns on shareholder equity were on the upswing during every year Gerstner has been CEO.

There are at least two ways to read IBM's annual report, however; either the hard drive is half-full, or it is half-empty.

The cautionary figures—absolute bad tidings to some cynics—appear in the breakdown of the company's business units. For accounting purposes, until 1998 IBM broadly lumped its products and services within nine separate categories. In 1997, six areas suffered revenue losses, two had healthy increases, and one was basically flat. Its main hardware lines—the RS/6000, AS/400, System/390, personal computers, and PC servers—were off. The System/390 mainframe line actually had a thirty percent increase in MIPS shipments (the standard measurement in computing power), but steep discounts and currency fluctuations caused revenue losses.

The arithmetic did not yield an encouraging outlook. Businesses that constituted nearly two-thirds of Gerstner's revenues were flat or down for 1997. In 1998, revenue in *all* the hardware segments continued to fall off. Its three major hardware segments saw revenues decline, from 4.4 percent to as much as 10.8 percent.

The Personal Systems Group lost nearly $1 billion. This includes "general purpose computer systems," consumer software (Crayola, Edmark, World Book Encyclopedia), Aptiva, IntelliStation workstations, Netfinity servers, PC 300 commercial desktops, and ThinkPads. This is real money, even for a firm the size of IBM. (One reason for this loss was IBM's insistence on using third-party vendors to sell its wares. It wasn't until spring 1999 that IBM finally announced it was offering all of its desktop PCs over the Internet.)

During an analyst phone call to report 1998 fourth quarter results, Doug Maine repeatedly told listeners how much he "loved" the seventy-five percent gross profit margins in software. But that isn't IBM's high-growth business. Software sales were down two percent in 1997, though they rebounded by six percent the following year (a net gain of only two points per year). IBM once was the world's largest software supplier, but in 1997 Microsoft finally caught it, edging Big Blue for the lead by $300 million. IBM has not had much success developing its own software. Much of its profits here come from software such as Lotus Notes, large system DB/2, and Tivoli's mainframe management applications. If Gerstner's and Maine's affection for this business is real, IBM probably will have to look for a new, major acquisition. Netfinity Objects, a small company IBM purchased to develop electronic commerce applications, is not enough.

In 1997, IBM managed to grow its top line only because of its Global Services and its OEM business. The OEM group's terrific results came primarily from sales of PC hard disk drives and computer chips to other companies that market IBM components under their own nameplates. Gerstner has grown the licensing business to a far greater level than many thought possible.

In one OEM deal, IBM has embraced the spirit of "co-opetition" to a larger extent than anyone might have thought five years ago. In 1999, Gerstner signed a $16 billion, five-year deal with Michael Dell to provide parts for his PCs. Though the pact was hyped at a well-attended press conference—it was billed as perhaps the largest such deal of its kind—the postgame analysis revealed that it could provide far less significant income than IBM hopes. Dell is not bound by any minimums, and even if he buys as much as Gerstner hopes—an average of more than $3 billion in gross sales a year—it is low-margin hardware that probably will not produce stellar profits. (A similar multibillion-dollar deal also was made with Acer.)

Gerstner has also had the same glittering success with services as he's had with licensing, with 1998 revenue growth at 13.5 percent. He will ensure that IBM continues as a problem solver and systems integrator for large customers. In some way, this is a return to the glass-house days when Big Blue dominated the IT industry. At the 1998 annual meeting, Gerstner recalled that "the outsourcing business had its antecedents in the services bureau that IBM built when I just got out of school." It is an indication that this is the IBM he likes to remember and wants to emulate. With IT more complex, he sees no end for the demand. "I think our services business can grow very nicely," Gerstner told shareholders in 1998. "I think we grew a Unisys last year," he said, referring to the Blue Bell, Pennsylvania–based services company that grew out of Sperry and Univac. The following year, in 1998, services hit $31.6 billion, growing a billion more than in the previous year.

Unfortunately, the gross margins in services are much lower than in IBM's other businesses. At the 1998 annual meeting, Gerstner said, "The profit margin in the business when we manage it well is very acceptable." Then, smiling, he added diplomatically, "I mean, I don't want to say they're highly acceptable because there are customers in the audience here. But . . . we just sort of make a good living out of it." Gerstner's answer was telling. Though the gross margins average about twenty percent, every contract is negotiated differently, and the field is more competitive than ever. Also, in the past, the profits tended to escalate in the later years of the contract. But now companies are driving harder bargains for shorter terms than the traditional ten years. Analysts do not think double-digit growth is sustainable for IBM—or its competitors—a few years out.

Since Gerstner has been running IBM, one can argue he has turned the company into a parts supplier and systems integrator (with a fairly healthy supply of software thrown in). It's not glamorous, but it works for now.

More than half the business—hardware sales—is now secondary in importance from a purely narrow, rigid view of the bottom line. But hardware is far from irrelevant. Gerstner is constantly advised by financial and technology analysts to sell the PC business. In the 1998 annual report Gerstner wrote, "The PC era is over. This is not going to say PCs are going to die off. . . . But the PC's reign as the driver of customer buying decisions and the primary platform for application development is over. . . . It has been supplanted by the network."

Gerstner also mentioned that the PC business was an "important turnaround story" for IBM in 1998. It's difficult to imagine what he's referring to here, other than the fact that IBM's PC Company incurred most of its huge loss during the first half of the year and seemed to recover in the second half.

At IBM, after all, PCs are a constant loser. If GE's Jack Welch were running the company, the PC business most likely would be long gone. But Gerstner does not view it as a discrete component. Large IT customers constantly ask Big Blue to supply low- or no-profit PCs, but accommodating them at any cost is a hollow excuse. IBM could complete any order with Compaq or Gateway or another supplier (and still get a piece of the deal). Gerstner sticks with the PC Company because it carries the company logo to places it normally wouldn't appear. Is this a good business decision, or merely the CEO's brand-encased ego getting in the way?

IBM will not have it easy now that its growth potential is in businesses with lower profit margins. Simple single-digit revenue growth—a small feat in itself for companies as large as IBM—does not necessarily return shareholder value. Though revenues increased $3 billion from 1997 to 1998, pretax income was virtually the same, even though there were no special charges.

For top-line improvement, Gerstner needs to keep nurturing his world-renowned research labs. He's managed this job far better than his predecessors. In the past, IBM had the expensive habit of funding almost anything with a molecule that moved, while few of its inventions became profit-making products. Gerstner has trimmed many of the blue-sky programs, to the consternation of several scientists who claim that he is sacrificing the long term for quarterly returns. Nearly half of the $35 billion in hardware revenues for 1998 came from products introduced in the last year. This has not always been the case, however, and often the company has not adhered to the standard acceptable ratios in high technology (where new products should account for half the revenues every three years). It is difficult and perhaps unrealistic to hold a huge enterprise like IBM to any holy R&D standard, especially when so much of its business is headed in another direction. Gerstner has said that being first is more important than being right, a clear reversal from IBM's old philosophy. But IBM still doesn't move fast enough. Gerstner continues to provoke, however. At an informal gathering of IBM researchers in 1998, he said, "I want . . . more than brilliant irrelevance. I want something substantive."

Gerstner gets much better grades than previous CEOs for seizing on potential moneymakers when he scours the work benches. He's rushed groundbreaking copper chips into IBM's new mainframes, which make the machines far more cost competitive and efficient; and even newer chip technology—silicon geranium—could prove to revolutionize cell phones. A "system on a chip" has been designed that combines both logic and memory circuits, and crowds as many as twenty-four million transistors on a single wafer. Despite Gerstner's reduction of the annual research budget by about $1 billion, IBM led the world in patents every year from 1993 to 1998.

Big and small, Gerstner is attempting to keep the company in the development game. IBM is building the world's faster supercomputer (ten trillion calculations per second) for the U.S. Department of Energy. A two-year project, the $85 million machine will track the nation's nuclear stockpile. At the same time, IBM has been the pioneering outfit in voice and speech recognition programming, which may or not be a next wave in personal computing. IBM's Via Voice software has garnered good reviews, but the competition is close behind. Microsoft has invested in a small software outfit with a competitive product, and the field is now crowded with a dozen or so makers. IBM's leadership role here probably is in jeopardy.

Gerstner is a scavenger in the positive sense of the word. He has looked everywhere within IBM to produce revenue streams, and not just to the future. In the last few years, he's mined the past, and he's benefited from great timing.

In 1995, the Year 2000 problem, or Y2K, was not widely anticipated by most computer users. Y2K refers to processing disruptions—not to mention apocalyptic nightmares—that will be caused when internal computer clocks cannot differentiate between the dates 1900 and 2000. There is some irony in the fact that IBM's early programmers began abbreviating the dates in a six-digit field (the year was in two digits). IBM and other forward-thinking companies knew problems could occur when the clock strikes midnight on January 1, 2000.

As the millennium bug issue became more widely publicized, experts lined up on either side. Peter de Jager was an early alarmist, and he became an expert and consultant after he wrote a seminal piece in the September 6, 1993, issue of *Computerworld* called "Doomsday." Y2K was largely dormant until three years later, when Nicholas Zvegintzov countered those who claimed the apocalypse was near. His piece, "The Year 2000 as Racket and Ruse" appeared in *American Programmer*. While the problem was real, Zvegintzov conceded, it wasn't complicated. "It's very clear what the implications are, but as a software problem, it isn't very deep," he said. Bill Goodwin, a programmer who worked on Wall Street in the 1970s, coped with it when he wrote software to accommodate thirty-year bonds. "I allowed for the year 2000," he said. "I took care of the problem right then."

Far too many corporations ignored it, however. At first, IBM approached Y2K from the defensive standpoint. One statistic Big Blue often recites is that as much as seventy percent, or the "vast majority," of the world's databases resides in IBM hardware and software. It's nearly impossible to go to a bank or a broker, book a reservation on a plane or log on to a Web site without coming into contact with something made by IBM. The odds are even higher in foreign venues. So IBM first worried about its Y2K legal exposure. (Apparently it still does. There is a disclaimer in the annual report that begins, "The company is also aware of the potential for claims against it," though it "believes that any such claims against it will be without merit." Lawsuits are just beginning to "trickle," according to a report in the *New York Times*. Among the targets were IBM, Lucent Technologies, and AT&T.)

The company published white papers and held discussion groups on the Internet far earlier than other technology companies. Then, when its customers began to worry about it, IBM shifted gears. The Gartner Group first estimated that businesses would spend $600 billion in the next few years to fix all that ancient computer code. (It has since revised its figure, upward of more than a trillion dollars.) IBM was one of the first companies to form special Y2K compliance teams within its services unit. It already has spent $575 million fixing its own Y2K problems. Helping companies to become "century rollover enabled" is now a double-digit problem with thirteen-figure revenue potential for technology solutions providers. IBM has booked all the work it can handle. The Y2K revenue stream, thriving at the time of this writing, will continue after the new millennium, but much of the business will dry up by the end of 1999.

With competitive pressure on every front, Gerstner's biggest challenge still looms. How good a rainmaker is he? The technology analysts read the balance sheet and wonder where he plans to make money.

One indication of where he sees future revenues and profits can be glimpsed from where he's spending money on marketing and advertising. He is trying to position Big Blue as the main backbone supplier for business transactions on the World Wide Web. With Wall Street and the rest of corporate America hyping the potential of electronic commerce, Gerstner has shifted the company's advertising effort in the past two years. "Are you ready for e-business?" read the headlines on full-page ads in 1998. The $200 million blitz eventually worked its way into products (e-business tools) and services (e-businesspeople). The full-page profiles of IBMers—their new titles are "e-business accelerator," "business intelligence specialist," or "knowledge facilitator"—include job descriptions and an appropriate saying (their "creed"). The business titles are a little hokey, but the ads are ethnically diverse, as they're obviously designed to generate cultural currency as well as new business. The direct sales pitch is that IBM can get your business online quickly and safely. The underlying message is that there's an eclectic mix of real IBMers who dress casually at work and, just like the folks in Silicon Valley, understand Webspeak.

Gerstner continues to invest in brand awareness because the future of e-business favors the younger, more agile competitors. He has some ground to make up here. When the trade journal *Information Week* surveyed two hundred IT managers, one question asked which company was considered the "most-trusted" vendor for e-business solutions. Microsoft was cited by respondents more than twice as much as IBM. There is certainly an e-business aroma to almost every move IBM has made in the last three years:

■   IBM is supporting Java with a massive effort that dwarfs most of its competitors.

■   It is porting its mainframe software to competitors' operating systems.

■   It is endorsing Windows NT. IBM also announced it would ship its Netfinity network servers with the upstart (and free) Linux operating system alongside Windows NT.

■   IBM has made dozens of small strategic alliances with everyone from France Telecom to Sun to facilitate Internet access for e-business.

■   IBM even began beta testing software for voice-enabled browsing on the Net.

Still, there is real skepticism about these and other initiatives. There are some who feel that Gerstner's e-commerce plans are nothing more than a veiled effort to push hardware. An IBM press conference held in New York City to announce new "e-business tools" in April 1998 appeared to support this view. With no substantive announcement as far as e-business went, it was nothing more than a bait-and-switch event. Senior vice president Dave Thomas clearly wanted to flog his new PC servers. Much of his announcement centered around a competitive ad he had produced that claimed IBM's servers were cheaper than Compaq's. He held up an ad that proclaimed Compaq's servers cost $19,000 more to run than IBM's. "And they're ugly," he remarked, though those three words—originally included in the ad—had been removed.

Yet this isn't a surprise. The Internet is still more bluster than business, still a venue that is clearly more appealing to insomniacs who have a lot of time to waste or like the idea of free research. While many retailers are selling goods on the Web, few companies are making any money. Despite the hype and the wildly high stock valuations for Web-based companies, it is not yet a viable stand-alone business model. The virtual mall is still more virtual than shopping mart. The auction sites—which are more like virtual flea markets or yard sales—appear to be far more popular than the stores.

"The question is, is there a strategy at IBM?" asks a former IBM senior vice president. "E-commerce is a name and not a strategy."

To be fair, Gerstner's strategy is every other large technology company's strategy at this point. Still, he gets credit for his willingness to lead the way in e-business with a couple of ill-fated ideas. He sees no upside in becoming a content provider like Microsoft. He launched infoSage, an electronic news service that was late getting into the game. The service used "push" technology, which means that depending on a user's profile, it could tailor the news to personal interests and deliver it to e-mail boxes. Gerstner shut it down, however. The reason, he said, was that he didn't want to compete with his customers. Also, IBM tried to create a virtual sales space with clothing firms like L.L. Bean and The Limited. It opened its version of an online shopping mall known as World Avenue. When its flagship client, the Limited's Express, could not muster any real business, IBM shut World Avenue's doors. The garment business was not yet ready for

Internet retailing, at least at a volume level that interested Gerstner.

Like other high-tech CEOs, Gerstner has faith in the Internet's future, though its role will probably be limited to back-office provider. For now, Big Blue is concentrating on selling what it knows best: robust, reliable hardware with annual downtime measured in minutes; scalable processors that customers can upgrade and expand along with their business; and secure electronic transaction technology for banks and other financial services. When electronic banking began to gain momentum, IBM formed a consortium with fourteen large banks to do online processing. The e-trading phenomenon became widespread in 1998. Suddenly, the Internet spawned a nation of day traders. When Gerstner spoke at a convention of stock brokers in November 1997, he predicted, "Your entire industry will be on the Net."

There is no doubting Lou Gerstner's ability to manage an enterprise as large, complicated, and forbidding as IBM. Few CEOs wanted the job, and few even thought it was doable without a breakup of its business units. He proved the naysayers wrong. This was inarguably the most dramatic corporate turnaround of the 1990s.

The question of leadership is one that is more difficult to settle. Lou Gerstner does not want to be remembered solely for rescuing Big Blue, for which even his harshest critics give him credit. Gerstner is sensitive to those who might summarize his career as that of an effective cost-cutter who merely got a teetering IBM back on track. Could someone else have done it? Of course. As well, and as quickly? Perhaps not. Could he have done it without Jerry York? Probably not.

As many as four years into the job, this legacy still concerned him. Early in 1997, during his annual worldwide pep talk to employees, Gerstner sensed a danger that IBMers might relax and become complacent. He said, "Now there's no place to hide. . . . We have no more excuses. We can no longer say we're still getting our act together. We can't say that we don't have our strategies figured out yet. We can't say we're preoccupied with fixing things inside. No. The stock market, the media, the industry consultants, our customers, have all said, 'You've got your act together.' They're all saying, 'We have high expectations for you again.'"

The following year, in front of the same audience, Gerstner said, "None of us at IBM is here, certainly not me, because we want to work on a perpetual turnaround. We're finished with the turnaround."

Doesn't it seem odd that he would even *mention* the turnaround in 1998? Hadn't he surprised even himself with the speed at which he and his workforce had risen to the task in 1994 and 1995?

The easy work has long been accomplished. To astute IBM observers, Lou Gerstner's second five years will be far more difficult than his first five years.

If one leads by example, and the boss's work habits set the standard, then Lou Gerstner is setting a very high standard for industriousness. What gets on his desk does not go unread. He tells employees he reads every e-mail. He sympathizes with their battles with the bureaucracy and the management "matrix." He encourages them to work around the infamous "silos" of rigid divisions of labor. He is known to take two briefcases home with him on weekends. What requires action is never tabled. Customer complaints that reach his office are dealt with swiftly (though they're delegated to senior executives).

His travel schedule would put CEOs with less mettle in a constant state of exhaustion, not to mention jet lag. Jerry York, a man who is known for taking on heavy workloads, is struck by Gerstner's energy and his thirst and capacity for work. "Lou pays the price," he said. "I don't know how he does it, he's on the road so much. Even if you have your own G4, after a while it gets very tiring."

Gerstner's passion for hard work and his willingness to lead are coupled with his aggressive, forceful, very direct style. There is no room for small talk on his agenda because everything looms large. His business life dominates his personality. The complete Gerstner package is perhaps simpler to those who think it's complex, and more complicated to those who dismiss it as simplistic.

This complete package is controversial and sometimes moody, and it is not for everyone, certainly not for every company.

In the past, his corporate directorships included one very long stint at the New York Times Company. He was elected in 1986 while at American Express. The Times is a public company, though one might not think so by the way it is run. The boardroom always had—and still has—a distinctly private ambience. The Sulzberger family controls the voting stock, and the company is run as if it were a public trust. Profits and shareholder return aren't ignored, but they are not as important as owning and controlling the destiny of the newspaper of record, the first place where historians turn when crafting the stories of our times.

The chairman, Arthur "Punch" Sulzberger, and his three sisters charted the course of the world's most influential newspaper and the company's other holdings, seeking and heeding little advice. Outside directors have limited input, but they relish their board seats for two reasons. "It's very prestigious to be on the Times board because of what the *Times* is," said one former *Times* news executive. "And there are some of them—I have no idea if Gerstner is one—who have the mistaken notion that they can influence the news reporting when the chips are down about something about their own company." A former *Times* business reporter put it this way: "He [Gerstner] was always pissed off at the *Times*" for what it was writing about him, but this was not unique. Other outside directors frequently complained about negative coverage their companies or industries received, the reporter said.

For most of ten years, Gerstner's relationship with Sulzberger's board has been cordial. But in the two-year period from 1996 to 1997, when Punch turned the mantle over to his son, Arthur Sulzberger Jr., it chilled considerably. Gerstner, whose corporate status had been elevated at both RJR and IBM, found that his more aggressive input was less welcome. He was aghast when the board did not even consider a formal succession proposal when Punch planned to step down. "The Times would much rather have somebody who's one of their own, who came up through the system and understands the place," said a close friend of Arthur Jr. "The Times would never bring in somebody like Lou Gerstner, and the fact that they didn't even think about it drove him crazy. Gerstner is a dynamic guy who's used to issuing orders." By far, he was the most dominating outside director.

Arthur Jr. is determined to operate The Times Company in the same collegial way his father did. Nonconfrontational, process-oriented, risk-averse, and genteel, where every decision is made at a deliberate, almost tedious pace. "He [Gerstner] was unhappy with the way things were moving" under Arthur Jr., said the former *Times* man. It did not surprise him when Gerstner resigned. The two were "like oil and water," he said. Another source put it this way: "They were like Martians to each other."

Gerstner's domineering boardroom style and impetuous behavior are likely to color his reputation until he retires. Though he claims his customer visits are one of his main strengths, his lack of charm among some of them has hurt IBM.

In 1997, J.P. Morgan had been planning for about eighteen months to outsource a portion of its IT. It spends $1.5 billion a year on technology worldwide, and Morgan wanted to contract out about twenty percent, or $300 million a year. The firm invited bids from all the companies that were eligible to get this business. Mike Szeto, the Morgan managing director and an ex-IBMer, even allowed his old shop a head start, breaking down Morgan's IT requirements on a quarterly basis. "They had this data six months before any of their competitors," Szeto said.

In fact, two key IBM senior executives, Ned Lautenbach and Dennie Welsh, both called Szeto, asking what they could do to give IBM an edge. "They just didn't listen," Szeto said. "It was a classic case of IBM's arrogance from twenty years ago. On the nine criteria we used to evaluate companies, IBM flunked on four of them." One criterion where IBM fell short was in its Terms and Conditions. Morgan wanted one simple form so that every one of its geographies could get the same T&Cs. IBM wasn't flexible on this. Computer Sciences Corporation, a major competitor, eventually won the business. Its chairman personally pitched Morgan, which helped to seal the deal.

While the Morgan account wasn't a crucial loss by IBM's standards, it was still a fairly substantial deal. Should Gerstner have made an appearance, given his reputation for being so customer-driven?

When J.P. Morgan awarded the contract to Computer Sciences, IBM "turned nasty," according to Szeto. IBM was also a Morgan customer, managing pensions, international currency trading, and a few other chores for Big Blue, totaling about $10 million a year. Gerstner, angry at the loss of the outsourcing contract, canceled its business with Morgan. He retaliated and punished the company in the same temerarious way he had punished *Fortune* magazine for publishing a critical article about him.

With J.P. Morgan and IBM unofficially not talking with each other, there was a halfhearted attempt to attain corporate peace. The Morgan CEO, Sandy Warner, and Gerstner had seen each other at a CEO outing, so a reconciliation breakfast meeting was arranged. The IBM CEO was still steaming, according to Szeto, who recalls, "The first thing that Gerstner said to Warner was, 'I don't even know why I'm here. I only meet with our top fifty customers.'"

Perhaps he was having a particularly bad morning. But there are other stories like this about Lou Gerstner. He is not especially well liked. Others who know him say that pomposity, arrogance, rudeness are descriptions that he cannot believe apply to his personality. It's as if he has no empathetic context because he has always lived in a world of single-minded pursuits of business goals. He believes in the work ethic, and he wants to win. But he craves respectability, and his impatience is disarming. He's like General George Patton, driven to win, to be sure, only without any philosophy.

For many years, he lobbied his colleagues for a sponsorship to join the Augusta National Golf Club, perhaps the most famous such club in America. While at American Express, the excuse for stalling him was that too many executives from that company already were members. But you cannot really apply for membership at a club like this, as Bill Gates found out when he wondered why being the richest man in the world wasn't enough to get in. You must wait until the membership committee selects you. Augusta sensed Gerstner's overeagerness and made him wait, though he was finally admitted.

Despite his penchant for privacy, he is a man who constantly works at his image. When Gerstner arrived at IBM, he had an opportunity to have an audience with Pope John Paul II. His staff prepared the advance materials requested by the Vatican. The writer who updated Gerstner's biography came to the place that asked for the CEO's "other interests." Not knowing much about Gerstner's leisure activities, he wrote "golf and gardening" because he had read somewhere that these were the only two things Gerstner had time for. Gerstner annually plays in the AT&T Pro-Am tournament. As a gardener, his primary interest has been asparagus, one of the most difficult vegetables for amateurs to grow. It takes a few seasons of turning over the soil and constant attention to produce strong, edible stalks.

When Gerstner reviewed his bio for the Vatican, he crossed out the reference to golf and gardening. It was the only change he made. Perhaps he didn't want the Pope to think he had time for any activity that might be construed as frivolous.

One wonders what the founders of the company would have thought about Gerstner and today's IBM. Certainly, he is not the leader that Tom Watson was, or even Tom Watson Jr., inspiring the IBM workforce by appealing to its sense of family. The Watsons ran IBM as if it were different from any other company. They were polite, warm, and endearing, and they kept this sensibility even as the firm grew to a very large size. They were models of corporate gentility. It was a company with a big heart. There was a sense of loyalty to workers, compassion. (Watson Jr., who applauded the board's choice of Gerstner, died shortly there-after, so we will never know his assessment of IBM's first CEO appointed from outside the company.)

Gerstner is long on passion for the business but short on com-passion for the workforce. Perhaps Lou Gerstner has been so mas-terful because he is the kind of CEO who demands far more loyalty from the people who work for him than he would ever give anyone else. There are few apologies here. It's nothing personal, it's just the way it is. The IBM that Gerstner walked into was a spoiled child of a bygone era in American business. It needed the discipline that per-haps only someone like him could impose. IBM's management is no longer polite, warm, and endearing because its CEO is not. Gerstner's method of inspiring the workforce is to issue bigger bonuses and to allow stock options to trickle down to lower-level managers. He's been good for the economy, too. Gerstner has cre-ated 70,000 new jobs since 1995, bringing IBM's workforce to 290,000. Unlike the Watsons, he doesn't attempt to dictate per-sonal behavior. He allows IBMers to imbibe at company functions and dress any way they feel is appropriate. Beyond this, he eschews or merely tolerates most other human resources devices, and in the end, it all comes down to customer wins, respectable revenue growth, shareholder returns. Pride in one's work is welcome, as long as it doesn't get in the way of any of those priorities.

The surgery was a success. IBM's heart is healthy, pumping steadily, but it is the same size as any other company's.

And now that IBM is like any other large enterprise in America, it takes a detached, shirtsleeve technocrat to run it. Gerstner is the consummate technocrat, a pragmatist.

That's Lou Gerstner and the IBM of today.

Full Disclosure

Some things about IBM never change, and one immutable fact is the company's policy toward book writers. Though there is no written decree, IBM never cooperates with authors who seek to examine the inner workings of its corporate structure. There have been dozens of books written about Big Blue, and they all suffer (or benefit) to some extent from the lack of official input. This book is no exception. IBM did not even sanction Tom Watson Jr.'s predominantly affectionate but unusually candid memoir, *Father, Son & Co.*, which appeared in 1990. Watson's book was well received partly because he was particularly forthcoming about IBM's past mistakes, his often protracted squabbles with his father, his rivalry with his brother, and even his brother's drinking problems. The company also didn't cooperate with Paul Carroll, a former *Wall Street Journal* reporter who charted its messy decline through the beginning of 1993 in *Big Blues*. As a daily newspaperman, he was accustomed to a modicum of access to senior executives until he announced his book. Then the doors suddenly shut.

So all of the books written about IBM have one thing in common: they're technically unauthorized views. Until IBM decides—if ever—to sanction a company history, any effort, including this one, will be frowned on by corporate officials.

While Lou Gerstner usually does three or four interviews a year with business reporters or TV anchors, company press officers turned down my request, citing his schedule. There were no openings on his calendar in the fifteen months I spent researching and writing this book. Later, an IBM source said that Gerstner had spoken about my forthcoming book, and the possibility of other books, at a corporate executive committee meeting with a dozen of his most senior staff. The CEO announced to them that he wasn't cooperating with me or any other author, but that they were free to make up their own minds.

This, of course, was a tactic I expected. While IBM wasn't sanctioning authors' projects, it also could claim they weren't inhibiting them either. Although IBM senior executives weren't barred from speaking with me, none agreed to an interview. The same was true of current board members. No senior IBM official would make himself or herself available unless Gerstner or David Kalis, his PR man, specifically requested it. On several occasions executive support staff confirmed this strategy. Seeing "no upside" in terms of their careers, as it was explained to me, they preemptively declined. Several IBMers informed me that as soon as my book was announced, I became persona non grata. Nobody was allowed to return my calls or speak with me. If their names were attached to a quote in my book, they ran the risk of dismissal.

Part of this attitude comes from the normal level of corporate paranoia that exists everywhere in American industry. When Tim Jackson decided to write a book about Intel, CEO Andy Grove originally decided to cooperate with the author. As soon as Grove realized that he couldn't control what was ultimately written, he issued a worldwide directive to shutter the gates. With few exceptions, American business is afraid that if it makes any overture to help an author, it is tacitly endorsing the project.

The IBM of today, despite more of an open-door policy toward journalists, is even more wary than the IBM of yesterday. The level of hysteria is higher because of the unusual personality of its CEO. Despite his high profile in American business, Gerstner has maintained a high degree of privacy. A security detail follows him almost everywhere in public, and he lives in gated communities, both in Greenwich and Hobe Sound. (When he made a visit to the Deep Blue chess team, a security guard even inspected the bathroom stalls in the basement of the Equitable Building in New York City.) He is fortunate to afford the level of privacy most others are not accustomed to having.

For the entire period of research, IBM did not put me on its press list. Officially, I was given access to internal documents that were either in the public domain or made available to other reporters at some prior date. I was not even invited to the annual meeting, even though it was open to journalists. I attended anyway because I own a very small amount of IBM stock in a retirement plan (16.19 shares). The rise and fall of IBM's share price had no affect on my reporting.

It wasn't until I explained to IBM communications personnel that some of the research I collected was unflattering to either Gerstner or IBM that the lowest level of cooperation was granted. At that point, Kalis asked me for a "wish list" of people I'd like to talk with. The only ones who were made available were a half dozen longtime friends or business associates of Gerstner, most of whom were somewhat reluctant and surprisingly inarticulate about explaining his many abilities and virtues. They either stuck to the previously published lore or made prosaic comments about his energy or his strategic genius. His enemies, of course, did not want to go on record for the most part. The threat of IBM's or Gerstner's displeasure was too much to contemplate. This is understandable because some of these sources continue to be involved with Gerstner on civic or corporate boards. Even among directors who do not enjoy cordial relationships, there is an unspoken agreement that one will not grant an interview about someone he knows without the subject's approval.

As a speechwriter for IBM senior executives from March 1996 through the end of 1997, I had a unique look at how the company works and doesn't work. Primarily, I wrote for Bob Stephenson, a senior vice president who is profiled in the book. If the proxy statement that discloses executive compensation is a reliable bellwether, then Stephenson has risen to become the third most powerful manager at IBM. After leaving IBM, I gave Stephenson several opportunities to do an interview or simply review, face-to-face, what I planned to write about him. He originally agreed, but then abruptly changed his mind and declined. The reader should be aware that my portrait of Stephenson is colored by the fact that I worked with him closely. I was struck by Stephenson's confidence and poise and his ability to lead a part of IBM that had greater revenues than most large American companies.

While at IBM, I also had substantial contact with other executives who are mentioned in the book. Among them are Sam Palmisano, Bill McCracken, and James Corcoran. (For a very brief period, I reported to Corcoran.) I also knew on a more limited basis Bob Dies, David Winn, Jim Vanderslice, Doug Elix, Jose Garcia, Linda Sanford, Bob Corbisiero, Bill Amelio, and Jim Firestone.

Although I never met Gerstner while at IBM, I heard him speak at several internal events and public forums.

The primary source material in this book comes from interviews with more than 150 former and current IBMers, competitors, business partners, and technology and financial analysts, some of whom I spoke with a half dozen times. I also spoke with many sources who knew Gerstner during his youth or worked with him at McKinsey & Co., American Express, and RJR Nabisco. Many of my former IBM colleagues helped immensely, especially when it came to delivering insights and distinctions between the old and new IBMs, or the difference in management style between former CEO John Akers and Gerstner. I also relied on hundreds of pages of documents, speeches, memos, and videotapes of IBM executives, including the CEO's. I'm grateful to the people who helped me obtain this material or provided it to me.

Several other IBMers refused to take my calls, no doubt fearing reprisals, even when I left messages saying my inquiries were purely social and not business related. They are undoubtedly fretting over what they said to me in the Somers cafeteria. They can exhale, however. None of what was repeated over lunch was included in this book unless it was information that I gathered independently as a journalist and ex-IBMer. I did not make notes for this book while working as an IBMer. I did not violate the nondisclosure agreement that I signed on entering and leaving the company. All documents marked IBM CONFIDENTIAL were left in my office and no copies were made. Any information I gathered after December 31, 1997, however, I considered fair game.

In the interests of full disclosure, the reader should know that at one point I proposed an entirely different book, and I wanted to write it while working for IBM. In April 1997, I was approached by a literary agent who wondered whether Gerstner might want to write about his transformation of IBM. Several publishers were interested in his story. At first I dismissed the idea, thinking there was no reason for Gerstner to recount his exploits until he retired. But then, about a month later, Bill Gates announced he was going after IBM's customers, and it created a stir in the business press. I had hoped this shot across Gerstner's bow might make him more amenable to such a proposal. So I wrote a four-page memo, explaining how a ghostwritten book could help explain where IBM fit in the new world of fast-paced, network-based technology. Also, Gerstner could crystallize and explain his management philosophy. If done well, I thought it could be a good business tool for the CEO and other IBMers who were waving the colors of the refurbished company. Also, such a book could help serve as a recruitment vehicle for Big Blue. Budding inventors, programmers, and engineers did not normally flock to IBM first because they knew of its past reputation for being stiff, difficult, bureaucratic, and generally risk averse.

The timing for an authorized book also couldn't be better. Many of Gerstner's peers had written books (or, like GE's Jack Welch, had given limited cooperation on management philosophy books), and this was a perfect opportunity for him to edge his way into the spotlight of important business leaders.

My proposal was ignored. I didn't even receive a no-thanks from IBM's corporate decision makers. (David Kalis said he never saw it, though my boss said to me on a number of occasions that he thought he had given it to him.) Seven months later, in one of IBM's periodic restructurings, I was downsized out of a job. Some cynical folks at Big Blue, who knew of my desire to ghostwrite a book for the CEO, still feel that my memo in part may have prompted IBM's decision to include me in its year-end purge. In other words, even the mere suggestion of such a project could have labeled me a potential troublemaker. I doubt if this was true, and even if it was, I harbor no grudge. It had no bearing on my reporting.

My manager's evaluation of my work was good, and it included the following comments: "Throws himself into the task at hand. Drives the organization to respond. Dedicated to achieving results. . . . Doug is passionate about his work and is committed to excellence. His passion is contagious." (The "bad news" was that I was impatient with IBM's often impenetrable bureaucracy.) Eight months before I was furloughed I received a stock option award of 700 IBM shares at 144½ strike price (1,400 shares after a split), but none were vested.

Just a few weeks after I was asked to leave IBM, management sent me a form e-mail message congratulating me on my recent promotion. (It was the first I heard about it.) It asked me to pick among a group of dates to attend manager's school. I thought this mix-up was amusing, even though the vice president who had issued me my pink slip was angry and embarrassed by it.

In the end, my manager checked the box in the IBM form that said my job was no longer necessary to the company's business. Of course, I asked if there was any chance of reassignment, but I was told that there were no speechwriting jobs open anywhere in the organization. Shortly after I left, a new speechwriter was hired to replace me.

Few nonfiction authors work in a vacuum, and almost all are indebted to those who helped shape a book. I'm no exception. For all those who gave unselfishly of their time to allow me to understand Lou Gerstner and the new IBM, I'm grateful. The list of those who helped is too long to mention everyone, so I'd like to offer my collective thanks.

This book had a serendipitous beginning, however, and I would like to mention the participants who made it possible. Steve Schlesinger, an author, friend, and former colleague with whom I worked in the Cuomo administration of New York, bumped into Cherie Burns on Upper Broadway in Manhattan. Schlesinger and Burns had worked together many years ago at *Time* magazine, and Cherie had since become a literary agent at Zachary Shuster. She had been musing about a Lou Gerstner–IBM book and asked if he knew anybody who might be interested in such a project. Steve touted me as a possibility, and Cherie followed up from there. She was cheerfully optimistic, especially when the original idea of an authorized book eventually turned into an unauthorized one. She convinced me it was too good an idea to let go of nearly a year after IBM turned a deaf ear.

Good editors are the most underappreciated people in all publishing ventures, and I can say without reservation that I was lucky to have one of the very best. Dave Conti, executive editor at HarperBusiness, shepherded the manuscript into print with a critical eye and unceasing enthusiasm. His former assistant, David Fortney, also made several suggestions that improved it. I would also like to thank my copy editor, Andrea Molitor, who did a magnificent job in catching the lapses in grammar, usage, and spelling.

My wife, Meg Perlman, and my son, Jake, put up with the erratic behavior and strange hours that authors typically exhibit during the last few months of completing their project. Their understanding and encouragement kept me going at full tilt.

Up in the Berkshires, Victoria Wright transcribed the tapes rapidly and accurately, and constantly graded my interviews. When a portrait of Gerstner began to emerge, she became fascinated with the man. She sent me an e-mail saying she'd transcribe the Gerstner interview gratis. Alas, I regret that I never got to cash in that coupon.

Notes

The author consulted the *New York Times*, the *Wall Street Journal*, *The Economist*, *Forbes*, *Business Week*, and *Fortune* for news and commentary about IBM. Zdnet's online service, the Computer Magazine Archives, was particularly helpful in pointing the author to a number of publications. It archived 86 magazines at its inception, and has since grown to 216. Of the dozens of trade publications that cover various aspects of the technology industry the author frequently relied on *ComputerWorld*, *Datamation*, *Information Week*, *Report on IBM*, *VARBusiness*, *Midrange Systems*, *PC Magazine*, *PC Week*, and *PC World*.

Chapter One

Although he did not attend, the author had access to a videotape of Gerstner's keynote speech at the November 1995 COMDEX show. The chapter's opening commentary comes from attending several COMDEX shows in Las Vegas and numerous conversations with city natives during the mid-to-late 1990s. Ancillary material about the chairman came from interviews, IBM's annual reports, and official biographies.

Chapter Two

An IBM corporate vice president and several other divisional managers who were present during the Akers-Gerstner transition recalled the company's ambience in 1993. The search for a new IBM CEO was perhaps one of the most highly reported in American corporate history. Most major publications had ongoing reports. Leslie Cauley wrote a particularly long and detailed piece about the search for the April 26, 1993, issue of *USA Today*. Gerstner himself revealed information about the interview process to the *New York Times*. Larry Bossidy and Scott McNealy were both quoted in *Times* articles. Judith Dobrzynski, a *New York Times* reporter who worked for *Business Week* at the time, described to the author how the magazine changed its cover when it received the late-breaking news that Gerstner had been chosen for the job. The author interviewed Graef Crystal about Gerstner's compensation package. He also interviewed a former IBM director who was on the board while the transition took place. Several sources who were present during the transition press conference described the activities, including Dan Mandresh, who told the author what he was thinking during the historic moment.

Chapter Three

Jim Burke read the letter he received from Tom Watson Jr., for the videotaped message he gave to the Harvard Business School Club award ceremony honoring Gerstner. In his testimonial, he said he was disclosing its contents for the first time. Lederberg's quote appeared in *Business Week* on October 4, 1993. Gerstner's new stock plan for executives was revealed in an interview he granted to *Fortune* magazine. Other details were gleaned from interviews with IBM managers. IBM released copies of Gerstner's e-mail reply to employees. The author interviewed several IBMers about the company's intranet. Several IBM sources used the phrase "understand his shorthand" for Gerstner's need to surround himself immediately with faces he knew.

The profile of Kalis was the result of interviews with at least a dozen IBMers, past and present, who worked with him. The profile of Kohnstamm came from the corporate biography, interviews with several IBM and Ogilvy and Mather sources.

York's background was assembled from interviews with York and several IBM sources and other financial officials from other companies who knew him. There have been several news articles about York, including a lengthy lead profile in the *Wall Street Journal* by Laurie Hays that described his turnaround efforts.

Richard Koppes, ex–general counsel of CALPERS, gave the author extensive details on how the pension fund operated with respect to IBM.

Gerry Czarnecki's quotes were made in several publications, notably the *New York Times*. Several sources, including an IBM vice president, revealed the circumstances of his short tenure as the senior human resources official of the company.

Chapter Four

The April 1993 annual meeting was widely covered by the nation's media. The comments and quotes were culled from news stories that appeared in the *Wall Street Journal* and the *New York Times*. The description of the IBM plan to break up the company came from several company sources and financial analysts Dan Mandresh, Steve Milunovich, and John Jones. An IBM vice president added details about Adstar and Pennant.

Financial restructuring details came from published accounts and a series of interviews with former CFO Jerry York. The contrast between the Akers and Gerstner administrations regarding management-employee relations resulted from an interview with Steve Schwartz and a former IBMer who worked in corporate communications. Details of the meeting where Akers had to disclose IBM's losses were disclosed by a source who attended.

The author interviewed all those present at the Gerstner meetings (Albert, Milunovich, Mandresh, Smith) with the exception of the chairman.

The material on Gerstner's actions on the IBM sales force and the creation of sales specialists came from a former senior IBM official.

On the matter of Amelio and Woolard and Woolard's tenure on the IBM board, the author relied on Amelio's account in his book and a subsequent interview with Amelio. Woolard, who declined several requests for an interview for this book, called the author to give his version of the account.

The sale of IBM's defense business came from published accounts and interviews with Mike Szeto.

Chapter Five

There are scant details about Gerstner's early years, primarily because the CEO does not like to provide them. In addition to interviews with childhood friends and acquaintances, the author relied on a visit to his high school, the neighborhood where he grew up, and public records. Chaminade High School's administrators granted interviews. Larry Karam, an attorney who graduated from the school, gave the author several details about how the school is run.

For Gerstner's years at Dartmouth, the author relied on several sources who knew him as an undergraduate. Harry Zlokower of the class of 1963, who edited the alumni notes in Dartmouth's magazine, was helpful in providing sources. The university's public relations department refused to cooperate in any cursory manner. The author received invaluable assistance, however, from Anne Ostendarp, who is in charge of special collections at the Baker Library.

The author relied on interviews from several McKinsey and Company principals for his tenure at the consulting firm.

Chapter Six

The Harvard Business School published two studies entitled "American Express Travel Related Services Company" (1985) and

"Lou Gerstner" (1985). The quotes from Gerstner appeared in these studies, conducted as a basis for class discussion.

Several sources were helpful in recounting Gerstner's years at American Express. Many interviews were on the record, and a former senior official confirmed many details during a background conversation. Gerstner appeared in many business articles as an executive with the company, and an extensive profile was published by Saul Hansell in *Instititional Investor*, December 1988. Jon Friedman, the coauthor of "House of Cards" gave the author insight about the intracompany tension that existed during that time.

John Medlin, the CEO of the Wachovia Bank, provided the author with details of the RJR board. Also, there were several published accounts of Gerstner's work heading the conglomerate. Paul Marks, recently retired head of Memorial Sloan-Kettering Cancer Center, was interviewed about Gerstner's board tenure there.

Chapter Seven

The Town Meetings were summarized and described by a number of IBM employees who attended them. The story about Gerstner's visit to the Burlington, Vermont, chip fabrication plant was recounted by a former communications aide who accompanied him on the trip.

Gerstner's aides regaled the press with stories about the CEO's impatience with IBM executives's presentation style. Many made them into published accounts. In the author's twenty-one months at IBM, he saw several presentations where presenters used overhead foils.

Sources on Bob LaBant included an IBM communications manager who saw a videotape of the meeting and one who attended. Quotes from the meeting appeared in *Information Week*, October 25, 1993.

For the material on Ellen Hancock, the author relied on interviews with both Lotus and IBM sources who had attended meetings with her. Several IBM managers described situations where they used the "FUMU" designation.

The author relied principally on four sources to tell about Ed Zschau's running of IBM's storage division: two current managers (one a vice president), a former senior executive, and a technology consulant who worked for the division. The "Had Enough, Big Blue?" poster anecdote appeared in *Business Week*, March 15, 1999.

IBM did not plan on releasing the story about reducing the excessive pay of executive secretaries until it was leaked to the *Wall Street Journal*. The author interviewed the *Journal* source.

PBCs and performance reviews are discussed constantly at IBM, especially during the year-end period where coworkers are asked to participate. The material describing the process was gleaned from subsequent interviews with IBMers after December 31, 1997.

Chapter Eight

IBM provided the results of some tracking studies on customer buying attitudes for the author. Interviews regarding the company's rebranding and advertising efforts were conducted with Shelly Lazarus, Steve Hayden, Bill Hamilton, Robert Chandler, Ken Segall, Brad Johnson, Howard Anderson, Jim Reilly, Steve Sonnenfeld, Chuck Martin, Bruce Bousman, and Charlie Tercek. Lazarus's quotes approximated Gerstner's comments to her as closely as she recalled. Material gathered from additional conversations with IBM sources who worked in advertising in the Personal Systems Group also contributed to this chapter. *Advertising Age* and *AdWeek*, two trade publications, provided background.

Chapter Nine

During several interviews Jerry York and Bill Amelio explained how IBM tackled the issue of process reeningering. Several sources, including Rick Thoman and Bruce Claflin, provided details on the revamping of the personal computer division. Because PCs represented IBM's closest relationship to the non-business public, dozens of additional sources had strong opinions about the way this division operated.

The attempted Apple-IBM merger was discussed in Jim Carlton's 1997 book on Apple and in several news accounts. The author also interviewed Jim Cannavino about it as well as other Armonk-based IBM executives, past and present, who had knowledge of the negotiations. An Apple director provided background information.

Chapter Ten

The author attended the meeting described that opens this chapter, and details were later confirmed by another source who also was there.

The Microsoft-IBM relationship involving the development of the OS/2 operating system was long, complex, and controversial. There are a number of accounts available to readers who are interested in the history, including the Manes, Carroll, and Gates books. It will be interesting to see how much more light, if any, the U.S. Justice Department will shed on Microsoft's involvement in this project when its antitrust investigation concludes. Claflin and York among other sources at IBM provided insight into Gerstner's views on OS/2.

The Cannavino quote about being the "V guy" appeared in the January 17, 1994, issue of *Business Week*. A March 3, 1995, *New York Times* business article reported that Gerstner was "complimentary but cool" about Cannavino's resignation.

Chapter Eleven

Mike Szeto allowed the author access to his copies of his merger and acquisition presentations made in 1994 and 1995 to both Lotus and IBM. Extensive notes were made from the documents, which were confidential to J.P. Morgan.

The author attended the Lotus 1–2–3 press conference in New York City in 1982.

The IBM takeover of Lotus has been reported widely in the press, mostly from the Lotus point of view. A notable exception was an account in the June 22, 1995, of the *New York Times*, where IBM officials cooperated with reporter Judith Dobrzynski. Wendy Goldman Rohm wrote an extensive article for *Upside* magazine in January 1996 chronicling the events that took place during the historic week. The author interviewed five former senior executives at Lotus, others at IBM who were present during the weekend press events, and Jerry Rosenfeld, formerly of Lazard Frères. Few were willing to go on the record even three years after the fact. Despite repeated requests, IBM's corporate public relations would not provide anyone who would officially discuss the company's involvement in the acquisition.

The author reviewed videotapes of the IBM press conference and the Lotus employee address at the Wang Auditorium made by Gerstner, Manzi, and Thompson. Sources present at the Iris meeting were interviewed about Gerstner's visit there.

Chapter Twelve

Two former corporate sources, a speechwriter and a communications manager, were the author's principal sources on the Harvard Business School Club dinner. A copy of the testimonials videotaped by Vernon Jordan and Jim Burke was obtained by the author. Direct quotes were taken from the tapes. A dinner guest was interviewed.

The author's profile of Stephenson was constructed primarily from comments Stephenson made during meetings or directly to the author between 1996 and 1997. Later interviews with IBMers who know him confirmed details of his background. The material on Corcoran came from interviews with a dozen or so sources who worked with him. The language about his hiring was used by two sources who formerly worked at Ogilvy and Mather, both of whom attributed it to Lazarus. Two IBM sources also confirmed it. The author was present when Corcoran made the remark about the "eight-hundred-pound gorilla," and it was later confirmed by another IBMer who also heard it at the same time.

Stephenson's remarks from the 1996 senior manager's meeting were transcribed from a videotape of the speech.

The material on Palmisano was compiled from his corporate biography and interviews with two aides who worked with him for several years. The anecdote about his signing a difficult account was reported in *Computer Reseller News*, November 25, 1997. Direct quotes from Palmisano were made at an internal meeting on April 24, 1996, where the author was present. A source later provided a transcript of the audio tape of the meeting.

Chapter Thirteen

Eli Primrose-Smith's comments were published in the June 1996 issue of *Marketing Computers*. Ron Palmich's quote about the Olympics being for "bragging rights" appeared in *USA Today*, June 19, 1996. Mall's quote about IBM "being undressed in front of the world" was in the Raleigh (N.C.) *News and Observer*. The author was present at a meeting where Scott Penberthy explained how the "WOM" worked. The *Datamation* comment was in the July 1996 issue. The *Fortune* quote appeared on September 9, 1996. The Kohnstamm reaction to the Games' negative publicity was published in *Think* magazine, Vol. 62, No. 1, 1996. The author was with Stephenson in the elevator when he asked about the headline.

Gelernter's comment appeared in the *Think* issue cited above. In an interview Jeff Kisselhoff provided details of the match. He summarized his experience in a piece he wrote for the "Electronic Newsstand" Web site, August 22, 1997. Gerstner's quote about the match was in the *New York Times*, May 8, 1997. Kasparov's *Time* article pleading for a rematch was in the May 26, 1997, issue.

The front-page business section story in the *New York Times* about Gerstner's retaliation to the *Fortune* article was on September 29, 1997. The *AdWeek* award citation was announced in an advertisement in the April 2, 1998, issue of the *Times*.

The Portchester (N.Y.) *Daily Item* described Pataki's ribbon-cutting ceremony at the new Armonk headquarters. The Gannett newspapers in Westchester published several articles on the building and the deals made with New York State government. The *New York* magazine review of the building appeared November 3, 1997. The author also attended several meetings held by senior executives in the building. Gerstner is quoted about the headquarters in the *New York Times*, September 17, 1997.

Chapter Fourteen

The author made several visits to the Palisades conference center between 1996 and 1997. The Education Summit was covered by the major news media, and IBM published a twenty-one-page "review" of the event. Clinton's quote from his speech appeared in the review. Gerstner's remarks were taken from the transcript of his speech. Gil Amelio described the summit in an interview and also in his book, *On the Firing Line*.

The author attended the 1997 senior manager's meeting. Gerstner's remarks came from a transcript of his speech and a source who heard it. "One Voice" was a special issue of *Think* sent to every employee. An IBM vice president who attended Microsoft's "Scalability Day" presentation described the event.

The international scandals affecting IBM have been variously reported in major news organizations, including Reuters and the Associated Press. The author relied on *Clarín*, a Spanish-language newspaper published in Buenos Aires, which followed the case closely. The affair concerning the sale of supercomputers to Russia was first investigated by the *New York Times* and was broken on October 27, 1997. The Gannett Westchester newspapers published several stories about the Argentinian bribery incident.

Gannett reporter Phil Waga wrote extensively about it from Buenos Aires on September 27, 1998.

Chapter Fifteen

The *Newsweek* piece, titled "The Hit Men," appeared on February 16, 1996. It was well known within IBM that Gerstner himself had mandated that all IBMers be connected to Lotus Notes as quickly as possible. In 1996, the trade press and some consumer publications ran countless articles on the network computer. The author retained several notes made about NCs for speech research, including the thin client and Redcliffe. He had access to both Stephenson memos sent to Gerstner. He was also familiar with the chart made by the Personal Systems Group to delineate user patterns. He was present at the meeting Palmisano and Dies attended.

The business strategy for the network computer was outlined by aides in Dies's division.

Material for the background on the Somers complex was provided by an IBM vice president. The sections on Donofrio and Bregman come from interviews with former aides who worked for them and their corporate biographies.

The author attended the 1998 annual meeting where Gerstner was asked about superconducting.

Chapter Sixteen

The author worked with the public relations manager who was responsible for the Aptiva Stealth. Interviews with him after he left IBM and others who worked in Raleigh on the product development formed the basis for this chapter. Several sources, current and former employees, at Ogilvy and Mather were interviewed. The author visited IBM's Raleigh facilities on several occasions. The mezzanine was described by a vice president in communications and a former IBM manager.

Firestone's remark about how IBM can "dazzle the world" was in the June 17, 1996, *Business Week*. The author attended the

September 26, 1996, press conference introducing the Stealth computer.

An IBM manager who attended the meetings with Stephenson provided details of the under-$1,000 PC. *New York Times* critic Stephen Manes reviewed the Aptiva E16 on December 2, 1997.

For years Armonk executives had been wondering how much brand leverage and direct business it received from exhibiting at the annual COMDEX show. After an internal study done by one manager, he concluded that the investment did not produce tangible returns.

Chapter Seventeen

Mandresh related the details of the two phone calls he had with Thoman during interviews. The material on Ricciardi comes from interviews with IBM sources who work in Armonk, a former corporate communications manager, and his company biography.

Anderson's *Network World* comments were published in the June 29, 1998, issue.

IBM's financial figures are widely published after each quarterly report is made available. Some figures were taken from the annual reports.

The author attended the joint IBM-Dell press conference.

The *Information Week* comment about its e-business survey appeared in the February 9, 1998, issue.

The author attended the IBM press conference that announced its new e-business tools.

Gerstner explained the company's abandonment of infoSage during a keynote speech he made at the Fall Internet World conference in 1996 at the Javits Center in New York.

The author obtained videotapes of Gerstner's 1997 and 1998 addresses to employees.

Bibliography

Amelio, Gil, and William L. Simon. *On the Firing Line: My 500 Days at Apple.* New York: HarperBusiness. 1998.

Burrough, Bryan, and John Helyar. *Barbarians at the Gate: The Fall of RJR Nabisco.* New York: HarperCollins, 1991.

Carlton, Jim. *Apple: The Inside Story of Intrigue, Egomania, and Business Blunders.* New York: Times Business and Random House, 1997.

Carroll, Paul. *Big Blues: The Unmaking of IBM.* New York: Crown Publishers, Inc., 1993.

Cringely, Robert X. *Accidental Empires.* Reading, Mass.: Addison-Wesley Publishing Co., Inc., 1992.

Daughen, Joseph R. and Peter Binzen. *The Wreck of the Penn Central.* Beard Books (paper), 1999 (originally published in 1971).

DeLamarter, Richard Thomas. *Big Blue: IBM's Use and Abuse of Power.* New York: Dodd, Mead and Co., 1986.

Downes, Larry, and Chunka Mui. *Killer App: Digital Strategies for Market Dominance.* Boston, Mass.: Harvard Business School Press, 1998.

Ferguson, Charles H., and Charles R. Morris. *Computer Wars: How the West Can Win in a Post-IBM World.* New York: Times Books and Random House, 1993.

Friedman, Jon, and John Meehan. *House of Cards: Inside the Troubled Empire of American Express.* New York: G.P. Putnam's Sons, 1992.

Gates, Bill, with Nathan Myhrvold and Peter Rinearson. *The Road Ahead.* New York: Viking, 1995.

Gerstner Jr., Louis V., Roger D. Semerad, Denis Phillip Doyle, and William B. Johnston. *Reinventing Education: Entrepreneurship in America's Public Schools.* New York: Dutton, 1994.

Grove, Andrew S. *Only the Paranoid Survive.* New York: Doubleday Currency, 1996.

Jackson, Tim. *Inside Intel.* New York: Dutton, 1997.

Maisonrouge, Jacques. *Inside IBM: A Personal Story.* New York: McGraw-Hill Publishing Co., 1985.

Manes, Stephen, and Paul Andrews. *Gates.* Garden City, New York: Doubleday & Co., 1985.

McKenna, Regis. *Who's Afraid of Big Blue? How Companies Are Challenging IBM—and Winning.* Reading, Mass.: Addison-Wesley Publishing Co., Inc., 1989.

Mills, D. Quinn, and G. Bruce Friesen. *Broken Promises: An Unconventional View of What Went Wrong at IBM*. Boston, Mass.: Harvard Business School Press, 1996.

Mobley, Lou, and Kate McKeown. *Beyond IBM*. New York: McGraw-Hill Publishing Co., 1989.

Rose, Frank. *West of Eden: The End of Innocence at Apple Computer*. New York: Viking, 1989.

Sculley, John, with John A. Byrne. *Odyssey: Pepsi to Apple . . . A Journey of Adventure, Ideas, and the Future*. New York: Harper & Row Publishers, 1987.

Sobel, Robert. *IBM: Colossus in Transition*. New York: Times Books, 1981.

Wallace, James, and Jim Erickson. *Hard Drive: Bill Gates and the Making of the Microsoft Empire*. New York: John Wiley & Sons, Inc., 1992.

Watson Jr., Thomas J., and Peter Petre. *Father, Son & Co.: My Life at IBM and Beyond*. New York: Bantam Books, 1990.

Wilson, Mike. *The Difference Between God and Larry Ellison: Inside Oracle Corporation*. New York: William Morrow & Co., Inc., 1997.

Index

Acer, 311, 315

Advertising: American Express campaigns, 99–101; Aptiva and related options campaign, 308, 312; Camel cigarettes, 113–14; e-commerce emphasis by IBM, 334–35; IBM ads pulled from *Fortune*, 270–71; IBM fear issue used, 158–59; IBM letterbox series, 158; IBM 1994 subtitles campaign, 139–55; IBM slogan, 154; OS/2 problems, 193; PC Jr. campaign, 10, 144

Akers, John: failed strategies, 13, 19–20, 26, 30, 56, 64; Gerstner's installation, 28–29, 34; IBM and American Express, 107; IBM board and, 20; IBM career, 29; management style, 59, 62, 118, 123; resignation, 19, 28; revenue loss under, 48; salary, 28

Albert, Sam, 67–68, 128, 321

Allaire, Paul, 322

Allman, George, 78, 81

Amelio, Bill, 162, 169, 170

Amelio, Gil, 72–73, 127, 155, 249, 278–79

American Express: advertising campaigns, 100–101; "cause-related marketing," 99–101; Gerstner as consultant for, 92; Gerstner as flag officer and biggest moneymaker, 102; Gerstner heads Travel Related Services, 93–94, 95–101; Gerstner leaves, 28, 107–9; Gerstner as president, 23; Gerstner's image, 97; Golub as CEO, 88; IBM and, 106–7; Kalis at, 37; Kohnstamm at, 41, 42; market share concerns, 96, 104–5; McKinsey as consultants for, 92, 97; Optima card and Platinum card, 104–5; Project Genesis, 105–7; Shearson merger, 101–4; team-building, 96–97; Thoman, Rick, at, 98–99; Vacation Packages division, 98; Weill-Gerstner clash, 102–4, 108; Welsh, Jerry, at, 98–99

Ammirati Puris Lintas, 140

Anderson, Howard, 143, 324–25

Andreesen, Marc, 77

Apple Computer, 179; advertising, 155; Amelio at, 72–73; classroom equipment, 278–79; Gates commandeering of graphical user interface, 191; IBM attempt to acquire, 177–83; IBM software deals, 208; market share diminishing, 155; Super Bowl ad, 141; System 7, 179

Armstrong, Mike, 74, 106–7, 323

AT&T acquisition of IBM Global Network, 323

Bachelder, Joe, 27, 28

Bagnasco, Adolfo, 288

Balaban, Bob, 200–201, 227

Ballmer, Steven, 141, 143, 189, 190

Ballou, Roger, 98, 103, 106

Barksdale, Jim, 220

Barnes and Noble, 286

Baxley, Jr., Robert, 85–86

BBDO Worldwide, 140–41, 155

Bechtel, Jr., Stephen D., 73

Beers, Charlotte, 141, 142, 145, 147, 148

Benjamin, Joel, 264

Binder, Paul, 85

Black, Cathleen, 73

Bossidy, Larry, 22

Boston Chicken, 235

Bousman, Bruce, 149–50, 152–53

Branscomb, K. C., 229

Braun, Mike, 318

Bregman, Mark, 302

Brown, Harold, 20

Buffet, Warren, 104

Burdick, Walt, 50

Burke, Jim, 20–21, 22, 23, 25, 26, 29, 34, 234

Business Week: campaign aimed at poorly managed companies, 30; Gerstner cover, 29–30

CALPERS, 48

Calvano, Jim, 99